Eat Sleep Sit

Eat Sleep Sit

My Year at Japan's Most Rigorous Zen Temple

Kaoru Nonomura

Translated by Juliet Winters Carpenter

KODANSHA INTERNATIONAL
Tokyo • New York • London

Originally published by Shinchosha, Tokyo, in 1996, under the title Ku neru suwaru: Eiheiji shugyoki.

Distributed in the United States by Kodansha America LLC, and in the United Kingdom and continental Europe by Kodansha Europe Ltd.

Published by Kodansha International Ltd., 17−14, Otowa 1-chome, Bunkyo-ku, Tokyo, 112−8652.

ISBN 978−4−7700−3075−7

First edition, 2008
15 14 13 12 11 10 09 08   10 9 8 7 6 5 4 3 2 1

Library of Congress Cataloging-in-Publication Data

Nonomura, Kaoru, 1959-
 [Ku neru suwaru. English]
 Eat sleep sit : my year at Japan's most rigorous zen temple / Kaoru Nonomura ; translated by Juliet Winters Carpenter.
 -- 1st ed.
   p. cm.
 ISBN 978-4-7700-3075-7
 1. Monastic and religious life (Zen Buddhism)--Japan--Eiheiji-cho. 2. Spiritual life--Sotoshu. 3. Eiheiji. 4. Nonomura, Kaoru, 1959- 5. Spiritual biography--Japan. I. Title.
 BQ9444.4.J32E34 2008
 294.3'675092--dc22
 [B]
                                         2008040875

www.kodansha-intl.com

CONTENTS

PART ONE

The End and the Beginning

Resolve

I awoke to the sound of rain. The long dark night, stretching interminably without beginning or end, I'd gone through alone. Yet at some point in the blackness of night I'd fallen asleep, slipping into what now seemed an unthinkably deep and quiet slumber.

It's raining, I thought. From between the covers I listened to the cold splat of rain on leaves in the garden, surprised to find myself so clearheaded. Apart from the unaccustomed interior of the room before my eyes, this was a perfectly ordinary morning, no different from any other.

When I left the old-fashioned inn, the wall clock was about to strike noon. After settling my bill, I placed my few remaining coins in the charity collection box on the counter and slid open the latticed front door. Fat drops of rain were still striking the cobblestones in the narrow lane outside. For a moment I hesitated, unwilling for the rain to stain the new split-toe socks in which my feet were awkwardly ensconced, but once I stepped outside it wouldn't matter anymore.

I was dressed in the standard travel garb of a Japanese Buddhist monk. On my freshly shaven pate was a mushroom-shaped hat of finely woven rice straw; my figure was draped in a black robe, with a wicker pack on my chest and another on my back; my legs and feet were encased in white leggings, white split-toe socks, and simple straw sandals. Thus attired, I plunged out into the rain.

The road to the Eiheiji monastic complex stretched peacefully through rolling hills that spread out in all directions like ripples on a lake. A single road. I pondered this. Roads come into being as people begin to travel with new purpose in places previously unmarked, each minuscule step helping to wear a path in the ground. This road in particular evoked that image for me. I started walking in silence, possessed of neither the means nor the will to fend off the falling rain, heading doggedly toward Eiheiji.

Branches of ancient trees intertwined thickly overhead, covering the leaden sky, while on either side, craggy rocks reminiscent of an ancient Chinese landscape painting jutted out of the hills. Everything in sight— road, trees, rocks—gleamed darkly in the spring rain, and through my feet rose the feel of the quickening earth. An eerie solemnity enveloped me and nearly took my breath away.

The notion of going off to become a Zen monk had hardened quickly to resolve. I told my parents about it one evening as we sat at the supper table.

"I've decided to go to Eiheiji."

"Oh, really?" responded my mother. "When are you going?" She sounded like she wanted to come along. The meaning of my "going" there had completely passed her by.

After I explained my decision, my parents' reaction was so muted that I felt rather deflated. They were of course surprised; but compared with having me forever popping off to unstable Asian countries or remote spots where no tourist ever set foot, my imminent death a continual worry, Eiheiji must have sounded far safer.

And so I went about my preparations to enter the monastery, settling first one matter, then another, sensing society's gravitational pull on me beginning to weaken little by little. It was comical, in a way: I'd grown weary of my life, had come to feel the entanglements of society so burdensome and disagreeable that I'd resolved to flee them by becoming a Zen Buddhist monk—and yet now that society's hold on me was slipping, I felt increasingly sad and sentimental.

In April, at the swimming pool where I swam a few laps every day on my way home from work, I would look out the big windows at the cherry trees in full bloom and murmur under my breath, *The last cherry blossoms.* On occasional clear days during the June rainy season, too-soon glimpses of summer's blue sky were oppressive. *This, too, is the last time*: the repeated thought made me want to gather all I saw in my arms and cherish it; and the subtle shifting of the seasons, gathering speed, filled me with sorrow and dread.

One weekend at the end of summer, Mineko came to visit me at my rented house in Zushi, a seaside town near Tokyo. Though it was past the season for sea bathing, we went for a swim. Afterward, we sat side by side on the veranda looking out at the little garden as if watching a movie.

"You know," she said, "when I heard you were going to become a monk, it didn't surprise me in the least."

"No? Why not?"

"I don't know. It just seemed so natural, I thought, well of course."

"Huh."

Mineko and I had been seeing each other since college. Our relationship was not clearly defined, but the times we shared were important to us both, the slight distance between us a sign of mutual consideration.

"This isn't a tragedy, is it?" she asked.

Caught off guard, I was speechless for a second. "Well—of course not."

"Anyway, I don't like it," she said. "And if this turns out to be tragic, I'll never forgive you."

I myself was confused. On the one hand, the prospect of starting my life over filled me with hope. On the other, I felt somehow like weeping out loud, as if it were indeed a tragedy.

Ice clinked in the glass of cold barley tea in Mineko's hand as she blurted out something else I hadn't seen coming: "Is it okay if I wait?"

"Wait for what?" I said, although I knew very well what she meant. "Can't wait to see me with my head shaved so you can jump up and down laughing, is that it? Forget it. Like I'm always saying, go find yourself some nice, respectable salaryman, fall madly in love, and get married on a desert island. I guess once I'm at Eiheiji I won't be able to go to your wedding, but I promise I'll say a sutra for your happiness."

Mineko was silent. Crying, I thought. The silence stretched on and on—the first such silence I'd ever felt between us. I was mixed up. I'd lost any determination I'd once had to make my way in society, could no longer live like others—I was running away. Mineko shouldn't concern herself about someone as hopeless as me. I wanted her to be happy. This was my fervent wish.

Without looking each other in the face, we went on sitting on the veranda and silently contemplated the sea, its summer sparkle starting to fade, as an occasional breeze swayed the maple branches in the garden.

By the time I was on the street that led up to the monastery gate, the rain had eased and the lead-colored sky was a shade lighter. On either side of the street, little souvenir shops crowded together like rows of inlaid stones, their colorful trinkets garish in the dull light. I lifted the brim of my rain-soaked hat to see what lay ahead, and stopped short. The giant cedars—there they were! The enormous trees, said to be seven centuries old, loomed imposingly through the rain. Below them would be the open gate to Eiheiji. I was here at last.

My decision to take the tonsure had been simple, a quick straightening of mental furniture. But ever since, like waves pounding the shore, the thought had kept coming back: *It's still not too late. There's still time to turn back.* Attachment to this world lingered in the recesses of my mind, periodically all but overwhelming me. And now, looking up at the cedars, I was engulfed by a final great wave. This was it, my last chance to retreat. My blood buzzed and I broke into a sweat, overawed by the majesty of the towering trees.

But in the end, I started walking forward again. I understood that I had no other choice. The flow of my life, at times crashing against

The End and the Beginning

boulders, and at times taking sluggish detours, had brought me this far. What could be more natural than to let that tide bear me on through the gate ahead?

As I walked on, I was surprised by the heaviness of my waterlogged sandals. The rain-swollen asphalt beneath my frozen feet felt oddly soft, as if I were sinking into wet earth with each step. And then all physical sensation, till now anesthetized, came rushing back. I realized I was wet and cold through and through. The straps of the wicker pack dug into my shoulders as if weighted down by countless anxieties and forlorn hopes. I was trembling in body and spirit. My feet grew still heavier, the drenching rain still colder.

I was just making my way past a tea shop when suddenly the door clattered open and an old woman hobbled out. She came straight over to me and declared: "Good luck, young man!"

That did it. Hot tears streamed down my frozen cheeks. I didn't know why I was crying. The tears came without stop. It was as if a dam had burst, as if along with the tears I was shedding all the disappointment and heartache, the regret and bitter longings I had dragged with me. I wanted to lift my voice and sob until the swirl of emotions within me was washed clean away.

I can still remember the heat of the tears coursing down my cheeks that day.

Drying my eyes, I found myself standing at the foot of the hill leading to the temple known as Jizo Cloister—first port of call for Eiheiji initiates like myself. As I looked up at the building, I felt no more distress. All that was left for me to do was climb this hill. Looking back, I realized it had taken many long years for me to reach this place. Scene after scene from my former life played before my eyes. When I finished climbing this hill, something of my life would end. One by one, the faces of my parents and friends rose and fell away in my mind. To each one I murmured, *Thank you* and *Goodbye*. And then I started up the hill.

Jizo Cloister

When I came to the top of the slope, following instructions I'd received beforehand, I struck the wooden gong next to the entrance three times with all my might. Each blow made a hard, dry crack that reverberated in the core of my being.

Jizo Cloister is a subsidiary temple where those who have applied to undergo training at Eiheiji spend their initial night, and receive preliminary inspection and instruction. It represents the first line of demarcation between the lay world and the Buddhist realm.

After striking the gong I stepped up to the entrance, where two others were already standing in stiff silence, eyes on the ground. Wordlessly I followed their example, positioning myself facing the cloister. What might happen next I had no idea. I took a deep breath and closed my eyes. In the emptiness spreading behind me I could hear the soft echo of raindrops splattering from the deep eaves to the stone pavement below. Now and then one or two more petitioners would come along and strike the gong, until finally there were eight of us. We stood motionless, our faces tight lipped and anxious.

At some point the rain cleared and soft sunshine leaked through the clouds, lighting up the temple walls. Then the door, till now tightly closed, abruptly opened. Before our eyes there appeared a monk, on his face a scowl so bitter that he might have been shouldering all the discontent in the world. Following the orders he barked at us, we each shouted out our name in turn, summoning all our strength to yell as loud as possible.

"Can't hear you!" he'd snap in reply. "If that's the best you can do, you'll never make it here! Turn around and go home!" Of course, he could hear us perfectly well. This sort of absurd exchange is a means of testing the petitioner's determination.

Again and again we raised our voices, yelling with such might that it seemed blood would spurt from our throats. As the shouting match continued, those whose responses won approval were permitted to take off their sandals and disappear behind the heavy door. Finally I was left standing alone. With every shout my voice grew hoarser, making it harder and harder to yell. How much longer could this go on, I wondered. The chill sun sank lower in the sky, its rays growing fainter, until it disappeared behind the temple eaves and I was embraced by the cold mountain air. When finally I was granted permission to remove my sandals, the mountain had begun fading into the blackness of night and my feet felt like blocks of ice. I slipped off my wet, stiff footwear and crossed the threshold.

The door opened on a plain, snug main hall. Just inside the entrance was an inkstone and a sheet of paper, where I was told to write down my name and address. The names of the other seven were already there, inscribed in order. Adding my name to theirs would mean severing my ties to the outer world once and for all. There was nothing I wanted more—yet in the moment before the first drop of ink stained the page, the brush trembled in my hand.

After watching me complete this task, the monk told me to sit in formal kneeling position on the tatami-matted floor and wait for further instructions. He then disappeared. The others were already seated in silence, facing straight ahead. Silently I folded my stiff legs under me and took my place behind them.

Time slowly passed. Had there been a clock on the wall, I would have lacked the presence of mind to look at it, but something else let me know the passage of time, like it or not: the steadily mounting discomfort in my legs. Slowly the tatami turned hard as stone and my legs became dead to every sensation but pain. I twisted in growing distress until, feeling faint, I happened to glance up and see that the other seven were struggling too. As the last to be let in, I'd been sitting here a shorter time than any of them. Their suffering was surely many times greater than mine. I straightened my back, ashamed.

All at once the ceiling light came on. While we were battling the pain in our legs, darkness had set in. The monk returned and began issuing brisk orders. Supper, it seemed, was the next order of business. Along one side of the main hall we arranged long tables in a three-sided

The End and the Beginning

square and sat down to a simple vegetarian meal served in individual red lacquered bowls. The largest bowl held rice, the second largest miso soup, the smallest a few boiled vegetables. Finally, a bowl containing yellow slices of pickled radish was passed around and we each helped ourselves with chopsticks, setting our portion on our rice bowl lid.

When he had made sure that everything was ready, our leader gave a brief explanation and instructed us to repeat with him something called the The Five Reflections, in time to the sound of wooden clappers. As the measured beat of the clappers rang out, everyone began to intone the chant. I was taken aback to discover that I was the only one who didn't know the words.

All this time I'd been too tense to feel hunger, but now, with a hot meal before me, I was suddenly famished. It tasted heavenly: rice mixed with barley, miso soup containing fried tofu, translucent slices of boiled radish. Yet there was no time to savor the food. All too soon, a large kettle of hot tea was passed around. I took it from my neighbor and began to pour tea into my empty rice bowl, then swore under my breath, realizing my mistake: without thinking, I'd eaten all of my pickled radish. Before the meal, we'd been pointedly told not to do that. You were supposed to pour tea into your bowl, rub the inside of the bowl clean with a slice of pickled radish, then eat the radish and swallow the tea. Well, I'd eaten mine already and that was that. I went through the motions of picking something up in my chopsticks and sliding it around the inside of the bowl, then drank my tea with an innocent air. The flavor of sweet-smelling roasted tea filled my mouth.

After our meal, several others came to inspect our belongings. We seated ourselves in two facing rows, laid our wicker packs in front of us, and began to empty them as told. Before coming, we'd been instructed exactly what to bring: two small wicker packs filled with designated items and a cushion for sitting. In the front pack went a mantle, document of heritage,[1] scroll,[2] copy of *Treasury of the True Dharma Eye*,[3] certificate of permission to enter the monastery, seal, health insurance card, and a set of bowls and eating utensils, as well as one thousand yen[4] to cover the cost of a funeral in case of death during training. In the second pack went a toothbrush and toothpaste, safety razor, two kinds of white socks (with split toes and without), and a sewing kit. We were to wrap the packs in a prescribed way, using gray cotton cloths, and bring them with us to Eiheiji.

Our packs and their contents were checked, and anything not on the list was confiscated. I had a handkerchief taken away and, looking around, saw others relieved of cash, watches, soap, and medicine. Someone's supply of tissues brought in anticipation of hay fever fared no better. All these things were placed in plastic bags, each one inscribed with the owner's name.

Then we were told to repack everything and wrap it all again in the gray cloths. Not just for wrapping, these cloths would also serve as facecloth, napkin, or dustcloth, as the need arose. We proceeded to wind them again around our wicker packs in a ritualized procedure that was both complicated and beautiful. When I had finished, I looked up and saw that one of my neighbors was making no progress.

"Why can't you do it?" yelled one of the monks in charge. "You didn't wrap these yourself in the first place, did you? Why the hell not?" He slapped the fumbler hard across the cheek, delivering a ringing blow that made all eyes turn that way. The hapless victim's eyes widened at this unexpected violence and he trembled, speechless, while the rest of us froze. The unfolding of events thus far had seemed unremarkable, an illusion that was now shattered as the terrifyingly dark reality of our situation set in. What sort of monstrous place had we stumbled into?

When our belongings had been inspected, we stood up for an inspection of our attire. Here, too, we'd been notified ahead of time what was required. The day of our arrival we were to dress in a plain black monk's robe and short mantle over a knee-length kimono of any plain color but white, with a long, black cloth belt, a stiff, wide sash, white leggings, white split-toe socks, and a deep-brimmed hat of finely woven rice straw. Underwear was to be long and white, cut off at the elbows and knees. Glasses had to have black frames.

When everyone was lined up properly, we disrobed in unison, item by item, following instructions. Every time we took something off, we learned the correct way of folding it. Finally we stood in just our underwear. After that in turn had been inspected, we took up our folded garments and, step by step, learned the correct way of putting each one on.

At Eiheiji, maintaining a tidy appearance in accordance with the rules of etiquette is an essential part of monastic discipline. Yet only two days before, all eight of us had been ordinary young men accustomed to modern, Western-style attire. Unlike Western clothing, which conforms to the shape of the body, traditional Japanese clothing is cut in straight lines: learning to wear it takes time. More than one of us struggled with the task and received a sharp reprimand.

Finally, after everyone was presentable, we were drilled in the basic procedures for rites and services, beginning with hand positions. First we were taught an expression of reverence, gratitude, or humility in which the palms are joined with the fingers aligned, the fingertips held just below the nose. Then we learned to make a fist with the left hand, place it in the center of the chest, and cover it with the open right hand, fingers closed. Basically, except when sitting or making a gesture of reverence, the hands were always to be in this position. Standing or walking with arms dangling loose was not allowed. We also practiced keeping our elbows raised high. The relative height of the elbows is one way of telling a senior trainee from a fresh arrival.

"What's the matter with you?" barked one of the monks. "Is that the best you can do?" One member of the group, stiff with nervousness and fear, earned a cuff for slowness. But he reflexively warded off the blow, raising his arm in self-defense at the last second.

"What'd you do that for? Who the hell do you think you are?" The outraged monk landed slap after slap squarely on the guy's face. The dull, jarring smack of flesh on flesh resounded through the hall. The struck cheek turned scarlet and started to swell before our eyes.

"All of you, listen here!" bellowed the monk. "You do not resist, is that clear?"

For the first time in my life I saw a completely unresisting person suffer a one-sided attack. After that, additional instructions were delivered tersely, and anybody who failed to carry them out properly was slapped or kicked without mercy. Addled, defenseless, and keenly aware of our vulnerability, we scrambled feverishly to learn.

Absolute submission was a must. Under no circumstances were we to look any superior in the eye, and the only words that could come out of our mouths were yes and no. All of us had received a modern education, had been taught to believe in the principle of equality as a human right. We had also learned that the basis of proper communication lies in looking straight at the other person and couching one's opinion carefully in appropriate language. These beliefs were stripped from us that first night. Each man's conception of his own existence, built up over the course of his lifetime, was casually and completely ignored.

Once the protocol had been drilled into us via shouts, blows, and kicks, it was time for bed. We took out the bedding piled behind sliding doors and laid it on the floor. I wanted only to go straight to sleep, but sleep refused to come. I turned restlessly again and again. Even had I been able to close my eyes and drift off, the day ahead promised new horrors. At the thought, my chest tightened and I felt as if I were suffocating—as if I'd fallen into icy water in pitch dark. Wherever I looked, there was no bank to crawl up on, no log to cling to. Flailing my arms and legs to keep my head above water took all my strength. Yet having come this far, I couldn't turn back. Entrance and exit alike were now painted over, blotted out. I was trapped.

As my mind whirled with these agitating thoughts, I glanced over and saw that others, too, lay unable to sleep, staring empty eyed at the dark ceiling. The thought that it wasn't only me that was suffering, that I had companions in agony, was my only solace.

I closed my eyes and listened. The low roar of water—whether the sound of rain or the crash of rapids against boulders, I couldn't tell—reverberated from afar through the darkness of Jizo Cloister.

Dragon Gate

"Your seniors got up early to make this ginger tea for you," said the monk in charge next morning. "It'll warm you up. Drink it thankfully, warm yourselves, and head for the Main Gate."

Pale amber tea was poured into my thick white teacup, giving off waves of steam that curled into the air. I brought the teacup to my mouth and, as a whiff of ginger met my nostrils, the horrors of the previous night dissolved into oblivion. The hot sweet tea slid down the back of my throat and through my insides, raising my body temperature ever so slightly.

The night in Jizo Cloister had been extremely short. My mind had kept traveling in meaningless circles, pursuing thoughts that could have no possible effect on my surroundings. Just as I was wondering if I was never to sleep again, the ceiling light came on and it was time to get up.

Beyond the windowpanes, the night was ink black, without a sign of morning. We washed our faces and had a simple chanting service, followed by breakfast and cleanup, then lined up as on the day before.

After a pause for the hot ginger tea, the heavy door of the cloister that had been closed since dusk was reopened and, packs in hand, we headed in a line outside.

As the predawn chill pierced my body, I shivered, awakened to the reality of this moment. I finished tying on my straw sandals, still sodden and cold to the touch from yesterday's rain, and stood up. On a sudden impulse, I turned and looked back. Yes—that was where I'd stood for so long the previous day, distracted, wondering whether I'd ever be let in. In the end I'd shed these sandals and crossed the threshold. The place was the same as yesterday, but I myself was changed. During the single night I'd spent behind that door, everything that had made me *me* had disappeared. Now, looking back, I could see no evidence that I'd ever even been there. My shadow, my footprints, and all other physical signs of my presence had vanished without a trace.

We fastened on our wicker packs, front and back, tied our hats under the chin, and left Jizo Cloister behind us, following after our leader in single file. Only the muffled rhythm of our footsteps sounded in the early-morning mist that hung in the woods. Every tree and bush seemed to be holding its breath, waiting for the moment of dawn just ahead. All nature lay in perfect stillness.

We went past bits of bluish white snow that lingered under shrubbery, and followed the path as it curved around to the left. After a while we found ourselves on the formal approach to the main Eiheiji temple, a pathway paved with rectangular stones. All around us was a dense forest of giant cedars. Our leader halted just before a slight step up in

Eat Sleep Sit

the path. A pair of stone pillars, one on either side, bore matching carved inscriptions:

> One drop of water in the bottom of the dipper
> One hundred billion people dip into the stream

The reference was to an incident in which Dogen, the Zen patriarch who founded Eiheiji in 1244, preached a sermon to a drop of water in the bottom of his dipper before returning it to the mountain stream.

Ahead, the stone pathway cut through the trees, straight into the Eiheiji compound. My heart thudded with excitement. Our guide explained: "This is the general gate to the temple, called the Dragon Gate. The name comes from an old saying that on entering the sea of Buddhist truth, even the smallest fish is instantly transformed into a great dragon. When anyone seeking to undergo monastic discipline steps through this gate, he changes into a dragon, and when he finishes his training here and reenters the world, he goes back to being a fish."

The Dragon Gate consisted simply of a rise in the path of an inch or two, directly between the two stone pillars. A person might easily pass by it unawares, seeing only a place where he might trip if not careful. But for me, that tiny rise loomed high.

Following in the footsteps of the others, I crossed over the dividing line and stepped into the sacred precincts of Eiheiji. Was I a dragon now too? Wondering, I tilted the brim of my hat and looked up at the dark canopy of cedar branches overhead. Cold blue air brushed my cheek.

Our conical hats formed a short, straight line as we continued on our way, surrounded by the seven-hundred-year-old trees. Throughout their unimaginably long life span they had stood sentinel, silently marking the progress of all who found their way here. Step by step, the outer world fell farther away, and the Main Gate drew closer. My pulse quickened.

Before long, the stone-paved pathway ended in front of the Imperial Gate, which is for the exclusive use of visiting emperors. We turned right along a narrower path beside a high wall. Here stood the workshops and storehouses of the army of carpenters who carried out all temple repairs and construction. The path took a turn upward and passed alongside another smallish gate called the Gate of Unimpeded Truth, continuing to zigzag until all at once the view ahead opened up. *This is it!* I thought wildly.

Before our eyes loomed the Main Gate, amid great cedars that soared heavenward from lichen blanketing the ground. My heartbeat thundered in my ears. With each step forward, the gate grew bigger. I pressed steadily on behind the others until all at once, with no time to sort out the confused welter of my thoughts, I found myself standing directly in front of the massive Chinese-style gate. Its tiered roof, having long withstood the harshness of the elements, projected an air of unassailable dignity. At the top was a board bearing the solemn words First Center of Soto Zen in Japan, copied from a scroll that Emperor Goen'yu had written and donated to Eiheiji in 1372. The stern gazes of the guardian deities known as the Four Heavenly Kings, enshrined on either side of the gate, bore down on us imposingly.

Our guide lined us up facing the gate and then went away, leaving us with instructions to strike the wooden gong hanging at one side three times apiece and wait for someone to appear. The others each took their turn, until only I was left. I stepped up to the gong. It was made of a thick slab of hard wood, yet the center was so hollowed out where it had been repeatedly struck that it seemed as if the next blow would smash right through it. How many seekers had struck it altogether, harboring what hidden emotions? I myself had dreamed countless times of standing here: sometimes a bright, auspicious dream of setting sail on a shining sea, sometimes a nightmare of mounting steps to the guillotine with nowhere else to go. Every twist and turn along the way had given rise to new hopes and disappointments; yet in the end here I was, standing before the Eiheiji gate, about to strike the wooden gong. I did not stop to wonder whether this was the right thing to do or a horrible mistake. Time, I thought, would tell.

I raised the wooden mallet high in my right hand, and brought it down again with all my might. The dry, clear vibration shattered the early dawn tranquility, echoing through the buildings of the temple compound.

Main Gate

It no longer bothered me to be kept waiting. The piercing cold in the woods and the icy paving stones that leached heat from my body through the soles of my feet mattered little now. It was rather the realization that I was about to be swallowed in an enormous current—swept away—that wrecked my composure.

As the frenetic pounding of my heart passed its zenith, however, I felt a sudden loss of energy, as if a knot of threads had somehow come easily undone. How long we'd been standing before the gate when this happened I don't know, but soon thereafter, a monk came out and began to walk slowly around us, radiating menace. With his every step, the wooden slats laid on the stone walkway creaked. There was no other sound to break the silence. When I felt his presence beside me, I tensed and held my breath.

After a short time he walked up to one person and inquired in a low, even voice: "What did you come here for?" The suddenness of the query left the addressee briefly at a loss, but he managed to reply in a loud voice: "I came for monastic discipline!"

"You did? What is monastic discipline?"

No reply.

"I asked you what it is."

Still no reply.

"You told me you came here for monastic discipline. Or was that some made-up answer you don't even understand?"

"No!"

"Then tell me."

The petitioner was unable to account for what he had said. Even had he not been rattled, the question was immense, not amenable to an easy answer.

The low controlled voice became a yell. "No one so spineless can come through this gate! Go home!" The wretched fellow received an unceremonious shove that sent him sprawling. After tumbling all the way to the bottom of the stone steps, he hastily picked himself up and climbed back to the top—only to be knocked back down without mercy.

"Didn't you hear me? Go on, go home!"

Another ignominious tumble. Again and again he was sent flying, again and again he crawled desperately back up, battered and sore. Even had he wanted to run away, family obligations made quitting unthinkable. Eiheiji is the central training center of the Soto school of Zen Buddhism, and the majority of its trainees are, like him, sons of priests at branch temples around the country—young men who are recent graduates of Buddhist universities, where they have enjoyed the pleasures of youth. Still bearing traces of that agreeable interlude, each one shaves his head, puts on a black monk's robe, and trudges to Eiheiji. Some, having gratefully received their father's tutelage, are full of solemn resolve to devote their lives to the priesthood. Others come with mixed feelings about the inseparable ties that bind them to their families.

In some ways it is probably very easy just to glide along on rails laid out before one was born, moving straight ahead without taking any byways. But anyone who has received a modern education with emphasis on the concept of "freedom" cannot help entertaining grave doubts about an environment where deciding how to live one's own life is not allowed, where one's only choice is to renounce all for the sake of family tradition.

There is a misapprehension that everyone who comes to Eiheiji has had a religious awakening and is embarking on the path of Buddhism in willing search of enlightenment, but this is emphatically not the case. Many are full of resentment at the burden laid on them. Hearts torn to pieces, they are forced to swallow their tears and scotch long-cherished dreams in order to come. Weighted down by the eager expectations of family and parishioners, seen off with flowery speeches of congratulation, they bid farewell to the freedom of their past lives and make their lonely way to the mountains of Fukui Prefecture. However much they might wish to run away, they have no other refuge. And so, however many times they are sent flying down the steps, they scramble right back up.

The rest of us were subjected to the same sort of harsh interrogation. Yelled at, slapped, kicked down the steps. Compared with the enormity of the Main Gate, our tumbling bodies were tiny and insignificant. Compared with the passage of centuries here, our short lives—a mere two to three decades at best—were a blink of time. And now, before this towering, imposing gate, we were being flicked away like so many motes of dust. Yet we endured it without resisting, hanging on desperately to our resolve.

In the end, the monk stood calmly in the center of the gate and indicated the wooden pillars on either side. "Can any of you tell me what's written here?"

On each pillar hung an oblong board engraved with flowing calligraphic writing in classical Chinese. The matched set dated from 1820 and was the work of Mankai Hakuyo, then abbot of Eiheiji. The boards' weather-beaten appearance told plainly of the intervening years, but the writing on them was magnificent, rendered with such spirit that the characters seemed poised to fly up into the air.

The monk read aloud the inscription on the right, transposing it into Japanese: "The tradition here is strict; no one, however wealthy, important, or wise may enter through this gate who is not wholehearted in his pursuit of truth." He then read off the one on the left: "The gate has no door or chain, but is always open; any person of true faith can walk through it at any time." He went on, "You should come through this gate only if you are prepared to give your all to monastic discipline. For the last time, ask yourself why you are here. Only those with the proper resolve should undo their sandals and come in."

For a moment, deep silence reigned. Then, spontaneously, we all began to remove our sandals. When we were barefoot, we formed a line and, setting our packs and hats down before us, prostrated ourselves three times in the direction of the Buddha Hall, straight ahead, to signal our arrival. With each bow I lowered my forehead to the wooden floor, offering myself in body and spirit. I felt deeply stirred in ways I could not have explained. Just as mist among the trees vanishes in the rays of the morning sun, I felt my heart growing lighter, as if a great weight had been lifted from my shoulders.

Finishing this ritual, at last we followed the monk through the Main Gate and on into the compound, turning now left, now right in the zigzagging corridors, proceeding ever deeper into the sanctified space. The dim recesses of the compound were eerily still. Everything I saw

The End and the Beginning

gave off a dull, heavy sheen; everything existed in solemn simplicity. As we made our way into the heart of Eiheiji, it felt as if the flow of time had reversed.

Temporary Quarters

The corridor ended in front of a sign in large black letters announcing that this was the reception area. We filed into two adjoining rooms on the left, partitioned by sliding doors. The inner room was an anteroom for new arrivals, where we took off our wicker packs, laid them against a wall, and then sat cross-legged facing the wall while we waited for our next instructions. In a small alcove hung an india-ink scroll. The eight of us sat in the eight-mat tatami room without making a sound, hardly daring to breathe.

Perhaps an hour later, the sliding doors clattered open and several monks, who would act as our instructors for the coming week, came trooping in. The tension in the room increased palpably. One of them addressed us roughly: "Listen. You guys know where you are now? This isn't the outside world anymore. Show us one sign you can't handle the life here, and you'll get thrown out on your ear. Is that clear?" Unsure whether to respond, we continued to sit in silence, holding our collective breath.

A shout rang out: "What kind of a way is that to sit!" Someone grabbed the fellow next to me by the collar and hauled him out of line. "Weren't you listening? If you can't do this amount of sitting, you'll never make it! Maybe you'd better pack it in right now!" About to be summarily ejected, the offender howled in protest. The monks all gave him a kick before releasing him. He scurried back to his place.

"The same goes for the rest of you," warned the voice. "So don't you forget it!"

With that, the door banged shut, leaving an unpleasant atmosphere in the room. Slack jawed with surprise, having failed yet again to make any concerted response, we silently straightened our backs.

Eventually, the monk who had met us at the Main Gate—our lead instructor—appeared and told us to enter our names, places of origin, and other information in a big ledger. It was an ancient tome, filled with the writing of many who'd come before us. One by one we carefully added our names to theirs.

After the considerable time it took to do this, a simple meal was served, exactly like the one at Jizo Cloister the day before. By this time I no longer had any sensation of hunger and had even lost the ability to distinguish between food that was tasty or otherwise. I scarcely felt any sense of having eaten as, the meal over, we quickly shouldered our packs and followed the lead instructor out of the arrival room.

We filed back out past the sign in the corridor, past a communal study area, and down the stairs by the Monks' Hall. As before, the compound was filled with heavy silence, as if everything were coated in lead. At the bottom of the stairs we turned right and walked to the end of a narrow corridor. By this time we had been up and down so many stairs and through such a maze of dim passageways that none of us had any idea which way we were heading. As we filed along, feeling lost and confused, the lead instructor came to a halt in front of a signboard marked *Tangaryo*. Temporary Quarters.

Originally the term "tangaryo"—literally "quarters to [enter in the evening and] leave in the morning"—referred to a room in a Zen monastery set aside for the overnight stay of wandering monks. While it still refers to quarters for new arrivals, today the word signifies a place of weeklong probation. Newcomers' fledgling commitment is tested as they are stripped of the self-centered attitudes they've brought with them from the outside world and drilled in the obligatory rules and manners of monastic life. Practically the entire day, from early morning till nightfall, is spent sitting in the full lotus position facing the wall. Only after a full seven days of this harsh initiation does one begin the life of an Eiheiji trainee.

We went into the room, which contained neatly aligned tatami mats and little else. Nine men who had arrived a few days before us sat facing the back wall without moving or speaking. The atmosphere was tense, and we stiffened automatically.

The lead instructor indicated where each of us was to sit. When this was settled, we were each handed two sutra books and other items we would need in daily life: two nametags, a pair of indoor shoes, two towels, two white cleaning cloths. The shoes were more like slippers, consisting of black rubber soles with two leather straps that crossed over the top of the foot. For us newcomers the straps were white; those of our seniors were black.

Each item was already inscribed with its owner's name. At Eiheiji, it is customary to use the given name, not the surname, and the characters used to write the name are pronounced in Chinese style, not Japanese. I received the brand-new name Rosan. Names are funny things. They're just a handy convention for distinguishing oneself from other people; yet once I was assigned a new name, I felt as if I were no longer the same person.

Next the lead instructor made sure we all had our equipment, and showed us how to lay out the various things we would be needing. Our split-toe socks, the clasps neatly fastened, had to be carefully folded and laid just so between the appropriate items, facing the appropriate direction. Of our two books of sutras, one went on the right, the other on the left. When we folded our mantle and laid it down, it had to be perfectly aligned with the other things, not a fraction of an inch out of place.

"I won't explain this again. Starting tomorrow, anything that's not laid out exactly right gets taken away. Okay? Now turn to the wall and sit." With these words, he left the room.

The eight of us were lined up in the order we had been admitted to Jizo Cloister: Daikan, Tenshin, Yuho, Enkai, Kijun, Choshu, Doryu, and me. Our week of initiation was underway. Whether I could last out the week, whether I could learn all the rules I had to, I wasn't sure. But I felt the rhythm of this new life, now finally starting, with my whole body. I was eager to put myself to the test. I would give it my best shot, and if I still ended up having to drop out midway, I'd be satisfied. At least I would have taken my own measure. That in itself would be something. I drew my cushion over, crossed my legs, took a deep breath, and quietly faced the wall.

Lavatory

At some point after we began sitting, the same bunch of monks who had burst in on us before showed up again to continue with their task of instructing us in the finer points of Eiheiji rules and etiquette.

Dogen, Eiheiji's thirteenth-century founder, laid down specific rules covering every aspect of monastic life. Monastic discipline consists in the scrupulous observance of those rules, and the least effort expended in doing so is, itself, nothing less than the Dharma—Buddhist truth. In other words, discipline at Eiheiji has nothing to do with attaining supernatural powers or doing special meditation, nor does it entail harsh penance or mortification of the flesh. Rather, it is to be found in the everyday practice of Zen rules. There is no differentiation between means and end. Monastic discipline is not something done in order to gain enlightenment; rather, the faithful observance of monastic discipline *is* enlightenment, in and of itself. It cannot therefore be left to others, but must be performed with one's own body and mind. In the words of Dogen: "Dignity is itself the Dharma. Propriety is itself the essence of the house."

To this day, discipline at Eiheiji is observed in strict accordance with Dogen's teachings. Now we eight, too, guided by our instructors, would attempt to bring our every movement in line with the same rules followed by so many before us.

Our first lesson concerned the rules of the lavatory. Dogen saw truth in every action of daily life and established corresponding rules of comportment; the act of elimination was no exception. In an essay in Dogen's *Treasury of the True Dharma Eye* entitled "Cleansing" he wrote out detailed rules for the elimination of bodily waste:

First, when you go to the toilet, always take your long cloth belt with you. Fold it in two and drape it over the crook of your left elbow. When you go in, hang the belt over the bar. Drape it the same way as over your elbow. If you are wearing a mantle, hang that over the bar alongside the belt. Hang them neatly side by side so that they will not fall down. Do not throw them over the bar carelessly.

Take off your robe and hang it beside the belt. Bind the robe with the belt and stand before it with your hands pressed together in reverence. Next tie back the sleeves of your kimono with the cord you have for that purpose.

Then go to the sink, fill a bucket with water, and carry it to the toilet stall in your right hand. You must not fill the bucket to the top. It should be no more than nine-tenths full. At the entrance to the stall, take off your footwear and change into slippers made of woven reeds.

When you are inside, close the door with your left hand. Next, pour a little water from the bucket into the toilet. When you have done this, place the bucket in its allotted place in front of you. Face the toilet in a standing position and snap your fingers three times. As you do this, your left hand should be clenched at your left hip.

Then, holding the hem of your garment, place one foot on either side of the toilet in the floor, squat down, and relieve yourself. Do not soil the floor on either side of the toilet, or in front or in back of it. During this time you should maintain silence. You should not chat with people on the other side of the wall or sing out loud. You should not spread snot or spittle around. You should not suddenly strain to defecate. You should not scribble on the wall. You should not poke the ground with the scraper.

When you have finished, clean yourself with the scraper. It is also possible to use paper, but not wastepaper. You should not use paper with writing on it.

Next, after you have used the scraper or paper, cleanse yourself in this manner: hold the bucket in your right hand and thoroughly wet your left hand. Using your left hand as a dipper, scoop up some water and rinse the part of the body from which you have urinated three times. Then, in the same way, cleanse the part of the body from which you have defecated. Wash everything thoroughly, as if doing Buddhist practice, and make each place clean. As you do so, you must not tip the bucket roughly or spill water.

When you have finished, set down the bucket, wipe the scraper and dry it. Using paper is acceptable. The parts of the body from which you have urinated and defecated should also be well wiped and dried. Next, with your right hand, straighten the hem of your garment, and leave the toilet stall holding the bucket in your right hand. Take off the reed slippers and change back into your own footwear. Go to the sink and return the bucket to its original place.

Next you should wash your hands. With your right hand, pick up the spoon in the ashes, spoon some ashes, and lay them on the tiles. Sprinkle the ashes with water and, using your right hand, wash the hand that had contact with feces or urine. Set your hand on the tile and scrub it as if to polish it. For example, rub as if polishing a rusty sword on a whetstone. In this way, scrub your hand three times. Then take a handful of sand, sprinkle it with water, and scrub your hand three times. After that, in your right hand take some bean powder, soak it in some water from the bucket, and wash both your hands, rubbing them together. You should wash all the way up your arms. Three times with ashes, three times with sand, once with powdered bean. Seven times in all is suitable.

Next, wash out the large bucket. Do not use bean powder, sand, or ashes for this, just hot or cold water. When you have washed it once, refill it with fresh water and wash both your hands. Always use your right hand to grasp the ladle. When you do this, you must not clatter the ladle or be in any haste. See that you do not scatter the bean powder, or spill water around and get the area wet.

Next, wipe your hands on the communal towel. You may also wipe them using your own towel. When you have finished wiping your hands, go over to the robe hanging on the bar. After placing your palms together in reverence, untie the belt and put the robe on. Then place the belt over the crook of your left elbow and apply fragrance to your hands. There will be communal fragrance hanging from the bar, made from scented wood in the shape of a vase. Rub the wood between your palms and the scent will transfer naturally to your skin.

To do these things is in itself to purify the Buddha realm and beautify the Buddhist paradise, so do them prudently, without haste. You must not be in a hurry to finish and leave. You must not forget the truth of preaching Buddhism in secret, in the lavatory.

Led by our instructors, we walked down the narrow, dim passage-way toward the lavatory building. Inside, the wooden walls and pillars had all been assiduously polished, and glowed a deep amber in the light from a small electric bulb. The lavatory building was divided into two rooms. Next to the wall in the first room was a bar to hang one's robe on, just as Dogen had described. This was the changing room. At the front of the changing room was a statue of Ucchusma Vajrapala, puri-fier of the defiled, behind which hung a framed quotation from Dogen's "Cleansing" essay. Off to one side was the door leading into the second room, which contained ordinary ceramic squat toilets.

The instructors lined us up and began to explain the protocol, which is as follows. On entering the changing room, you press your hands together in the gesture of reverence in front of the statue, bow your head, and silently chant. (This is one of the three places in the compound where speaking aloud is forbidden; the others are the bath and the Monks' Hall.)

> As I eliminate bodily waste,
> I vow with all sentient beings: may we
> remove all filth and destroy the poisons
> of greed, anger, and foolishness.

After that, you remove your robe, leaving the kimono. You fold the robe into a neat rectangle and hang it over the bar. If you intend to urinate, you take your belt and tie the robe to the bar. But if you intend to defecate, you leave the robe folded over the bar as it is and use the belt to tie your sleeves out of the way.

Next, you take off your shoes, line them up neatly next to the wall, and change into toilet slippers. To urinate, you proceed straight to the gutter at the back of the inner room, which is set in the floor by the wall, with a step up in front of it. When you come up to the gutter, you stand facing it and snap your fingers three times, signifying purification. After that you step up with your right foot first, laying your left hand on the handrail—specifically, the fourth and fifth fingers of the left hand. (Those two fingers, known as the "defiled fingers," may not be used to touch any sacred object, as they are the ones used in the toilet.) Then you squat down to urinate; urinating from a standing position is not allowed. When finished, you step back down, right foot first, and again snap your fingers three times.

To defecate, first take up a pail of water from the sink in the inner room. The pail is made of stainless steel and holds a generous cupful of water. Holding it with the defiled fingers of the left hand, you proceed to a toilet stall and rap on the door. If there is no response, you go inside and set the pail down in its allotted place. Facing the toilet, you snap your fingers three times before squatting down to defecate. Afterward you chant silently again before cleansing yourself with the water in the pail just as Dogen specified. (Eiheiji has dispensed with the scraper.)

> As I cleanse myself with water,
> I vow with all sentient beings: may all
> enter on the supreme path of Buddhism
> and escape the world of delusion.

When you have finished cleansing yourself, you silently recite another chant, flush, and snap your fingers three times as before.

> As I flush away waste,
> I vow with all sentient beings: may all
> possess patience in body and spirit
> and attain utter purity.

Then you take the pail with you out of the stall and over to the sink, fill it with water, and set it back where it first was. When you have done all this, the last step is to wash your hands at the sink, which has a basin containing disinfectant mixed with cresol. You disinfect your hands, rinse them in water, and wipe them on a communal towel hanging up at one side. Then you return to the changing room and put on your shoes and robe. After tidying yourself, you bring your hands together in reverence and bow once more to the statue of Ucchusma Vajrapala before leaving the building.

"When you desire to go to the toilet, you should allow plenty of time, not waiting till you must rush." This counsel appears in *Rules of Purity for Chan Monasteries*, an eight-volume work by the Chinese monk Changlu Zongze, compiled in 1103. In other words, always have time to spare so that your demeanor in the toilet will not be rough and unbecoming.

But what if the urge came on suddenly? Would there be time to go through all this rigmarole? Would this method of cleansing always suffice? Only after experiencing monastic life did I discover that on a strict vegetarian diet, the need to evacuate the bowels does not occur with sudden urgency. Stool consistency, moreover, comes to resemble that of a small herbivore.

In 1227 Dogen returned to Japan after five years of study at a number of monasteries in China. Shortly thereafter, at Koshoji, the first Soto Zen monastery in Japan, he said this:

I did not go to many monasteries, but I happened to meet with the head of the one on Mount Tiantong.[5] Seeing that his eyes were horizontal and his nose vertical, I was no longer deceived, and came home empty handed.

In other words, he studied under a famous Chan master in China, saw that the man's eyes were horizontal and his nose vertical, and came home armed only with that knowledge, unburdened by sutras or Buddhist statues. Eyes horizontal, nose vertical: for human beings, what could be more natural, or more true?

Soon after that, Dogen began to write this essay on cleansing. Certainly, defecation is not something that people talk about willingly in public. Yet however valuable the act of eating may be, without the corresponding physiological process of waste elimination, the life of the individual could not be maintained. This too is completely natural. The natural, human act of elimination is, like all of life itself, replete with truth, and this is what maintains the harmony behind the existence of all things. This knowledge must have welled up fervently in the youthful Dogen as he began to write.

Facing the Wall

We sat. No one moved. Legs crossed, backs perpendicular to the floor, eyes on the wall in front of us: for now, nothing was asked of us but to sit like this. Until now, I suddenly realized, I had spent my life exerting mental and physical strength in a desperate attempt to fill the emptiness of passing time. Now I was turned around, literally, in the opposite direction. Without exerting my mind or body in the least, losing even the awareness of myself sitting, all I had to do was just sit and not think.

But having until a couple of days ago been soaking in the ease of the world, I found "just sitting" to be far from simple. The more I tried not to think, the more my mind wandered. And that was far from the worst of it. Before long, such pain shot through my legs that I felt my bones grate in protest. The pain slowly spread from the bones to the flesh, until entertaining random thoughts was no longer possible. Uncertainty as to the limits on this pain—how long we would be required to stay this way—only served to amplify it.

But uncrossing my legs was not an option. Nothing could have been easier—but then the faint sense that I was starting to make some kind of progress would evaporate. I would lose sight of everything. And even if I turned back now, I had no means of retrieving the past I'd cut myself off from.

Inwardly I scoffed at my pain: "Bah. Compared to the suffering of birth-and-death,[6] this is nothing."

Buddha Bowl

By the time the instructors came back, the pain in everyone's legs was at its peak. As soon as they came in, they ordered us to get up, bring in the long narrow tables piled up out in the corridor, and arrange them in the room. We quickly fell to the task, happy to be released from the torture of sitting, staggering on still-numb legs as we followed directions. When we'd finished, we got out our bowls as instructed and took our places at the tables.

The set of bowls and eating utensils known as *oryoki* includes everything needed at mealtimes. Nested into a large bowl are four others of successively smaller size, including a rice bowl, a soup bowl, and a pickle bowl. The smallest bowl is actually a saucer that fits snugly under the rounded bottom of the largest bowl to hold it steady. Usually the bowls are made of black lacquered wood. Originally they were made of pottery or iron; wood was deemed unacceptable because it stains easily. But at some point it was decided that lacquered wood did not violate any Zen precepts, and today its use is standard.

The set also includes what is called a "water board," a small board of lacquered wood that is used to protect the tatami mat from wet cloths and the like, and a place mat that folds in thirds, made of stiff paper coated in black lacquer or persimmon tannin. A small bag holds a spoon, chopsticks, and a cleaning stick, all made of lacquered wood. The spoon has a long, narrow handle and the chopsticks are squared to keep them from rolling; the cleaning stick, which is tipped with white cloth, is used at the end of the meal to rub off any bits of food adhering to the bowls and to wash them clean. All of these items are tied up and stored in a prescribed manner, along with a lap cloth and a drying cloth, in a dark gray cotton wrapper.

The term "oryoki" refers formally only to the largest bowl, which is not a mere eating bowl but has great symbolic significance. In a an essay in *Treasury of the True Dharma Eye* called "Buddha Bowl," Dogen stated that this bowl was handed down from the Buddha Sakyamuni to the ancestors, and to explain its significance he refers to the ancestors' everyday practice. Some have interpreted this to mean that the bowl is the body and mind of the buddhas and ancestors, others that it is their life. Yet others have maintained that the bowl is the physical transformation of the buddhas and ancestors, or that it is one with them—the embodiment of Buddhist teaching. Accordingly, we were taught to handle this bowl with special reverence, being careful always to hold it in both hands and never under any circumstances to allow it to come into contact with the defiled fingers of the left hand. We also learned that it is taboo to touch it directly with the lips.

In Zen monasteries, the practice of eating is done according to strict rules, not to satisfy hunger or appetite, but to carry out the teachings of Buddha. The act of eating is itself a Zen discipline.

Dogen attached particular importance to the act of eating. He spoke of the oneness of eating and the Dharma, or Buddhist truth, stating that the rules of conduct for meals are intrinsically the practice of Buddhism. So to conduct a meal in the proper way is not simply a matter of good table manners, but nothing less than the dignified enactment of Buddhist truth. At the same time, strict norms and detailed rules of etiquette are necessary to ensure that all can gather in the Monks' Hall without the slightest lapse or disarray and get on smoothly with the ceremonial meals. During our seven-day initiation we would have to thoroughly master these rules. This was to be our most difficult hurdle.

To begin with, the bowls and other implements had to be correctly laid out in a ritualized procedure. From the first untying of the knot in the wrapping cloth until everything is arranged in its proper place, the hands must move with smooth precision, carrying out the allotted tasks in the prescribed order without a second's wasted motion.

After untying the wrapping cloth, first you take out the water board and set it in front of your knees with the drying cloth and utensil bag on top. Then you open the lap cloth and place it on your lap. Next you unfold the mat, lay it down, and set the stack of nested bowls on top of it, at the left edge. You then lift out the top three bowls and place them in the center of the mat, leaving the largest bowl where it is. In the same way, lift out the remaining two and set them on the right, leaving them stacked. Now the bowls are arranged horizontally on the mat before you, in descending order of size from left to right; the largest, on the left, is for rice, the middle one is for soup, and the smallest, on the right, is for pickles. After that you take out the spoon, chopsticks, and cleaning stick from the bag and lay them in their proper positions at the top of the mat, each facing in the proper direction. From beginning to end, every gesture must be performed in correct, flowing sequence without interruption. The bowls are to be set out quickly and in absolute silence.

Next we learned the proper way of receiving food. No one serves himself; instead, food is always distributed by a server. Every detail of the ritualized procedure was spelled out for us: the gesture of respect beforehand, the manner and timing of offering one's bowl to be filled, the gesture of respect afterward. The Monks' Hall, where mealtimes would take place once we had finished our probation period, is one of three places of meditation where talking is forbidden, the other two being the toilet and the bath—so all communication with the server must be wordless. To indicate that the amount of food you've been served is sufficient, you lightly raise the index and middle fingers of the right hand. To indicate that you've been served everything, you lay your chopsticks across your bowl of soup.

When eating, you use both hands every time you take up or put down the spoon, chopsticks, or cleaning stick. Every time you handle a bowl, you do so using two hands. You eat with elbows held out to the sides, back straight; slumping over or leaning to one side is not allowed. You must not make any noise while eating. Above all, you must not drop any of the implements, a particularly grave offense.

Extra helpings are offered only once. Each person is allowed a second helping of rice and soup only. If you want an extra helping, you indicate this by first licking the tips of your chopsticks, using your hand to shield your mouth, and then laying the chopsticks on the mat with the tips pointing right. Otherwise, you set your chopsticks on top of the soup bowl and raise the index and middle fingers of the right hand as the server passes by.

When you have finished eating, you place your chopsticks on the mat with the tips facing left. A kind of tea, made using any rice that has burned at the bottom of the cooking pot, is then served, which you receive in the rice bowl. Its purpose is to soften sticky residue on the inside of the bowl. After tipping the bowl to wet the entire inner surface, you empty the tea first into the soup bowl, then the pickle bowl, and finally you drink it. Then you take the cleaning stick and, using the cloth-wrapped tip, scrub clean the inside of each bowl in turn. Next, plain hot water is served, which again you receive in your rice bowl and use to wash the inside of the bowl with the stick. When you have finished washing the rice bowl, you pour the water into the soup bowl, place the rice bowl in it sideways, and wash the outer surface and bottom; then you wipe it dry with your cloth and replace it on the left edge of the mat.

Next you wash the spoon and chopsticks, wipe them with the cloth, and put them back in the bag. Then, following the same procedure as before, you transfer the water into progressively smaller bowls, washing and wiping each one, and nesting them as you go. Finally, after washing the pickle bowl, you wash the cleaning stick in it, wipe it, and replace it in the bag.

Now the server brings in a small bucket and makes the rounds of the room. Everyone empties the remaining water in his pickle bowl into this bucket, leaving just a mouthful, which they then drink down. Then the smallest bowl is wiped and laid on top of the rest, the mat is folded and put away, and the lap cloth, utensil bag, water board, and drying cloth are all put away following the proper procedure. Finally all is tied up in the wrapping cloth, and the meal is over.

The oryoki set is the crystallization of the pure, fundamental essence of the act of eating. To reflect this essential purity, each item must be handled with supreme economy of motion. Movements of hand and bowl alike must occur in an irreducible minimum of space and time, without aimless and unnecessary fluttering.

The entire meal takes place in the space on top of the small mat. The bowls are laid out on it, the food is served and eaten on it, the utensils are washed on it; and in the end, the mat is folded and put away so that nothing remains. It is a marvel of concision. Yet precisely because this way of eating is so pure and so concise, considerable training is necessary to master it. Mealtimes would be punctuated with angry voices: "Look here! How many times do you people have to do it before you get it right! Listen to me. Until every one of you gets it right, nobody sets foot in the Monks' Hall! This initiation can go on for a month or even two for all I care. Is that clear?"

All one can do is physically absorb the flow of such a meal, sear it into memory through action. That is all—and for us it was the beginning of it all.

Evening Service

At some point the light streaming through the windows shifted, the shadows in the room began to lengthen, and we each put on our mantle and left the temporary quarters. Out in the covered walkway, the approach of evening was apparent in the pervading stillness. Only the sound of our footsteps could be heard.

The entire Eiheiji complex is connected by corridors and covered walkways that are fitted with stairs as necessary, following the natural configuration of the mountainside. We went through one corridor after another, following twists and turns until we arrived at the Buddha

Hall. Dedicated to the veneration of Sakyamuni Buddha, this hall is the heart of the temple. It is made entirely of stout zelkova timbers and has a stone floor in keeping with the architectural style of China's Song period (960–1279). On the central altar is a triad of the Buddhas of the Three Times: Amitabha, the Buddha of the past; Sakyamuni, the Buddha of the present; and Maitreya, the Buddha of the future. The frieze is intricately carved with the three auspicious trees—pine, bamboo, and plum—as well as engravings based on a variety of Zen teachings.

When we arrived, the hall was already filled with orderly rows of monks, and the evening service of sutra chanting was just about to begin. Such services take place three times daily at Eiheiji: morning, noon, and night. Unless the day in question is the death anniversary of a Zen patriarch, or some other special event, evening service is always held in the Buddha Hall. The passage to be recited is fixed according to the day. On days of the month ending in a one or a six, it is from the Peaceful Practices chapter of the Lotus Sutra. On days ending in two and seven, it is the Universal Gate of Bodhisattva Avalokitesvara chapter; on days ending in four and nine, it is the Life Span of the Tathagata chapter; and on days ending in five and zero, it is the Mystic Powers of the Tathagata chapter. On days ending in three and eight, there is a special ceremony for the reciting of buddhas' names, and so no sutra chanting takes place.

When we came to the entrance, we did not go inside but lined up on reed mats that had been spread outside. All at once, a monk came flying out of a doorway off to one side, carrying a box about the size of a desk drawer, in which were sutra books. He came to the end of our line and proceeded to dash by at amazing speed, holding the box in outstretched arms. Following our instructor's example, we each snatched up a sutra book as the box flashed by. My hands were stiff with cold, and in my fear that I might bungle it I almost did, but I managed to grab one. Relieved, I looked beside me and saw that Doryu, having missed his chance, was standing flustered and empty handed. When the monk came to the end of the line, he turned back toward Doryu with a look of annoyance, as if to say, *You moron*. Then he came back and thrust the box at him again before disappearing inside the Buddha Hall.

Before long the chanting struck up, and we each opened the accordion-pleated book in our hand and began to recite in harmony with the voices filtering out through the open doors. Not having the slightest idea how to pronounce the Chinese characters aligned on the page before me, I moved my mouth with the rest, giving myself over to the music of the chanting. The area all around was enveloped in an indistinct blue darkness tinged with lingering daylight. Reddish light streamed through the space between the heavy doors of the Buddha Hall, along with the sonorous drone of chanting. I shivered at the sublime sound.

With its stone floor and high ceiling, the Buddha Hall has power to invest the human voice with transcendent spirituality. This, of all the buildings in the Eiheiji compound, is where sutra chanting sounds the most beautiful.

Evening Meal

After the evening service we returned to the temporary quarters and, carrying our cushion under one arm, picked up our set of bowls and went out again, holding the bowls carefully in both hands. Next we were taken to the Outer Hall, a sort of anteroom to the inner sanctum of the Monks' Hall, which we, with our provisional status, were not yet entitled to enter. Along one wall of the long, narrow Outer Hall are seating platforms fitted with tatami mats for the practice of seated meditation. Each platform is edged with a ten-inch-wide wooden area where bowls are laid out at mealtimes and food is served. This space is held sacred; touching it at any time with the feet, the buttocks, or the defiled fingers of the left hand is taboo.

On the opposite wall, away from the Monks' Hall, are windows covered with translucent paper to let in the light; beneath them are folding shelves to hold buckets, trays, and the like brought in from the kitchen. The Outer Hall also contains a number of musical instruments: at one end are a large drum and bell; at the other hangs an enormous wooden gong in the shape of a fish, suspended from the high ceiling; and on a pillar by the entrance is a wooden gong like the one at the Main Gate.

When we arrived, we each laid our cushion and bowls at our assigned place on the platform before carefully seating ourselves in the prescribed way. First you drew your cushion up to the edge of the platform and set your buttocks on it; then, supporting your weight on your fingertips (using all but the fourth and fifth fingers of the left hand), you hoisted yourself into place and crossed your legs, taking care that your feet and buttocks never touched the wooden edge. Under no circumstances was stepping up permitted, even if you could do it without coming into contact with the edge. The practice of eating is such an important part of Zen discipline that you assume the same formal cross-legged posture for it as for sitting in meditation.

As we clambered awkwardly up on the platforms and settled into place, a small door opened and, one after another, in came monks bearing buckets and trays. Without a word they went straight to work, drawing out shelves along the far wall, setting down the buckets and trays, and laying out small tables on the floor. I watched them, entranced, until suddenly the sound of the wooden gong at the entrance announced the start of the evening meal.

The Zen term for the evening meal—*yakuseki*—literally means "medicine stone." Originally Buddhist monks in India ate only once a day, and the meal was required to be finished before noon. This rule was enforced with surprising strictness: past noon, monks were forbidden even to swallow bits of food stuck between their teeth or oil left on their tongue or lips. Eventually, in Chinese Chan monasteries the number of meals per day was increased to two, one in the morning and one at noon. In the evening it was the practice to place a heated stone on the belly to soothe pangs of hunger. This stone was called the "medicine stone." Only the name survived to later ages, eventually becoming the accepted term for the evening meal.

In a Zen monastery the evening meal is not a formal meal, and so does not involve the sacred Buddha bowl. The procedures for the evening meal and the morning meal differ considerably. Back in the temporary quarters we'd been drilled in all the fine points, but it was so complicated that we were thrown into hopeless confusion and no longer had any idea what to do or which rules were for when. Yet here we were, about to be put through our paces.

Five or six instructors stood planted in front of us with arms folded and eyes gleaming, on the lookout for miscues. In this tense, forbidding atmosphere, drawing on indistinct memories, we proceeded cautiously to lay out our things.

"What do you think you're doing?" Somebody was getting yelled at before his bowls were even out of the wrapping cloth. It was Daikan, at the other end of the row. Arms crossed, the monks all went over and glared daggers at him.

I managed somehow to spread out my kit and put the bowls where they were supposed to go. But I was stiff and clumsy with nervousness, and when I took my chopsticks out of their bag, I almost dropped them.

Daikan still hadn't got it right. Now, with all the instructors lined up in front of him observing his every move, he was falling completely apart. "No! You're the only one who can't do it! Pay attention!" Another vicious slap across the face. Helplessly, he pressed his shaking palms together. "What do you think you're doing? Fine, stay like that till you die. If you can't lay out your bowls, you don't eat. Remember that!" As this little drama unfolded, the servers went quietly about their business, oblivious.

Daikan wasn't the only one to earn the instructors' wrath. "No! No, no, no! Come on!" As the meal progressed, the yells grew steadily louder and more menacing. The sound of slaps rang out ceaselessly.

"What's this? You don't want to eat? Fine, then don't!" Tenshin had mistakenly laid his chopsticks across his still-empty bowl. The servers passed him by without stopping.

Enkai had the opposite problem: miso soup being poured into his bowl spilled over the edge and ran down onto the tatami while he watched aghast, not knowing what to do.

Doryu got punched in the stomach and dropped his bowl.

Daikan finally managed to lay out his bowls properly by copying his neighbor, but from then on his every move earned him another slap or punch. In the end, he was grabbed by the scruff of the neck and dragged down off the platform. As he lay on the floor in fright, the instructors kicked him.

Yuho, Kijun, and Choshu somehow managed to keep up with the servers, but their bodies were rigid with effort, their eyes wide open and unblinking as they hurriedly crammed food into their mouths and gulped it down without chewing.

For all of us, the acts of eating and drinking were carried out in a state of abject terror. The least mistake brought an instant cuff from one of the eagle-eyed senior trainees standing watch. The food had no taste; there was no sense of enjoying a meal. The pace was fast and it took intense concentration to keep up. *Now the chopsticks. Next the lap cloth.* You had to confirm each step mentally before you could act.

If you paused to savor the food, before you knew it, second helpings were being served and you had to rush to get your share. If you took time eating that, next thing you knew the servers were coming around with tea, then hot water. Even after we'd memorized exactly what to do and the routine grew familiar, there was never any time to linger over our food.

Eat carefully and you fell behind. Rush and you ran the risk of dropping your chopsticks or bowl. Washing up was fraught with danger, too. You had to turn each bowl in hot water with one hand while scrubbing its sides and bottom with the other, and the slippery bowl was in constant danger of skittering from your grasp. When wiping and stacking the bowls, if you got them out of order they wouldn't nest properly. I have to say that when I finally tied the wrapping cloth I felt intense relief, nothing more.

Our first meal using the bowls, conducted in this highly charged atmosphere amid the unceasing scramble to keep up, was over before we knew what had happened. It left us in the state of mental numbness that follows extreme tension. Amazing feats of physical strength may be possible under duress, but the human mind, by contrast, shuts down to the most primitive, instinctual level. Extreme stress and fear had instantaneously frozen the minds of some of us, leaving us literally at wits' end, unable to do a thing. In the end it was not with our minds but with our bodies that we memorized the compact and intricate form and motions, clenching our teeth as we were slapped and knocked about.

Night Sitting

We returned to the temporary quarters and sat in our accustomed places feeling let down and empty, as if we'd left behind somewhere the ability to think. Nothing cheerful came to mind, nor could we possibly have worked up any plan of action. The one thing we were sure of was that this oppressive, stifling gloom would never lift; never in this place would we know the freedom—now a distant memory—of utter physical relaxation untrammeled by doubt, of simply stretching out lazily in the stream of time.

As if to keep us from wallowing in our woe, the order came quickly for us to pick up our mantles, which we had just taken off, and put them back on. Clutching our cushions to our chests, we shuffled out of the room again. The sun had long since set; the temple compound was sunk into deep, ravine-like blackness. Here and there the dim light from a naked bulb formed mysterious shadows in the dark. We threaded our way through the depths of the darkness until we came to the Walking Corridor. Located next to the Monks' Hall, it is a place for walking at a slow pace during the interval between sitting periods. Such walking is not a time of rest, but is itself another important part of meditation.

The corridor was empty except for raised seating platforms that had been set up along one side. Its emptiness made it all the more impressive. Dangling from the high ceiling was a bulb in whose dim glow the solid timbers of the walls and floor took on a beautiful dark brown sheen. There was something warm and human in the color, I thought. We set down our cushions on the platforms and seated ourselves as instructed.

Dogen wrote out the method of practicing sitting, the heart of Zen discipline, in the "Rules for Sitting" essay in *Treasury of the True Dharma Eye*. The rules are still strictly adhered to at Eiheiji, just as he set them out.

The study of Zen means the practice of sitting.

First, to practice sitting, you need a quiet place. Use a thick mat, and do not let in smoke or drafts. Keep out the damp. The place for sitting should be carefully and properly maintained. It should be warm, and not too dark in day or night. In winter it should be heated, and in summer it should be pleasantly cool.

Leave behind all attachments and bonds, and keep yourself entirely at rest. Do not dwell on thoughts of good things or bad. Sitting is neither contemplation nor meditation. Do not think of it as a means for attaining enlightenment. Rid yourself of superficial notions of sitting and lying down.

Eat and drink in moderation. Use your time well, and do not waste it. Like one whose hair is on fire, make use of every moment, sitting down quickly and devoting yourself to the practice.

When you practice sitting, wear a mantle and use a cushion. Don't sit on the entire cushion but only on the front, placing it under your buttocks. This is the way of sitting that has been passed down from buddha to buddha and from ancestor to ancestor.

There are two ways of sitting, the full lotus and the half lotus position. In the full lotus, the right foot is placed on the left thigh and the left foot on the right thigh. The soles of the feet should be laid horizontally on the thighs, in perfect symmetry. In the half lotus only the left foot is placed on the right thigh.

Wear your robes loosely and sit up straight. Next, put your right hand on your left foot, your left hand in your right palm. The tips of your thumbs should be touching. Hold your hands close to your body.

Hold yourself erect as you sit. Do not lean to the left or right, and do not bend forward or backward. The ears should stay even with the shoulders, and the nose and the navel should be aligned. Hold your tongue against the roof of your mouth. Breathe through the nose and keep your teeth and lips together. The eyes should be open, neither too wide nor too narrow.

When you are ready to begin, take a deep breath.

Sitting this way, you become immovable. Surpassing existence and nonexistence, you free yourself from constrictions of thought. This is the way of Zen sitting.

At Eiheiji, the half lotus position is not allowed, and as the instructors walked around and observed us, they were on the alert to make sure our legs were folded properly.

Suddenly an accusing cry rang out: "Hey! Why aren't you sitting in the full lotus position?"

Doryu answered in a low, shaky tone: "Um, I broke my leg once, and I can't cross my legs the right way."

The End and the Beginning

"You what? Can't cross your legs? Where do you think you are? This is Eiheiji! You've got to be able to sit properly. All right, starting tomorrow, you will tie your legs in place. Is that clear?"

I couldn't believe my ears. The man had broken his leg! Was it necessary to go so far? That was when it finally sank in. This was indeed Eiheiji—the premier Zen training center in Japan, famed down the centuries for the rigor of its discipline. Nothing here, including meditation, bore the least resemblance to the fanciful pictures my mind had painted before coming. I was forcibly reminded that once a man sets foot in this holy place, he must devote himself to the discipline truly as if his life depends on it. At the thought my blood buzzed, and sweat trickled down my back.

In the stillness time passed quietly by, until through the darkness came the deep sound of a bell, echoing through the hall in great waves that seemed to reverberate in the earth beneath us and linger in the silence, deepening the beauty of the pervading tranquility. When the ringing of the bell died away, our first experience of night sitting at Eiheiji was over. We went straight back to our quarters, brought out the heaps of bedding from behind the sliding doors in the rear of the room and spread them out while the instructors yelled. Then it was time to go to bed. All at once the lights went out and the room went black. The far-off sound of a handbell signaling time to sleep gradually faded away.

The first night in Eiheiji. The day had passed with a frenzied momentum. I'd been thrown into a panic, worn to a frazzle in body and mind.

Any resentment I felt, however, was directed purely at the sluggishness of my mind and the clumsiness of my hands and feet. Nothing to do but give a long, deep sigh.

Time and again I sighed and turned over. Once I happened to lock eyes with Doryu, who lay in the bedding next to mine. The oldest son from a temple in northern Japan, he had just graduated from university this past spring. The previous day, when we were scheduled to appear at Eiheiji, he'd flown in and gone not to Eiheiji but to a hotel in town. He'd gotten the days mixed up, thought he was a day early. When his family realized the mistake, they hastily sent word to him at the hotel. Without even unpacking, he tumbled into a taxi and sped over to Jizo Cloister, where he was the last to arrive. Despite this initial blunder, he'd managed to win admittance and take off his sandals before me even though I'd started out third in line, thanks to a booming voice out of keeping with his small stature.

He smiled at me somewhat stiffly and said in a low tone, "Some place, eh?"

Unable to come up with a suitable answer, I gave a slight smile.

"Think it'll be more of the same in the morning?" he asked.

"Yeah, probably," I said. "More of the same from now on." Even as I said the words, I hoped deep down I was wrong.

"Huh. When you think about it, there's no Saturday or Sunday here, so you could be right."

No Saturday or Sunday. The hardships of a life like this would be somehow bearable, I thought, if I could know that in a few days' time there would be a respite. For the first time I realized that the pattern of life in Eiheiji was not interrupted by weekends. And of the stupendously long time stretching ahead, a single day had gone by. I found it suddenly hard to breathe.

Doryu went on, "You know what a friend of mine said? That tough as it is in the beginning, after that it only gets worse."

"Worse? What happens after this?"

"I don't know. Didn't ask."

It would only get worse. I felt myself suffocating. I no longer wanted to think about anything, but my mind was flooded with worries. "Hey . . ." I wanted Doryu to tell me more about what his friend had said, but he was already snoring softly. Well, good for him. How anyone could fall asleep so easily at such a time was beyond me. My disconcertment soon gave way to loneliness as I felt myself left behind, alone in the total darkness.

More of the same from now on.

Was this the life I'd gained in exchange for giving up everything? Was this what I'd been seeking? What would this way of life do for me? I didn't know. All I knew for sure was that thinking about it now would do no good.

Enough. My task now, I told myself, was to go straight to sleep. I closed my eyes.

Eat Sleep Sit

PART TWO

Etiquette Is Zen

Morning Service

At 3:30 a.m. I awoke to the insistent ringing of the handbell that sig-nals morning in Eiheiji. The moment my eyes opened, I trembled at the thought that sleep was over and a new day had begun. But as the ringing of the bell gave way to the roars of our instructors, there was no time to dwell on thoughts like that. We leaped up, put away our bedding, and dressed, before being shepherded back to the Walking Corridor.

When we got there, monks were filing into the Monks' Hall for the early morning session of sitting, which was about to begin. The sight of dozens of black-robed monks moving in utter silence through the dim corridor created a mysterious aura.

At Eiheiji it is customary to practice sitting wearing the mantle, except at this morning session, when it is left folded in its envelope. We each laid our envelope carefully on the platform before hoisting our-selves up and folding our legs into position. Then, just like the previous night, we sat.

After a while the soft padding of feet heading into the Monks' Hall died away, and then the bell and drum in the Outer Hall were each sounded in turn. Just as the last reverberation died away, the great bell in the bell tower at the foot of the compound rang out. This impeccably timed succession of sounds charged the predawn air with electricity.

Sitting with my legs folded and my back straight when my every muscle still retained the lassitude of sleep was, I found, exhilarating. It felt as if every cell in my body were slowly recovering sensation and motion in synch with the steady reawakening of nature all around. Then, little by little, we were enveloped in an intense silence broken only by the occasional sharp whack of the monk's stick on someone's shoulder, my own body stiffening each time I sensed it was about to fall.

Early morning sitting lasts normally for a single session of forty minutes, the length of time it takes for one stick of incense to burn down. When the time was up, a metal gong in front of the kitchen, known as the cloud gong, signaled the end of this early morning session. The gong was struck several times at measured, unhurried intervals, easing the palpable tension in the air and slowly returning things to normal. When its last reverberations had died away, the bell in the Monks' Hall rang out once, and sitting was over. We each placed our folded mantle on top of our head, pressed our palms together, and chanted:

> The great robe liberates us from blind passions.
> Departing from all form, it builds up merit beyond measure.
> Now we wrap ourselves in the teachings of Buddha
> so that everywhere, all living beings may be free.

After getting down from the platform we formed a line and followed the other monks out into the covered walkway. Before early morning sitting began, the temple had been swathed in the black of night; now it emerged in the morning twilight, filled with shadows the mysterious color of the moment when night turns to day.

We walked single file up a corridor fitted with stairs, climbing up toward the Dharma Hall at the top of the incline. From the recesses of the shallow blackness ahead came the gurgle of water and a magical sound as of a velvet hammer striking a silver ball. I caught my breath.

This bell, I soon learned, hung high outside the entrance to the Dharma Hall at the top of the stairs, and it was rung by an altar attendant. The sound lingered on and on, as if the sound waves were resisting time's passage. Accompanied by the reverberation of the bell, we removed our footwear beside the entrance and stepped up into the hall.

The Dharma Hall in a Zen temple is where the abbot delivers lectures, and where various ceremonies and services take place. The one at Eiheiji has 380 tatami mats, with a great central altar enshrining an image of Avalokitesvara, the bodhisattva of compassion. On either side of the stairs leading to the altar is a statue of a white lion, while the ceiling is hung with an octagonal canopy in ancient Chinese style. The monks filing into the room ahead of us took their places on either side of the altar, lined up in neat rows facing the wide central space directly in front of it. When they were all in place, we eight went in next, lining up behind them. After that the officiant came in with his attendants, and the morning service finally got underway.

The service begins with an offering of incense from the officiant, followed by a triple prostration of worship to the image of the bodhisattva from the congregation. To perform it, you first unfold the rectangular

Etiquette Is Zen

cloth draped over your left wrist and spread it out in front of you. Then, after bowing your head and holding your hands palm to palm in a standing position, you kneel down on the cloth, lay your forehead and the backs of your hands on the floor, and then raise your upturned hands level with your ears. This is called "receiving the feet of Buddha in worship." It signifies that the feet of Buddha have come to rest in the palms of your hands; to symbolically lift him in your hands is a form of worship.

The act is repeated three times. Wearing layers of wide-sleeved, unfamiliar clothing, topped by the capacious mantle draped over one shoulder, I found it wasn't easy to alternate between standing up and pressing my head to the floor. I struggled to keep up with the smooth, fluid movements of the others. Every time I knelt, my mantle got in disarray, and every time I stood up, I trampled the hem of my robe. The pleated sutra booklet tucked into the folds of my kimono seemed in constant danger of toppling down onto the tatami. Certainly this first clumsy attempt was far from a pious act of devotion.

The canon includes three types of sutras: those which are sung in Sanskrit; those which are sung in Tang- and Song-period Chinese; and those which are sung in Japanese. The idea of Buddhist monks "singing" these may strike some as peculiar, but sutra chanting is indeed a form of sacred music similar to Christian hymns. The sutra books we'd brought with us had phonetic markings to indicate the pronunciation, but the sounds we were hearing for the first time were so unfamiliar that even with a crib sheet to follow, it took considerable practice before any of us could articulate them smoothly.

We were taught to "chant with the ears," not the mouth. The idea was not to open your book and sing out randomly, but to listen to the voices of others and try to blend in. Even if not used in a particularly musical way, the human voice in combination with others forms a rich tapestry of sound that moves the listener's heart. Although there was no special melody, because of the very simplicity of the vocalization, the slight variations in each voice produced a mysterious resonance with beautiful overtones.

The reading of sutras has two meanings or purposes. One is to encounter the thought of the founder, a form of reading that closely resembles study. The other is to gain spiritual merit, which is done purely by chanting; questions of meaning and content are secondary in this case. The act of chanting a sutra is considered to have intrinsic merit. The chanting that takes place each morning falls into this category.

The morning service usually begins with the Universal Gate of Bodhisattva Avalokitesvara chapter of the Lotus Sutra and proceeds in order through the Heart of Great Perfect Wisdom Sutra, the sutras The Harmony of Difference and Equality and Precious Mirror Samadhi, the Great Compassionate Mind Dharani,[1] the Life Span of the Tathagata chapter of the Lotus Sutra, and the Dharani of Good Fortune that Averts Calamity.

The chants flowed from one to the next in the prescribed order without pause, each participant knowing his place and performing his role, doing neither more nor less than required. The service held a sublime and solemn beauty in which individual feelings had no place.

Etiquette Is Zen

Morning Meal

When we had finished the morning sutra chanting and returned to our room, we were immediately hustled out again, bearing our cushion and set of bowls. It was time for the morning meal. As always, we were rushed from place to place in confusion. We moved along in unresisting silence, without looking back or stopping along the way.

The knowledge that another meal was about to begin filled us with heavy gloom. Those who had been battered the most yesterday evening looked especially dismal, as their thoughts homed in on what might befall them now.

When we arrived at the Outer Hall, the air was filled with deep reverberations from the cloud gong, summoning us to eat. We clambered up in our places with the same awkwardness as on the previous night, and then someone began to strike the large, fish-shaped wooden gong hanging from the ceiling. The dry, clear sound continued in a fixed rhythm of alternating fast and slow beats, giving way to the deep tones of the cloud gong again, which yielded in turn to the "thunder drum" at the other end of the hall. Before the meal ever got underway, these varied sounds and rhythms cast an aura of solemnity over the occasion that was completely unlike the previous night's supper.

The morning meal at Eiheiji consists of rice porridge accompanied by pickled vegetables and, for flavoring, unhulled sesame seeds mixed with salt. There were a number of differences between this formal meal and the informal meal of the previous night. First, this time an offering was placed before the statue of Manjusri, the bodhisattva of wisdom, enshrined in the center of the Monks' Hall. Second, this time we would use the large Buddha bowl, which we had not done before. And third, the progress of this meal was punctuated by the above-mentioned musical instruments as well as by a variety of chants.

Each stage of the meal was heralded by a different instrument or chant. The beating of the fish-shaped gong was a signal for servers to enter bearing special cloths and set about polishing the wide wooden edge of the seating platform. The moment that sound stopped, the cloud gong started up as if in response, a signal for us to begin laying out our bowls. The deep drumbeat then signaled time to begin the offering to Manjusri, ending exactly as the offering finished. Simultaneously we each then held our hands palm to palm and chanted the Verse upon Hearing the Meal Signal:

> Buddha was born in Kapilavastu,
> enlightened in Magadha,
> taught in Varanasi,
> entered nirvana in Kushinagara.

This was followed by the Verse for Setting Out Bowls:

> Now we set out Buddha's bowls.
> Along with all living beings,
> may giver, receiver, and gift alike
> be freed from desire and enter the realm of selflessness.

Then we removed the wrapping cloth and began to lay out our bowls, chanting:

> We pay homage to the three treasures.[2]
> Let each heart be sincere.
> Now let us pay homage to the precious Names.

After that we joined together to chant a recitation of the Ten Buddha Names:

> Vairocana Buddha, pure embodiment of the Dharma.
> Lochana Buddha, complete embodiment of the rewards of practice.
> Sakyamuni Buddha, of myriad manifestations in this world.
> Maitreya Buddha, of future birth.
> All buddhas throughout space and time.
> Lotus of wondrous truth, the Mahayana sutra.
> Manjusri Bodhisattva, great wisdom.
> Samantabhadra Bodhisattva, great activity.
> Avalokitesvara Bodhisattva, great compassion.
> All honored ones, bodhisattvas and great bodhisattvas.
> Wisdom beyond wisdom.

After this, the leader would chant this verse on rice porridge:

Rice porridge has ten benefits.[3]

Therefore it is rich in benefits to the practitioner.

Its rewards are boundless, leading ultimately to ease and joy.

While this was being chanted, servers distributed first the porridge, then the pickled vegetables, and finally the sesame seed and salt mixture. When this was done, the leader would use wooden clappers as a signal to begin reciting The Five Reflections, which may be paraphrased as follows:

First, we must not forget the blessing of nature in the food we now eat, nor the efforts of many that went into its making.

Second, as the purpose of eating is the practice of those things we ought to do, we must consider well whether we deserve this food today.

Third, even if the food is to our liking, we must not eat it greedily. There must be no delusion or error in our approach to food.

Fourth, food is medicinal in nature; we take it to keep the body from withering and dying.

Fifth, we take this food now so that we may fulfill the true way.

Etiquette Is Zen

After this came the Verse for Raising the Bowl, during which we each placed our spoon in the now-filled Buddha bowl, laid our chopsticks over the bowl of pickled vegetables, and raised the Buddha bowl to eye level.

> The first bowlful is for the three treasures.
> The middle one is for the four benefactors.[4]
> The last is for beings in the six realms.[5]
> May they all be nourished.
> With the first bite may all evil be ended.
> With the second may every good be cultivated.
> With the third may all beings be saved.
> And may we realize the way of Buddha.

As soon as this chant finished, we took a mouthful of porridge before emptying the bowl of seasoning into it and proceeding with the meal.

Unlike the abbreviated evening meal, at the formal morning meal we were so busy with all these chants and accompanying gestures that it took quite a while before we actually ate anything. We still hadn't fully absorbed the lessons of the night before, and now an entirely new set of procedures was being added on top of them, leaving us more confused than ever. Again the instructors hovered before us with eagle eyes, on the lookout for the slightest deviation from protocol. I glanced at the head of the line, where Daikan was getting yelled at again. Beside him, Tenshin was earning glares for clumsiness. "It's only you two who can't do it!" cried an instructor impatiently. "Come on!" Just like last night, it started up again—the disagreeable sound of the slapping of flesh against flesh.

Even for meals, we were lined up in the same order we'd been admitted to Jizo Cloister that first night. In general, those who are first to remove their sandals are later the most severely tried, and come in for the bulk of the instructors' attention. Doryu and I, at the end of the line, had time to review what came next while Daikan and Tenshin were getting bawled out. That time when I was locked out of the cloister at night, left to stand in front of the gate all by myself, I'd come near panicking, but later I came to realize that being last was actually something to be grateful for.

After the extra helpings had been served, we set to scraping our bowls with the cleaning stick. There was no hot water this time; unlike with sticky cooked rice, there was no need to soften the already-soft porridge.

When we had finished cleaning our bowls, it was the servers' turn to be served, and then to clean up. When they were done, the leader started up the Verse for Rinsing Bowls, and we joined in:

The water with which we now wash our bowls
tastes like ambrosia.
We offer it to the many spirits
that they may be satisfied in body and mind.

During this time the pail made the rounds of the hall and everyone discarded their leftover water. Then we put away our things and wrapped them up again. The servers once again polished the area where the food had been served, and finally the leader began the final chant:

> To live in this world
> as in complete emptiness without hindrance,
> a lotus untouched by mud.
> Purification of mind is the all-transcending truth.
> Now we bow in devotion to the inestimably holy Buddha.

Then he clapped the wooden clappers, and the morning meal was over.

"That's it for me," muttered Tenshin. "I feel like I never want to eat again."

Though I didn't say so aloud, I fervently agreed.

Whichever way we turned, it was as if all around us was impenetrable black, a darkness so extreme that we lost sight even of ourselves. If, in the midst of that blackness, we gingerly wiggled a hand or a foot, we received a swift cuff. At all times, not only during formal meals, eye contact with the senior trainees was forbidden; the price of looking one of them in the eye by mistake was a slap in the face. When you passed a senior in the corridor, failure to join the palms in respect was punished on the spot with a blow. There were exhaustive rules for eating, walking, sitting, speaking, and every other human activity, and the slightest deviation from them met with instant physical reprisal.

There was never a second's relaxation. Amid this swirl of events, in some dimension far removed from our own will, we surrendered ourselves to this great current and were carried away, we knew not where.

Cleaning the Corridors

As soon as the wooden clappers had been sounded to mark the end of the morning meal, the great drum in the Buddha Hall was struck to signal time to begin polishing the corridors. Swiftly, yet maintaining a fixed pace, the monks in the Monks' Hall picked up their bowls and filed out in order. We left the Outer Hall in the same way, hurrying back to the temporary quarters. Of course, we did not run—running inside the temple is forbidden, and to do so while carrying the sacred bowls would be particularly egregious.

On returning to our quarters we put away our bowls and quickly changed clothes. Cleaning the corridors is usually done in work clothes consisting of a short kimono-style top and baggy trousers, which we were not yet entitled to wear. We went in "temporary-quarters style." This meant removing the mantle and outer robe, leaving only the kimono, which was tucked up at the waist and fastened with a cord so that the hem reached just to the knee. Then the long cloth belt was crisscrossed over the back and tied to hold the sleeves out of the way. It had to be fastened so tightly that there was barely room to slide a finger under it. Our feet, naturally, were bare.

"Hurry it up!" scolded an instructor. "What's taking so long?"

The garments removed had to be neatly folded in the proper way and laid down just so in the proper place. Everyone's appearance had to be neat and tidy, with nothing amiss. Yet there was no time to spend lingering over our toilet. We finished as quickly as we could and rushed back out again.

Although running is generally forbidden at Eiheiji, for cleaning floors it is de rigueur. Anyone who took his sweet time would be sent sprawling by a swift kick. There is one place, however, where running is never tolerated, not even while polishing the floor: the Walking Corridor. However fast the monks might be tearing along, when they came to this corridor they would slow to an ambling pace, taking off again like jackrabbits as soon as they could.

The floor cleaning would begin at the highest point in Eiheiji, outside the Dharma Hall. Every trainee monk in the temple raced up the stairs in the sloping corridor at top speed, cleaning cloth tightly in hand. The sight was truly awesome. There were no stragglers.

I also dashed up the long staircase as fast as I could. When I finally reached the top, I had used up nearly all my strength. For an instant I felt dizzy. But the real test of endurance lay ahead. We were each to take our tightly wrung out cloth and clean the floor of the corridor stretching all the way to the Founder's Hall, Dogen's mausoleum. Slow, painstaking polishing was not required. The point was to do the corridor end to end with alacrity. When that was done, we had to go back to the staircase that descended from the Dharma Hall to the Buddha Hall at the foot of the hill, and clean it. We worked stooped over, not on our knees, holding the cloth in both hands and moving it back and forth in wide swipes across each step as we flew to the bottom in the blink of an eye. Once there, we turned and charged back up to the top to start all over again. We novices had to do this five or six times in succession. If the pace fell off by even a little, we were yelled at, kicked, sent flying. I thought my heart would burst.

After that we did the floor from the Buddha Hall to the Monks' Hall, and finally the long hallway that ran past the Main Gate. That one we had to do again and again, back and forth and back and forth until the instructor said we could stop. The cleaning cloths we had wet and wrung out before starting could not be remoistened; by now they hardly slid over the boards, necessitating an increased expenditure of energy just as our strength was dwindling. Our breath came in gasps, our legs shook. Still the signal to stop did not come.

Enkai sank to his knees, unable to move. He was immediately grabbed by the crisscrossed belt on his back and dragged off; afterward I realized this was why the belt had to be tied so tightly. Meanwhile, others were being kicked.

Countless times I thought, "I can't take this anymore. When I get to the end next time, I'll rest." But always I was stopped in the nick of time by another voice inside me protesting, "You came here by choice. Throw in the towel now over a little thing like this, and what was it all for?"

How many times did we tear back and forth? By the time the instructor's voice called time to stop, even though this was a freezing morning with patches of snow in the shadows of trees, we were soaking in sweat. Emitting clouds of white breath, we staggered into line in front of the Main Gate.

"All right now," barked the instructor. "Let's have no complaining. This is just the beginning. Is that clear?"

Just the beginning? What a thought. Horrified to realize that this would be our morning routine from now on, hearts sore with anxiety, we hurried back to our quarters.

Dignified Dress

Exhausted from cleaning the corridors, we had only a moment's rest before it was time for another quick change. At Eiheiji there are elaborate rules for how to dress for every daily activity, and we were constantly changing into proper attire. This had to be done swiftly and neatly, a task hampered by a host of detailed rules dictating the precise way to take off and put on every garment. In putting on the robe, for example, there are rules governing what part of it to handle first, how to unfold it, which sleeve to thrust your arm in first, and what posture to assume as you do so.

Monks at Eiheiji ordinarily wear white undergarments, topped by a plain kimono of any color but white: we could wear gray, brown, dark blue, or black, as we liked. On top of this goes a loose robe, with long wide sleeves that are not just decorative but can be used to cover the palm of the hand when picking something up that must not be touched directly. The inner part of the sleeve, moreover, just around the shoulder, has a cord attached that can be tied around the neck to bind up the wide sleeves out of the way. The robe is always black at Eiheiji, but there is no particular regulation on the material it should be made of. Silk is not used, however; usually it is a thin synthetic fiber.

After the robe is on, you put on the belt. This belt, which is used to fasten the sleeves out of the way when using the toilet (for defecation), and when polishing corridor floors, is some four yards long, and is wound twice around the waist and tied in a special knot.

For sitting, lectures, and other formal occasions, on top of all this goes the mantle or *kesa*, which derives from an everyday sari-like garment of ancient India that was transformed into something sacred. In an essay in *Treasury of the True Dharma Eye* entitled "The Transmission of the Robe," Dogen wrote in detail about the origins and benefits of this vestment, as well as its varieties and materials. He also gave instructions on how to wear it, how to sew it, and even how to wash it. The mantle symbolizes the transmission of Buddhist teachings from master to pupil, which is called "passing on the robe." During his stay in China, Dogen saw monks place their mantles on their heads and hold their palms together in reverence. He wrote that this holy sight filled him with such irrepressible joy that he wept until the collar of his robe was soaked with tears.

Concerning the materials for the mantle, he specified that it should be made from pure materials, and decreed that the following ten types of discarded cloth are especially pure:

Etiquette Is Zen

Cloth chewed by an ox.

Cloth gnawed by rats.

Cloth scorched by fire.

Cloth soiled by menstruation.

Cloth soiled by childbirth.

Cloth discarded at a shrine.

Cloth discarded at a graveyard.

Cloth discarded in petitions to the gods.

Cloth discarded by king's ministers.

Cloth laid over the dead.

Monks would gather scraps of such discarded cloth and patch them together. Dogen expounded further on the meaning of such rags, known as *funzoe* (literally "excrement-sweeping cloth"):

When collecting discarded bits of cloth, some will be silk and some will be cotton. But once they are used to make a mantle, they are neither silk nor cotton but funzoe. Cloth that is funzoe is not silk, nor is it cotton.

If a human being should become funzoe, that person would be no longer a living creature, but funzoe; and if a pine or a chrysanthemum should become funzoe, it too would no longer be vegetation but would indeed be funzoe.

Only by grasping the principle that funzoe is neither silk nor cotton nor jewels can one understand funzoe and come face to face with it. Those who are convinced that a mantle is silk or cotton cannot begin to understand funzoe. Even if someone wore a mantle of rough cloth all his life in a spirit of humility, as long as he was distracted by the material and appearance of the cloth, faithful transmission of Buddha's teachings would never be possible.

There must be a complete departure from human desires. Put another way, only when the wearer's understanding of the mantle transcends the physical can the garment be a true expression and symbol of the transmission of Buddhist teachings. Therefore, just as we did with our set of bowls, we approached the mantle in a spirit of reverence.

The color of the mantle is limited to black for novices, but eventually, depending on the rank and position we achieved in coming years, we would wear other colors too. The mantle is draped so that the right shoulder is exposed, a style of dress that dates back to ancient India. The exposure of the right shoulder indicates respect for others. The mantle is never put on while standing, but always while kneeling and facing a wall. During sitting, sermons, and at informal times, instead of the usual mantle a bib-shaped, short mantle is worn around the neck.

The mantle is paired with a bowing cloth made of the same material. This is a rectangular cloth placed under the knees at worship, deriving from a prayer mat used in the time of Buddha for meditation. When not in use, it is folded lengthwise and placed in the sleeve under the left wrist for easy access during worship. Different ways of unfolding it are used depending on the formality of the occasion.

The feet are bare during sitting, at meals, and at most other times. During memorial services and other ceremonies, sometimes the monks are barefoot and other times, depending on the occasion, they wear formal socks, those that do not have split toes.

The monks' attire for cleaning and other miscellaneous chores is black, loose-fitting kimono-style shirt and pants. This is informal attire, and sometimes the short mantle is worn with it for decorum.

Soon after we started to change our clothes, an uproar broke out. "My mantle is gone!" shouted one. "My cushion's not here, either," said another. "How about you, Rosan?" asked Doryu, peering at my things.

I did a quick inventory, but fortunately everything was there. I breathed a sigh of relief. "Looks like I'm okay," I said.

"What's going on?" cried someone else. "I'm missing my mantle, my cushion, and my sutra book!"

In the midst of this consternation, suddenly the lead instructor appeared and we hastily got in line. "Did you forget what I said yesterday?" he said sternly. "I taught you the right way to put away your things, and I said that anything that wasn't put away properly, I'd confiscate. Don't be sloppy. You want your things back, you'll have to come see me. One at a time. Is that clear?"

He'd been as good as his word: everything put away amiss had indeed been confiscated. Apprehensive about what lay in store, those with missing property left the room with faces set like stone.

Washing the Face

"Washing the face is done not only to remove grease and grime. It is the living truth passed on by the buddhas and ancestors. If you pay respect to others or receive respect without washing your face, you commit a grave sin." In the essay "Washing the Face" in *Treasury of the True Dharma Eye*, Dogen went on to lay out meticulous instructions for the act.

To wash your face, wear your monk's robes, take a towel, and proceed to the sink area. The towel should be a single width of cloth, and the color must not be white. White is forbidden.

When you use the towel, observe the following procedure. Fold it in two and hang it in the crook of the left elbow. One half of the towel is for wiping the hands, the other for wiping the face. Do not use it to wipe your nostrils or a running nose. Do not wipe your armpits, back, abdomen, navel, thighs, or shins, either. If any of those are soiled with grease or grime, they should be rinsed with water. If the towel becomes wet, hold it over a flame and then dry it in the sun. Do not take the towel with you into the bath.

The sink where you wash your face is in the washroom behind the Monks' Hall. When you arrive at the sink, place the towel evenly around your neck. Then pass both ends of the towel under each armpit to the back and cross them; bring the ends to the front, the left end from the right and the right end from the left, and tie them. This way, the collar of your robe will be covered and the sleeves tied up out of the way, exposing the arms from elbow to palm.

When washing your face in the washroom, take the face-washing basin, go to the hot-water pot and dip up hot water, and place the basin on the washstand. When washing your face in the bathhouse, scoop hot water from the tub with the face-washing basin.

Next, use a toothpick. In the great temples of China, toothpicks have long gone out of use, but they are used at Eiheiji. To do so, take the toothpick in your right hand and nibble on the fat end. Do not chew more than one-third down the length of the toothpick. When it has been well softened, use it to brush the front and back of your teeth. Brush and rinse many times. You should also thoroughly brush the gum at the root of each tooth. Rub the toothpick back and forth between each tooth and clean the area thoroughly. The mouth becomes clean by repeated rinsing.

Next, scrape the tongue. There are five points to be observed. First, do not exceed three times. Second, if the tongue bleeds, stop. Third, do not make any rough movements that soil your robes or feet. Fourth, when you throw away the toothpick, do not discard it where people walk. Fifth, throw it away discreetly.

After that, rinse the mouth again. Using the thick of the thumb and the first two fingers of the right hand, rub the inside of the lips, under the tongue, and around the jaw until smooth and clean. If you have just eaten something oily, you can use bean powder.

When you have finished using the toothpick, throw it away out of sight. Then snap your fingers three times. In the washroom by the Monks' Hall there is a receptacle for the purpose; elsewhere, you can throw it somewhere out of sight. The water you used to rinse your mouth should be discarded outside the basin.

Now wash the face itself. With both hands, scoop up hot water from the basin and wash everything: the forehead, both eyebrows, both eyes, the nostrils, the ears, the top of the head, and the cheeks. Scoop up plenty of water and then give the face a rubdown. Do not allow tears, saliva, or mucus to get into the water in the basin. When washing this way, you must not use hot water without limit, or spill it outside the basin, or use it up quickly.

Wash until the dirt and grease are gone, and do not omit to wash behind the ears. Do not put water inside the ears, however. Rinse the eyes thoroughly to cleanse them of dust. Next wash the head and even the nape of the neck. This is the way of the buddhas and ancestors.

When you have finished washing your face and have discarded the water, snap your fingers three times again. Next, wipe your face with the towel. Wipe it with the end of the towel and dry it thoroughly. Then put the towel back where it was, folded in two across the left elbow.

Tell yourself this in private: even though you were born in this degenerate age of Buddhism[6] and live on a remote island, the good deeds of previous lives have not been exhausted; you are able to receive the teachings of ancient times accurately and pursue the way of Buddha without stain. Is this not a matter for rejoicing?

At Eiheiji, as described by Dogen, just behind the Monks' Hall is a place called the washroom, and this is where the face is washed. It has a large sink with shelves where wooden basins are kept in low piles. It does not, however, have a pot of hot water as Dogen described; today face washing is done at Eiheiji with cold water.

When it came time for us to wash our faces, first we each tied back our sleeves. With a wash towel in the crook of the left arm, and everything else we needed in the right hand, we set off.

Current practice differs from Dogen's instructions in another way: today toothbrushes are used in place of toothpicks. When Dogen visited the temples of China, he found to his distress that no one there knew about toothpicks, and that monks and others had such bad breath that even from a considerable distance the odor was unendurable. It was a great pity, he wrote, that the true way had been utterly forgotten. He added this about the toothbrushes in use there:

> Although for the most part toothpicks have fallen out of use, a few people did clean their mouths. They took a bit of cow's horn, carved square, and attached one-inch cuttings from a horse's tail, lined up in a row just like a horse's mane. This is what they used to clean their mouths. Such a tool is hardly fitting for monks to use. It is no different from the tools used for cleaning dust off the soles of one's shoes and combing the hair. Though different in size, they are all equally impure.

As this passage shows, the toothpick has a special value to Zen practitioners far beyond the imagination of laypeople. Dogen's "Washing the Face" essay also includes the following story: after a meal, Buddha used a toothpick and tossed it aside. Before everyone's eyes it grew to a great tree reaching all the way to heaven; its branches trailed like clouds, eventually producing flowers the size of wheels, then gigantic fruits. Roots and trunk, branches and leaves, all shone like jewels, with a light so bright it put the sun and moon to shame. The fruit was sweeter than nectar and gave off a fragrance that filled the air in all directions. The branches swaying in the wind played a melody so graceful that it was like listening to a holy sermon.

Dogen had much else to say about the use of toothpicks by the buddhas and ancestors. Those who know how to use a toothpick properly are, he stated, the true heirs of Buddha. An encounter with a toothpick is nothing less than an encounter with absolute truth—and if anyone questions what this means, he added, "Just tell them you had the good fortune to see Dogen using a toothpick."

When we arrived at the washroom, we went to the sink and laid our toothbrush and toothpaste on the shelf in front of us. After that we took a basin, turned on the tap, and filled it slowly to the brim. This is all the water that can be used at one time. Then we silently recited a verse:

Toothbrush in hand,
I vow with all sentient beings: may all

minds attain truth
and may we be naturally pure.

After this we put the toothpaste on the toothbrush, and then silently recited another verse:

Brushing my teeth in the morning,
I vow with all sentient beings: may all
gain the teeth that conquer evil
and so bite through the afflictions of man.

Then we began to brush. This is done with the head held low, and must be done discreetly and soundlessly. When finished with the brushing, next we scooped water from the basin in one palm and rinsed off the brush. We each put our toothbrush back on the shelf and silently said:

Rinsing my mouth,
I vow with all sentient beings: may all
approach the gate of pure truth
and ultimately achieve liberation.

Then we rinsed our mouths. We scooped up water from the basin in both hands, noiselessly rinsed out the mouth, and then carefully spat out the water near the drain to keep from dirtying the sink. After this, one more verse was said before it was at last time to actually wash the face:

Washing my face,
I vow with all sentient beings: may all
attain the gate of pure truth
and remain forever undefiled.

Partly because it is behind the Monks' Hall, the washroom is an especially quiet part of the compound. The ceiling is high and so are the windows. There, in the soft light streaming down from above, I too washed my face in the clear, knife-cold water of early spring that flowed from the mountains. Seeing the small amount of water in the basin made me feel it was extremely precious. Bending over, I scooped some of it up in my hands, which promptly went numb with cold, and washed my face all at once. It felt as if my skin were being sliced away. Taking in the harshness of the shock, I splashed myself again. The cold, clear water trickled over the contours of my head, quickly evaporating into white steam that rose into the cold air.

The practice of face washing laid out by Dogen involves cleansing and purifying the body, the mind, and all things: to cleanse the body and mind is also to cleanse the world around oneself. The face should not be washed because it is dirty, or left unwashed because it is not. The truth encapsulated in the practice of washing the face transcends ordinary concepts of the pure and the impure.

Verses

"Yes. It's *nyanni, sanpo, ansu inshi, nyanpin, sonshu nyan.*"

"Okay. Enkai, you're next. Let's hear it."

We'd been assigned a new task to perform while sitting: memorizing the various verses to be chanted through the day. These are something like sutras in the form of short poems. We recited them as we performed all sorts of daily actions from setting out our bowls and washing our face to using the toilet. At Eiheiji, without saying the appropriate chant at the appropriate time it's impossible to eat, or wash your face, or relieve yourself. And so we were forced to memorize them all.

I was a little fearful that after coming so far I might not be up to this task. Never had I felt so disheartened on account of my age, which was thirty. Most of my fellow applicants were kids fresh out of college, their powers of recall undoubtedly superior to mine. More than that, they were like the proverbial boy near the temple who knows the sutras without trying. Perhaps they couldn't recite every verse from memory, but a substantial portion was embedded deep in their minds like a familiar lullaby. This put me at a great disadvantage.

It wasn't just the sheer number of verses to be learned that was daunting. The Chinese characters with which they are written are pronounced in ancient Tang- and Song-period style, and mastering these unfamiliar, enigmatic readings was also a struggle.

Our progress was checked by our instructors, who would show up unannounced several times a day, notebook in hand, and test us one by one, noting down the result. They kept this up until we had all earned a pass in every verse.

Most applicants to Eiheiji come straight from Buddhist universities, and in a sense these sessions were extensions of college seminars. Not all of those born into temple families follow the same path, however. A few go to live in a Zen training monastery at around age sixteen and undergo monastic discipline while commuting to high school. In our group Choshu had done this, getting his high school diploma just before coming here. Still a teenager, he'd learned the basic verses by heart long ago and could carry off the various other tasks required of us with equal aplomb. He had far and away the best record of us all.

But I couldn't afford to sit back in admiration. Sitting cross-legged facing the wall, I opened the book containing the verses and said them over and over in my head.

Noon

Among all the thinking that human beings do, the question "Why?" has always been predominant. Undoubtedly it has played an enormous role in helping to bring about what we call progress. But in the course of each day's round of activities at Eiheiji, the question "Why?" is virtually meaningless. Delving into the rationale for every single action would mean that nothing ever got done smoothly. What is essential is to accept without question what you are taught to do, and throw yourself into it entirely. There is no room for subjectivity.

And yet the urge to search for meaning and purpose in all things is an instinct embedded deep within us; resisting it was not easy. At odd moments my mind, untethered, would fill with nagging doubts: "What am I doing this for? What's the good of it all?" Then I would be stuck in an endless process of trying to solve unanswerable riddles. Tormented by this unsettled state of mind and tortured by the inescapable and mounting pain in my legs, I continued to sit, sometimes on the verge of passing out. And so the morning passed. At noon we put our mantles back on and headed for the Buddha Hall.

The midday service was about to begin. As we had done the night before, the eight of us lined up on reed mats outside the entrance and joined our voices with those resounding within. As with the evening service, midday chanting always took place in the Buddha Hall, unless it was the founder's memorial day or some such special occasion.

The spring sun, its rays still weak but gaining daily in strength and luster, came filtering through the tops of the cedar trees into the Buddha Hall. It felt surprisingly warm. I'd forgotten that sunlight could be so warm. Since I first set foot inside Eiheiji, everywhere I'd gone had been far removed from the sun. The temporary quarters, the Walking Corridor, the Outer Hall, the washroom and toilet, were all set off by deep eaves. These rooms were dark and filled with pools of bitterly cold air.

I drank in the warm sunshine, marveling at nature's blessings. I wanted only for this pleasant interlude to last on and on. Yet the things we find most pleasant pass the most quickly, and the midday service was over in the blink of an eye. We went back to our room, grabbed our bowls, and set off for the Outer Hall. It was time for the noon meal.

In my old life, I ate without reflecting in particular upon the act of eating as such. I ate when I was hungry and stopped eating when I was full. Any thoughts I had on the subject concerned how to get the tastiest food possible, no more. But here at Eiheiji, eating was a major undertaking. It was not a question of hunger or satiety, or of food tasting good or bad. The point lay in the act of eating itself. Eating was the Dharma, the essence of Buddhist teaching, and vice versa. In his text *Rules for Eating Gruel* Dogen wrote out detailed instructions for how to eat:

> Do not eat from the center of the bowl. Do not seek extra vegetables or rice unless you are ill. Do not cover up the vegetables with rice in order to obtain more. Do not look into your neighbor's bowls or compare portion sizes.
>
> Pour all your physical and mental strength into the act of eating. Do not roll the rice into a big ball. Do not fill your mouth with a large amount of rice at once. Do not eat spilled grains of rice. Do not chew noisily. Do not slurp. Do not lick anything.
>
> Do not eat with your arms hanging loosely at your sides. Do not eat with your elbows on your knees. Do not spill rice and then peck at it like a chicken. Do not touch your food with dirty hands. Do not stir the food in the bowl and slurp it up noisily. Do not pile up food like a pagoda. Do not fill the bowl so full that it overflows.

Etiquette Is Zen

Do not pour soup on your rice to eat it. Do not put vegetables on top of the rice or mix them in. Do not fill your mouth with food and chew it for a long time like a monkey.

Do not finish eating before everyone else and then sit with your arms folded watching them eat. Do not rub your bowl and drool longingly when it is not time for a second helping. Do not ask for a second helping when you still have rice and vegetables in your bowls. Do not scratch your head and get dandruff in your bowls. Keep your hands clean.

Do not sway about, put your arms around your knees, sit with one knee raised, yawn, or blow your noise loudly. When you feel a sneeze coming on, cover your nose with your hand. When removing particles from between the teeth, cover your mouth with your hand. Place uneaten vegetable bits, seeds, and the like in the shadow of your bowl in such a way that your neighbors will not be offended. Even if a neighbor offers you his leftovers, do not accept them. If you must communicate with someone, do not speak in a loud voice but use gestures in silence.

If there are bits of food stuck to the sides of your bowl, wipe them off with the cleaning stick. Do not scoop up big spoonfuls of rice, spill rice in other bowls, or get rice all over the spoon. Do not talk with food in your mouth. When eating, do not make noises with your tongue or throat. Do not breathe on your food to warm it, or blow on it to cool it. If you find unhulled rice, peel off the husk and then eat the rice. Do not throw it away or eat it as is. If you find some unpleasant foreign object in the rice, do not eat it or bring it to the attention of others. Even if you eat something by mistake, never spit it out. If you have leftovers, do not save them but give them to the server.

When the meal is over, stop wanting more, and do not go on drooling. Do not noisily scrape the inside of your bowl with the chopsticks or spoon. Do not abrade the bowl and damage its finish. When you take a mouthful of hot water, do not swish it in your mouth noisily, or spit it out in the bowl or anywhere else. Do not wipe your face, head, or hands with the lap cloth. At meals, always observe the principle of not letting even a single grain of rice go to waste. It is for this reason that the Dharma is eating, and eating is the Dharma.

When Dogen returned to Japan after completing his studies in China, he observed monks eating at Kenninji, the oldest temple in Japan, and lamented that they ate "like wild beasts." That is how he came to write this text, which went on to acquire great significance as the basis of meal etiquette in Japan. The instructions written here are matters of common sense today. But for us neophytes, the days ahead were to bring all these matters home as never before.

Basically, the noon meal is just like the morning meal. The main difference is that instead of the chant on rice porridge, the leader chants as follows:

We offer this meal
of three virtues and six flavors[7]
not only to Buddha and the community of monks
but to all living beings.

After this chant, we were served rice, soup, and pickles, in that order, and finally a side dish. When all the food had been served, we recited The Five Reflections as in the morning. There was then one more ceremony, observed only at the noon meal: we offered the food we'd been served to hungry ghosts, chanting this verse together:

Hungry ghosts
I now offer you this.
All hungry ghosts everywhere,
together partake.

As we began the chant we would press our palms together, then dip the tip of our right index finger in our soup. With that fingertip we would then moisten the end of the cleaning stick, and place seven grains of rice on it. After that we moistened our finger in the soup again and wiped it on the lap cloth. The reason for moistening the stick was to keep the grains of rice from adhering to it.

As soon as second helpings had been dished out, the server went around with a pan and something resembling a small wooden hoe, and collected these grains of rice. They were scattered in a special place out behind the Monks' Hall, and eventually would make their way into the bellies of wild birds.

About the only difference between the morning meal and the noon meal was this collecting of rice grains, but even so the meal did not go smoothly for us. Just as before, we all performed shakily, heart in mouth, swallowing our food without tasting it.

The Chinese scholar Cheng Ming-tao (1032–85), on visiting Ding-lin monastery and observing the mealtime ritual in all its solemnity, commented that "the etiquette and music of the ancients are here in their entirety." Our style of eating might not have been quite as bad as that of wild beasts, but neither were we anywhere near summoning up the etiquette and music of the ancients.

Stick

Before my eyes loomed a wall of wood, polished in silence by many hands across the years. The grain of the wood stood out distinctly, like vertebrae in the spine of an emaciated old man. Countless times I traced the pattern by sight. It was just like this labyrinth with no exit that I'd fallen into: again and again my eyes would trace the pattern, only to end up right back at the start, or to be brought up short at the edge of the wall with no place to go.

At such times I would glance out the window, where the warm sunshine of early spring poured down on the tree branches. By contrast, how cold it was inside! The air sank heavily, as if frozen, and as I sat motionless, my arms and legs slowly went numb. I tried spreading the wide sleeves of my robe over my crossed legs, but the material was too thin to restore any heat to legs that were chilled to the bone. I longed for the sun. If I raised the window in front of me and leaped outside, its warm brightness would instantly envelop me, body and spirit. Captivated by this fantasy, I went on sitting.

The pain in my legs grew fiercer day by day. Sometimes it hurt so much that I drove fingernails into the flesh of my legs and drew blood. But the pain racking my legs was so violent that the jabbing fingernails felt only like strokes with the fleshy part of the finger over a thick layer of cloth. My legs had become abominable foreign bodies that did nothing but torment me.

Our days in the temporary quarters wore us down mercilessly through physical agony such as this, combined with the mental agony of fear and anxiety. And by allowing no latitude for personal feelings whatever, but forcing us to fit ourselves body and spirit into an unforgiving, constricting mold, the experience obliged us to give up all attachments. The days of initiation blended into one mind-bogglingly long day that allowed not a second's loss of vigilance.

Even so, time crept by until at last it was the seventh day. Although this was the final day, in the absence of any calendar, newspaper, television, or radio, we had completely lost track of time and were no longer sure how long we'd been there. Nor was the seventh day anything out of the ordinary: dawn came as usual, noon came as usual. But toward evening, the lead instructor came by and informed us that this ended our stay in the temporary quarters; the following morning there would be the ceremony of Entering the Hall. Until now we had been restricted to the Outer Hall, but tomorrow we would be allowed inside the sacred precinct of the Monks' Hall. The ceremony would mark an important step on our journey to acceptance as bona fide monks-in-training here.

Somehow, although we were still far from proficient, we had managed over the past seven days to learn the required etiquette and memorize the various incomprehensible chants. We had been continuously reviled, punched, and kicked, and yet without the resulting tension and fear we could hardly have learned so much in the short space of a week. Having one another to share these hardships with, too, had undoubtedly enabled us to come this far. Realizing that the severe initiation period was finally over, we traded looks of silent joy. Written on each face was the satisfaction of knowing that together we had gritted our teeth and accomplished something.

After that we had supper as usual and went to the Walking Corridor for night sitting. The session ended earlier than usual. We went back to the temporary quarters and, told to sit facing the wall again, took our usual places. In a short while the lead instructor reappeared with a flat wooden stick in his hand. He walked slowly back and forth behind us, and then began to talk in an unhurried, deliberate voice.

"Seven days have gone by since you people knocked at the gate of Eiheiji and started sitting here. Before that you lived in society in complete freedom, so your life here must have been painful. But this is

Eiheiji. Remind yourselves of this ordinary fact. And don't forget, it was you yourselves who knocked at the gate. Since you did the knocking, you have to get rid of wishful thinking and apply yourselves seriously to the discipline here. Eiheiji is the basic training ground of Zen. We treat everyone who comes here the same, no exceptions. Anyone who can't get rid of the wishful thinking he brought with him will get thrown right out.

"One more thing. Your initiation may be over today, but if you think you can relax now, you're making a big mistake. As long as you're still in this room, you haven't even gotten started. Now is when it finally begins. Is that clear? All right, starting with you on the end, one at a time, reflect out loud on your actions during the past week."

His speech finished, the lead instructor went and stood behind Daikan at the far end of the line. After thinking for a while, Daikan made a short statement of reflection. The lead instructor listened, made a few comments, and then brought the stick in his hand down hard on Daikan's shoulder. The sharp sound of the hard-grained wood hitting his shoulder instantly tautened the atmosphere in the room.

After that came Tenshin, Yuho, Enkai, Kijun, Choshu, and Doryu, until finally it was my turn. I took a deep breath and thought back on the long seven days before speaking: "Everything I encountered during the seven days of initiation was entirely new to me, and it was all I could do to take it in. The harder I tried to do well at what I was taught, the worse I did. I was made thoroughly aware of how hopelessly incompetent I am."

"To suffer for your own sake is a fine thing," replied the lead instructor. "Go on suffering after this, too."

I accepted his words, held my hands palm to palm and lowered my head to one side. Instantly, the stick slammed down hard on my right shoulder. I felt an invigorating vibration pass through my whole body.

The words spoken by the lead instructor that last night of initiation—"suffer for your own sake"—would come back to me over and over during the life of discipline ahead, always stiffening my resolve.

Tomorrow at long last I would enter the Monks' Hall. That night, like that first night in Jizo Cloister only one week ago, I was restless, unable to sleep. The thought of what would happen the next day filled me with equal parts joy and anxiety. The self-evident fact that whatever happened, time would continue its flow, made me happy. That simple fact gave me strength.

I can do this. As I lay sleepless, looking out the window at the expanse of sky, that is what I told myself.

PART THREE

Alone in the Freezing Dark

Entering the Hall

The induction ceremony took place in the Monks' Hall directly after the morning meal. When we headed for the Outer Hall for breakfast that morning, as well as our bowls and cushion we also took along formal socks and a bowing cloth. When we had finished the meal, we slipped the socks on and laid the cloth over our left wrist before getting down from the platform. Then we lined up, and the lead instructor looked each of us in the eye. After that, led by Daikan, who was carrying incense, we finally passed through the front entrance and on into the Monks' Hall, single file.

And so at last we set foot in the sacred heart of Eiheiji. The hall stretched before us in the dim light, cut off from the outside world by double walls. The air inside was of inordinate transparency. The room was laid out with startling simplicity, its silence deep with meaning.

Daikan set a stick of incense in the incense burner in the center of the room, while the rest of us waited tensely in line. Various kinds of incense are used, for various purposes, on the many occasions that mark the seasons of life in a Zen monastery; Daikan's action here signified a kind of solemn oath. As soon as he finished, we each spread out our bowing cloth and performed a triple obeisance. Every time I knelt and lowered my forehead to the floor, I felt a chill permeate my body. The solemn dignity of the moment was overwhelming.

Then we lined up again and circled clockwise around the central altar, each one bent forward from the waist with his hands held palm to palm and his head bowed. Circumambulation, a form of worship going back to ancient India, is the act of moving around a sacred object. Moving in a clockwise direction also suggests the east, the symbolic source of life, and beyond that the south, also associated with the sun. Our circumambulation thus signified walking toward the source of life and into the sunlight. We held our palms together, heads bowed, as we circled in silence. When this ritual was over, we filed silently back out into the covered walkway.

Outside, all was radiant. Everything that met my eyes shone brilliantly in the rays of the new-risen sun. The buds on the old plum tree in front of the Buddha Hall would surely swell to bursting in the spring sunshine of this long-awaited day. Rays of sunlight slanted through the latticed windows of the walkway, falling warmly on our feet as up, up we climbed behind the lead instructor. When we could go no higher, we turned to the left and went past the well containing spring water from Mount Haku, arriving finally at the Founder's Hall, where Dogen's spirit and ashes are enshrined.

The Founder's Hall faces the sprawling temple grounds, surrounded by tall trees. At its entrance is a huge incense burner, inside which the ashes are smoothed over and impressed with an oblong bar. Slender sticks of dark green incense placed in the groove made by the bar release wisps of fragrant smoke that silently mark the passage of time. Before entering the Founder's Hall, we each rinsed out our mouth and washed our hands with water from the basin, and then we purified our garments in the smoke from the incense burner.

Within the Founder's Hall is a worship hall paved with stones in the ancient Chinese fashion. Polished to a high luster, the stones reflect the soft light seeping through paper-covered windows, heightening the atmosphere of sublimity. Straight ahead hangs calligraphy by the Emperor Meiji, reading *Joyo*—a name posthumously given to Dogen in 1879. Below that, between circular pillars, stately vermilion stairs lead up into a dark recess where there is a sanctuary enshrining Dogen's ashes. The stairs, which only a handful of people with exalted qualifications are allowed to climb, exuded a mysterious air.

We lined up in front of the entrance and then, just as we had done at the Monks' Hall, we entered in single file, with Daikan bearing incense at the head of the line. When he had finished offering it, we all performed a triple obeisance, and the ceremony here was safely over.

The ceremony of Entering the Hall is one in which applicants who have been drilled in the rules and regulations of monastic life, and granted access to the Monks' Hall, go about paying formal respects to the founder and all his successors, including current teachers and monks-in-training. Although we now had access to the inner sanctum, we still maintained our provisional status, and would go on doing so until the day we went through a ceremony of registration.

Next it was time to make the rounds of the various residences, starting with the one next to the Founder's Hall, where we lit incense in the incense burner in the alcove, bowed low three times, and called out

Alone in the Freezing Dark

a greeting in unison. The lead instructor read out our names, and we were done.

From there we went to the Dharma Hall, the abbot's quarters, and Administration, and then further down the slope to Accounts, the kitchen, Buildings and Grounds, the Memorial Hall and the repository and exhibition hall for temple treasures. By the time we were done, it was nearly noon. So many places, I couldn't help marveling, and so many people in each one! Everywhere we went the air was taut with energy, and each person seemed driven by a sense of urgency that I found strangely beautiful and awe inspiring.

At one point in this ceremony, as we were en route to our next stop, an event took place that shook me. I was following silently behind the lead instructor, the special excitement I'd felt earlier beginning to wane as the number of ceremonies piled up, when we came upon some people going in the opposite direction. It was a group of old women, here presumably on a retreat. As soon as they caught sight of us they quickly pressed back against the wall to make room, and stood reverently with hands pressed together as we went by.

With a start, I realized for the first time that I had taken on the identity of a monk. Shaving the head and wearing monk's robes—neither action, taken in itself, is particularly difficult. Run a razor over your head, pass your arms through the sleeves of a robe, and voilà. But seeing those old women press their hands piously together as they faced us, I understood the immensity of what I had done. I was suddenly ashamed of the way I'd let little things upset me during the initiation period, of all the complaining I had done. I locked eyes with one of the old women at the end of the group. Her wrinkled hands were pressed together in veneration, and on her face was a beatific smile. Tears rose unbidden to my eyes. *I'll try hard. I've got to.* That was all I could think. My heart swelled with new resolve.

Monks' Hall

Now that our initiation was over and we'd been formally admitted to the Monks' Hall, this room became the focal point of our lives. At all Zen temples, the Monks' Hall forms the center of monastic discipline. The one at Eiheiji is built in ancient Song-dynasty style. The main entrance consists of heavy doors that slide open to the left and right, with paper panes on the top half to let in the light. Those doors open into the Outer Hall, where until now we had taken all our meals. Straight ahead, on the opposite side of the Outer Hall, a thick woven curtain marks the entrance to the hall proper. To enter, you roll the curtain up like a slatted blind and fasten it on a large metal hook. At the back end of the hall is another curtain of the same type, which instead of rolling up, you slip past through the spaces on either side. In general, entering through the front is restricted to formal occasions.

Behind the back entrance is the washroom for face washing. The Monks' Hall is flanked on the left by the Walking Corridor, and on the right by a narrow passageway known as the North Side Corridor. In the center of the Monks' Hall is a miniature shrine containing an image of the bodhisattva Manjusri with his hair arranged in five knots, the sword of wisdom in his right hand, and a lotus blossom in his left. Before the shrine is the "set of three" arrangement consisting of a censer, a candlestick, and flowers; before that is a low box-type seat of lacquered wood where the officiant sits to perform ceremonies. The shrine is surrounded by low wooden platforms, each covered with a tatami mat measuring roughly six feet by three. Each platform has a wooden edge where meals are taken, as in the Outer Hall, and storage space in the wall, with two shelves. The upper shelf is for sutra books and bowls, the bottom shelf for bedding.

As suggested by the saying, "Awake half a mat, asleep a whole mat," each person's tatami mat represents the personal space allotted to him in the Monks' Hall. For a trainee monk his mat is indeed the universe. The hall at Eiheiji is equipped with eighty-two mats, so it is capable of accommodating eighty-two monks-in-training.

After the induction ceremony, over each of our mats a black placard was hung up, inscribed with the occupant's name. Our group was assigned the line of mats along the wall next to the Walking Corridor.

In the "Rules of the Newly Built Meditation Hall" essay in *Treasury of the True Dharma Eye*, Dogen laid down detailed rules for comportment in the Monks' Hall. Following these time-honored rules, we too ate, sat, and slept on our mats.

> Let only those who earnestly desire the way and who have cast
> aside fame and profit enter this hall. Those without a mind of truth

must not enter. If such a person should enter the hall, he must be carefully examined and then expelled. Let it be well understood: once desire for the way arises, the desire for fame and riches will disappear in a moment.

All those in the hall should blend like milk and water, earnestly seeking the way of Buddha together. Although there is now the relation of teacher and student, later all alike will be buddhas and ancestors. Therefore, let all as one encounter that which is difficult to encounter and practice that which is difficult to practice, never forgetting the mind of truth. This is the mind and body of the buddhas and ancestors. All will definitely become buddhas; all will definitely become ancestors.

Those in the Monks' Hall have already left home and village behind. Relying on clouds and water, they aid one another's welfare and pursuit of the way. The debt thus incurred is greater even than the debt owed to father and mother, who are one's parents only for the duration of this life. Those in the hall will be friends in Buddhism for all eternity.

Do not willingly walk beyond the gates. Take your inspiration from those people who, long ago, went to live in far-off mountains and practiced ascetic discipline in distant woods. They not only left the world behind but cut all ties with it. Now is the time to rid yourself of wicked thoughts. If, at a time like this, you were swayed by things of the world, how regrettable that would be! Things of this world are impermanent and fleeting. This life of ours is as ephemeral as the dew, and what roadside grass it may fall upon we cannot know. It is truly pitiable.

Inside the hall, do not read books, not even Zen writings; only seek and clarify the truth, and practice the way of Buddhism wholeheartedly. Turn to the light shining through the windows, and let ancient teachings illuminate your mind. Do not waste a moment. Focus your thoughts single-mindedly.

Have nothing to do with the wrongdoing of others. Do not look on others' misdeeds with venom. If you neither find fault with others nor take pride in your own good deeds, you will come naturally to esteem the high and the low. Do not emulate others' wrongdoing. See to your own virtue. Buddha said to restrain the misdeeds of others, but this does not mean you should despise them.

If two monks quarrel, both of them shall be expelled. They impede not only their own Buddhist practice, but that of others as well. Anyone who looks on a quarrel without restraining it is to receive the same punishment. In all things large and small, report to the supervisor of the hall. Disturbances in the relationship between master and pupil eliminate the distinction between host and guest.

Do not go out on your own. An excursion could coincide with the end of this life. It sometimes happens that life ends in the midst of pleasure. Should that happen, you would surely feel regret.

Do not bring alcohol into the hall. Do not enter the hall drunk. Anyone who forgets and does this should pray and repent. Also, do not enter the hall reeking of leeks or onions.

Anyone who drops a utensil on the floor during the morning or noon meal must keep the oil lamp in front of Manjusri burning for twenty-four hours.

Do not blow your nose or spit loudly in the hall. Such actions show that one is not imbued with proper discipline, and are lamentable. Let us regret the subtle lapse of time that steals away even the life of training. Think of the mind of a fish that swims in a small amount of water.

Do not fail to observe all of the rules laid down by the buddhas and ancestors. Write the rules of the monastery on your flesh and bones. Let it be your desire to spend your life peacefully on the path of Zen. The rules above are the body and mind of ancient Zen masters. They must be revered and kept.

Zen, it has been said, aims to compress human physical needs to the barest minimum and to direct the human spirit to a higher sphere of activity. Diligent study to this end is concentrated within the walls of the Monks' Hall, a place that was, I thought, the epitome of self-denial. Row upon neat row of mats, one to a man, with shelves for bedding and bowls: that was all. Each occupant had cut off every tie with society and abandoned whatever riches and position were his, wordlessly turning his back on the stream of events in the world in order to sit, eat, defecate, wash his face, brush his teeth, sweep, polish, and pray.

I pondered the strangeness of it all. Monks take the human capacity for desire and turn it around so that, by observing the self that remains unsatisfied, that seeks no satisfaction, another, different self can obtain fulfillment in a different dimension. What convolution! Perhaps it's a kind of instinctual thought process unique to our species, one that comes into play precisely because we are so proficient at using every possible means to satisfy our longings that we don't know when to stop. Of all the creatures on the planet, we are capable of the most convoluted thought processes, a piece of good fortune that is perhaps also our misfortune.

When I saw the spare austerity of the orderly rows of mats in the Monks' Hall, I sensed the struggles that had taken place on each one, where previous occupants had struggled in agony, choking back bitter tears. I was flooded with a complicated sadness that I myself could little understand.

Common Quarters

At Eiheiji, some two hundred monks-in-training lead lives of strict discipline. Everyone belongs to one of a number of units called residences, each of which is responsible for a different set of specialized tasks. As is customary, new arrivals were assigned first to the common quarters, where our primary duties would be bell ringing and cleaning, under the close supervision of a second-year trainee.

In the Monks' Hall it is forbidden to look at writing of any kind. The common quarters is located behind the Monks' Hall, and it is here that monks can study the scriptures and biographies of ancestors. Its layout is the same as that of the Monks' Hall, with curtains at the front and rear, and a central statue—not of Manjusri, but of Avalokitesvara. All around this image are low platforms, as in the Monks' Hall, but here they are set lengthwise against the walls as in the Outer Hall, and the wall area behind each one is fitted not with storage space but with a reading desk.

We moved our things into these new living quarters. As before, we had to put them away in the prescribed places and in the prescribed way. When we'd done this, we followed our new instructor out of the residence and down a dark stairway beside the washroom to our work area. Here the floor was made of wood; in the back was a large sunken hearth and a miscellany of objects including an antique water heater, shelves, and low desks piled up in a corner. The walls were covered with a jumble of rules and announcements on big and little pieces of paper, creating a chaotic impression.

When we went in, we were instructed to get out the desks and line them up. We worked together quickly to get the job done. Next we were told to seat ourselves, and were each given a notebook and two pens, one red and one black. Our new instructor, holding a set of ledgers bound in heavy black paper, stood in front of us and launched into an explanation:

"This morning you finished your induction, and now you belong to this residence, the common quarters. These are the common quarters' work ledgers. They set out the various tasks you'll do while you're here. The first thing you need to do is to copy out the contents of these

Alone in the Freezing Dark

ledgers into the notebook you were just given. After that, memorize everything. When you're ready you'll be tested, item by item. Until you pass the test, you're useless around here, so look sharp.

"Even though you haven't passed the test yet, starting tomorrow you will participate in the day's work. Any mistakes you make will impact the whole community, and can even bring the temple routines to a halt. Keep that thought in mind, and do your best not to make any mistakes. While you're here, your day will begin two hours before the wake-up bell. Get your studying done in those two hours. Is that clear?"

Two hours before the wake-up bell? That meant we were now required to get up at 1:30 a.m. *For crying out loud*, I thought reflexively, *that's the middle of the night!* A hell of a time to be getting out of bed. This was serious. How long would we have to endure such torture? For a second, everything before my eyes went dark.

But eventually, knowing there was nothing for it but to comply, I swallowed my dismay and began copying from the ledgers the instructor had left behind.

The work ledgers were divided into different sections, with detailed descriptions of the various tasks. One of the first sections we'd be tested on was the list of instruments. "Instruments" refers to the various percussion instruments struck during the course of the day at Eiheiji. Since silence is the norm, each day begins and ends with the striking of an instrument. Every ceremony or activity is also heralded, and punctuated, by the striking of one or more instruments. It takes thorough familiarity with the various instruments to get through the day at Eiheiji.

We'd been told to begin by memorizing the names of all the instruments in proper order. Even though for now we were required to know only the names, it was no easy task to commit to memory an array of strange-sounding words, none of which held any meaning for us or brought any picture to mind:

shinrei senmenban shijo koten kyosho koten shokaijo daikaijo densho hozensho koten kyoku chohan ho ahappan dairai shinku unpan butsudenku saisho chohan ho ahappan dairai unpan unpan sodoban kairoban konku koten konsho kinhinsho chukaisho shijo koten sodoban josho hozensho kaichinrei

This is the sequence of bells, drums, and gongs sounded at Eiheiji during the course of a single day. On rest days, the sequence and combination differ; naturally, we had to memorize that pattern too. As I copied the words over, I muttered them to myself. *Shinrei, senmenban, shijo, koten . . .* It was tough going.

With the laundry list of names still far from fast in my mind, it was soon time for the evening meal. Afterward was normally the time for evening sitting—but today we instead went to pick up the various things we'd had sent to Eiheiji before coming. Except for the cushion and the wicker packs we'd brought with us on the first day, everything else had been sent ahead. The items to send had been clearly spelled out: two quilts of subdued color, a pillow, sneakers or split-toe heavy-cloth shoes with rubber soles, rubber boots, wooden-soled sandals, black work clothes, extra underwear, and a calligraphy set.

The instruction booklet we each had received from Eiheiji before leaving home told us what to bring and what to have delivered, how to dress on the first day, and what the initial procedure would be. It also included a section for the applicant's family that listed the following points:

- No one may leave the temple except in case of emergency.
- Please do not send snacks.
- No visiting is allowed.
- Contact by telephone will be indirect.
- Until further notice, mail cannot be sent or received.
- Money is not needed (except for one thousand yen to cover expenses in case of death), so please do not give the applicant any.
- Messages from the applicant will be relayed by the superintendent of monks.
- Should the applicant become acutely ill, he will be taken to a hospital and treated or hospitalized in accordance with a doctor's instructions, so please do not worry.
- Those with chronic conditions should have them attended to before coming. If there is a recurrence, the applicant will be examined by a doctor and sent home.

After a number of similar reminders and cautions, the section concluded with the following words:

> You undoubtedly will be concerned about your relative's well-being, but please know that the more you try to provide for him, the longer his suffering will continue. We ask that you do nothing for a time.
>
> Please faithfully observe all the above instructions. Every effort is made to maintain the health of the monastic community, so there is no cause for worry. However, please understand that when those who cannot rid themselves of immature or selfish ways fail to follow the rules, severe punishments will be meted out in accordance with temple regulations.

In the quiet of the night we trailed behind the instructor, heading further and further down the dark, roofed stairways. Our packages lay in a heap at the very bottom of the compound. When I found my own things in that jumble of boxes, and laid my hand on them, I felt a twinge of nostalgia.

I'd packed these things one warm afternoon when long rays of sunlight were streaming through the window. As I'd written my name on each item, my mother stood next to me, telling me to be sure to pack carefully so as not to forget anything. I responded to this conventional advice by saying I wasn't a child anymore. She looked pointedly at my awkward scrawl and said I was worse than a child, and we both laughed. The awkward scrawl and the tightly fastened knots were both there, just as I'd last seen them on that afternoon.

Each of us hauled our heavy burden back up the long stairway to the common quarters. When we got there, we were instructed to put our things next to the place we'd each been assigned, for inspection. As on the first night, anything not on the list was confiscated and put into a plastic bag marked with the owner's name.

When the inspection of Tenshin's things began, the instructor did a double take and yelled in a mixture of amusement and dismay, "What the hell is this! Are you out of your freaking mind?" Folded inside the quilts and tucked all around the other items were scads of chocolate bars, cookies, sweet buns, bean-paste jam, and other goodies. Tenshin himself clearly knew nothing about it and was flustered, while the rest of us could hardly keep from laughing out loud. Yet this was nothing but a loving gesture by a mother determined that her boy would not go hungry at Eiheiji.

Tenshin certainly gave the impression of having been raised by warm and loving parents who saw to it he lacked for nothing. His family ran a large, prestigious temple; he was, somewhat surprisingly, the second son. Most of the trainees at Eiheiji are eldest sons of a head priest, destined to succeed their father one day, but every so often a younger son makes his way there as well. Once I asked Tenshin what had led him to undertake this rigorous life even though he wasn't his father's heir. His answer was simplicity itself: "No real reason. After college there wasn't anything I especially wanted to do, and the life of a salaryman looked hard, so my folks said 'Well, why not go to Eiheiji, then?' So here I am."

Most of the other second and third sons I talked to had much the same story to tell. To them, the rigors of life at Eiheiji seemed less arduous than the life of a white-collar worker.

His anger vented, the instructor set quietly about removing all the snacks from Tenshin's belongings and putting them into a plastic bag.

When the inspections were over, night sitting was over in the Monks' Hall as well, and before long the bell signaling time for bed began to resound in the corridors. We each lugged our inspected and approved quilts over to our mat in the Monks' Hall. From now on, this was where we would sleep. Doing so meant that we would have to sleep according to the numerous rules laid out by Dogen in his text *How to Train in Buddhism*:

> When going to sleep, lie always on your right side, never on your left. Your head must always point in the direction of the buddha statue. If you place your head toward the wooden edge of the platform, it will naturally point in the right direction. Do not sleep facedown or with the knees raised. Do not sleep faceup with the legs crossed or stretched out. Do not sleep with your kimono pulled up, or naked, or in other unseemly ways like a rascal. Do not undo your sash.
>
> When you finally go to sleep in this way, do so focused on a point of light in your mind.

At Eiheiji, the word for lights-out—*kaichin*—means literally "opening the pillow." It goes back to the old days in Zen monasteries, when monks used to sleep on folding wooden pillows. Today the practice of unfolding the pillow for sleep survives only in this word. A bell announces bedtime at 9 p.m. At this signal the trainees all head to the Monks' Hall and, standing in front of their own mat, perform a triple obeisance to the shrine in the center. After this each one turns to his own place, bows once, and mounts the platform. Then he removes his mantle and robe, folds them in the prescribed way, and puts them on the shelf. There are no nightclothes at Eiheiji; everybody sleeps in the same kimono he wore in the day.

No mattresses are used at Eiheiji, either. Instead, each person has two quilts, which must take up no more than the allotted space. Before lying down you align them so that they overlap slightly, then roll them into a tube, which you tie snugly at the bottom and loosely at the top before wriggling inside. Finally, you tie the covers once more around your chest, lie on your right side, and go to sleep. This position is chosen because it is the same position in which Buddha entered nirvana. Lying faceup is called "corpse sleep," and lying facedown "debauched sleep." They are frowned on equally.

Night in the Monks' Hall. Under the high ceiling, in freezing darkness, I closed my eyes. In the awful stillness, only the faint ticking of the wall clock could be heard. The sound was hateful to me: at any moment the clock would strike ten, yet from now on we had to get up at 1:30 a.m. I was painfully aware that I needed to get to sleep, yet the ticking hampered sleep, growing steadily louder, pursuing me relentlessly.

What was the meaning of that "point of light" at the end of Dogen's notes on sleeping? As I lay there that first night, even if there had been a glimmer of light in the darkness of my mind, I was incapable of perceiving it. Before I might be able to comprehend the meaning of Dogen's light, there would be many more sleepless nights to endure.

Wake-up Bell

No sooner had I dozed off than I was shaken awake. I looked around, but nothing had changed from when I crawled inside my covers. The same velvety blackness lay over all. Could it be one thirty already?

Without meeting one another's eyes, we each silently stowed our bedding, dressed hurriedly, and left the Monks' Hall. In the darkness of the corridor, the light from the unshaded bulbs was strangely harsh and disagreeable. This thought was on my mind as I descended the stairs to the common quarters workroom, where light was already streaming from the door. Inside, one monk was busily tending a charcoal fire, while others huddled around it, warming themselves.

As on the day before, we pulled the desks into place and continued with our task of copying from the work ledgers. I wasn't sleepy now; but with my mind sunk in gloom, unable to foresee how much longer this would go on, I was incapable of a single positive thought. Around me, some of the others had their notebooks open and were studying, some were speaking earnestly in low voices, and the rest lay curled on the floor, fast asleep.

The freezing-cold air of the dead of night; the low sputter of the charcoal fire; a lingering listlessness in my limbs. My mind a jumble of these sensations, I propelled my pen over the paper.

After an hour or so, we put away our desks. This morning we were scheduled to accompany the trainee whose turn it was to sound the first bell of the day as he flew around the compound announcing time to wake up. Our job was to memorize the route.

When we got back to our room, he was ready and waiting. Quickly we got ready too, putting on formal socks and tucking up our kimono and robe at the waist so they came above our knees. After binding up our wide sleeves, we crisscrossed our belt tightly over our chest, the way we did for polishing floors. When we were dressed, we went to the stair landing beside the Buddha Hall.

Partly because the Eiheiji compound is so huge, the ringing of the wake-up bell is done simultaneously along two routes, one above the Monks' Hall, the other below. This first morning we would take the upper route, starting from the landing by the Buddha Hall. I stood in the open with my skin prickling in the cold night air, tense with determination. The monastery lay wrapped in silent darkness, on the verge of being roused from slumber. At any moment the wooden gong in the Outer Hall would be struck a single time, the signal for our mission to begin. We waited, hushed and listening, a faint excitement in our hearts.

Crack! The hard, clear sound of the gong ripped through the darkness. Instantly we dashed up the stairs in the corridor to the Dharma Hall, the insistent ringing of the handbell ricocheting off the walls around us. Then we shot past the Dharma Hall, went through Heaven's Gateway Corridor to the abbot's quarters, and turned in front of the abbot's room, flying past the Patriarch's Interview Hall, past Administration and the Seat of Enlightenment Hall, racing down the stairs at the end of the passageway and past Accounts, then down another flight of stairs, and on to the kitchen, where we ran clockwise around the great pillar there and then made a mad dash for the Main Gate. We ran this long course through the dark-enshrouded compound at top speed, without pause. It was all any of us could do not to lag behind; committing the course to memory was impossible.

At the Main Gate, our leader turned and shook the handbell strongly in the direction of the Buddha Hall, straight ahead. Then the gong in the Monks' Hall was struck a second time, at which the leader set down his bell and we performed a triple obeisance facing the Buddha Hall. After that, we sprinted to the Monks' Hall, the handbell now silent. It was over in no time, without a moment along the way for us to catch our breath. We were limp with exhaustion, our hearts pounding as if to burst.

The next day we took the lower route, starting next to the toilet. Just as on the day before, we were off and running at the sound of the wooden gong. We dashed down the corridor, slipped into the Memorial Hall and raced clockwise around the large fish gong there, then darted back out into the corridor, tore past the Visitors' Meditation Hall, swung right in front of the auditorium and raced to the basement. Then we ran to the right, crossed in front of the lesser kitchen, came to another set of stairs and tore back to the first floor, ending in front of the general office, where the bell received a final vigorous shaking.

Since the lower route ran downhill, we had anticipated an easier time than the day before. In fact, it was far more difficult, because at the end, when all our strength was used up, we had to run back up the long, long staircase to the Monks' Hall in one spurt, panting for breath.

There was one place where the bell was not to be rung. That was on the upper route going past the Dharma Hall, from the beginning of Heaven's Gateway Corridor till we had passed Administration. A red carpet was laid there, and beyond it the floor was covered with rattan. As yet unfamiliar with this part of the temple, we scampered at top speed through the dark compound with only the feel of the different floor coverings underfoot as our guide. At this early stage in our training, we had yet to set foot inside the Dharma Hall, let alone these other lofty places. It was therefore impossible to go back and physically review the routes that we had taken the past two days. Instead, we put our heads together and shared our recollections of where the corridors turned and forked, where there was a pillar, and so forth.

Starting the next day, we took turns ringing the morning handbell ourselves for real. And committed all sorts of unimaginable errors. We took wrong turns and ended up completely off course, hit dead ends and came to a sudden standstill. We rang the bell where we weren't supposed to, slipped and fell when going around the fish gong, lost our footing on the stairs.

Kijun's failure was more complicated. While he was running the lower route, the handbell clapper fell out. Like many Eiheiji trainees, he was the eldest son of a temple priest and a recent college graduate; apparently well brought up, he seemed to have no ambition or selfish desire, and carried out whatever task he was assigned with singular devotion. In terror that he would be taken to task for failing to do his job, he promptly raised his voice and went around making like a bell at the top of his lungs. It must have been hilarious.

Yet we were all in deadly earnest. At three thirty in the morning the temple grounds were still enveloped in darkness, the sky ablaze with stars. Eiheiji's day begins with the hammering pulse of a lone runner tearing at full speed around the compound, his heart at the bursting point.

Bell Tower

No colors of dawn showed yet in the ink-black sky. A mournful rain fell in long silver threads from the leaves of the ancient cedars to disappear into the lichen below. "Damn this rain . . . ," I muttered to myself, facing the great bell in the bell tower. Today, tolling this bell at various times during the day would be my task, beginning now, in the early morning.

The tasks assigned to the common quarters, eleven in all, were rotated among us every day so that we all had an equal chance to carry out each one. Briefly, the eleven tasks are as follows: ringing the hand-bell announcing time to rise, striking the cloud gong by the kitchen, beating the drums in the Outer Hall and the Dharma Hall, working all day in the Monks' Hall as supervisor, assisting the Monks' Hall supervisor, working all day in the common quarters as supervisor, working all day in the common quarters office doing miscellaneous chores, preparing meals in the kitchen and overseeing the progress of meals in the Monks' Hall, assisting with preparation and overseeing of meals, overseeing special meals by loudly calling out the various steps, and tolling the great bell in the bell tower.

The bell tower at Eiheiji, located below the Main Gate, is designed in the dignified and beautiful style of the Kamakura period (1185–1382). The enormous bell hanging inside it is five feet in diameter, ten feet high, and weighs some five tons. It is a gracefully curving bell embossed with images of flowers and birds, grasses and trees.

At Eiheiji it is not enough to strike an instrument in the prescribed way; you must also dress in the precise way stipulated for the occasion. This means changing clothes every time you strike a different instrument. To toll the great bell I was decked out formally with mantle and formal socks, and I also had with me a bowing cloth and a watch.

For this first tolling of the day, I was supposed to start walking toward the bell tower as soon as the wake-up bell sounded. I prepared myself ahead of time, stood waiting for the ringer of the wake-up bell to sprint by, and then took off. In front of the bell tower, just under the long wooden beam with which the bell is struck, there is a box-shaped seat just like the one before the altar in the Monks' Hall. I knelt on it, spread out my cloth, and performed a triple obeisance. Then I recited this chant:

> May all suffering be eradicated.
> May all living beings in this world
> hear the sound of this bell and
> enter into the way of enlightenment.

The first peal must sound just as the last chime of the time-telling bell in the Outer Hall fades away. But wouldn't you know it, on this day of all days it was raining. The more I strained to listen, the more the sound of raindrops tapping branches and water splashing on rocks blocked off all other sounds. Yet for centuries, this great bell had been tolled day in and day out, in every kind of weather; it was unthinkable that the sound of the time-telling bell wouldn't carry this far. I comforted myself with this thought, but I felt uneasy anyway, this being my first time.

And worse luck: today the one striking the time was, of all people, Tenshin. The other day when he was supposed to be sounding the cloud gong by the kitchen to announce the end of the sitting session, for some reason he was off in the Monks' Hall taking part in the sitting session with everyone else. One of the senior trainees, realizing the signal hadn't been given, hastily ran over and did it for him. Even then, Tenshin didn't notice his mistake, unconcernedly continuing to sit to the very end. Who knew what scrape he might get into today? Just thinking about it made me more anxious.

When I finally caught the distant sounds of the drum and bell through the rain, I came to myself. Aiming for the exact moment when the last reverberation ended, I grabbed the rope hanging from the big horizontal wooden beam, yanked it toward me with all my might, and rammed the beam into the side of the bell. The wavelets of sound caused by millions of raindrops falling into the darkness were overtaken by an immense billow of tone that rolled out from the great bell, shaking the predawn temple grounds.

After every tolling, I was required to kneel and bow down. As soon as I released the rope I prostrated myself, overawed by the commanding presence of the bell.

At dawn the great bell was to be tolled eighteen times, at intervals of one minute and fifty seconds; hence the need for a watch. Lined up on the lacquered seat in front of me were eighteen small stones, to be slid off one by one as visual confirmation of the number of tolls remaining. Moreover, of the eighteen total, the fourteenth had to be soft, and the seventeenth and eighteenth had to be a soft-loud sequence signaling the end.

All of the tasks in the monastery were interconnected. If the drum and gong in the Outer Hall were not sounded properly, the monk waiting by the bell tower could not do his job. If the fourteenth toll were not properly soft, the one whose signal that was to do his job would be stymied. Any misstep was not just an individual blunder, but had the potential to bring to a halt the monastery's entire cycle of activity. There was no room for mistakes.

Tolling the bell softly, moreover, was tricky. It meant manipulating a tool intended to produce a loud sound in such a way that it produced a soft one. If the sound was too slight to carry through the compound, it served no purpose, and if it was so loud that it was indistinguishable from the rest, it was equally a failure. After the thirteenth toll, I checked my watch. When the moment came, I gingerly hauled back on the rope and then jerked it awkwardly forward. Holding my breath, I watched the rope leave my hands and drift forward with the beam, slowly approaching the bell. Gently it touched the round spot embossed with a lotus blossom, setting off a slow, quiet reverberation. Success!

The next most difficult thing about this job was timing the interval of one minute and fifty seconds between each toll. You began when the second hand was on twelve; after the second toll, you waited for the second hand to sweep all the way around once, and then struck the bell when it pointed to ten again. After that you let it go once around again, and struck the next time it reached eight, and so on.

This was harder than it sounds. If all I'd had to do was keep an eye on the second hand, it might not have been so bad, but I was tense and jittery to start with, knowing I couldn't mess up. At times my mind would go blank: had the second hand already made its circuit? Which number had it pointed to the last time I pulled the rope? That wasn't all, either. I was supposed to shift the stones in front of me each time I did my triple obeisance, but the more I thought about it, the more unsure I became:

had I remembered to do it the time before last? Suddenly I would have no idea how many times I'd struck the bell. Such doubts could lead to increasing confusion, until the situation turned chaotic.

Alone in the dark bell tower before dawn, chased by the second hand on my watch and fishing nervously for memories that evaporated behind me one by one, I managed somehow to toll the bell eighteen times, do my last prostrations, and leave.

My next job was to go to the Buddha Hall to signal the time. I bowed my head in respect to those on their way to morning services, then headed for the Buddha Hall, watch at the ready. Behind the central altar are a drum and a bell, the drum a large one like the one in the Outer Hall, the bell a smallish one about a foot in diameter. Various combinations of drumbeats and bells sound the time periodically during the day. The drum is used to sound the hour, the bell to sound the minutes. No distinction is made between a.m. and p.m.; either way, one o'clock is represented by a single drumbeat, five o'clock by five. To indicate minutes, each hour is divided into two half-hour segments, from ten minutes before the hour to twenty after, and from twenty after to ten before. For the former, the bell is rung once, and for the latter, twice. Thus 5:10 would be five drumbeats and one bell, and 5:40 would be five drumbeats and two bells. There is one other little twist: 5:55 is not five drumbeats and one bell, but six and one.

All these rules had to be learned by heart. It was forbidden to carry out any sort of task while referring either to the contents of the work ledgers or to any sort of notes. Successfully carrying out a complicated task like the tolling of the morning bell was thus an enormous challenge. There were no dress rehearsals. When the time came, you had to go to your assigned station alone and do the best you could with nothing but memory as guide.

Because the instruments gave off such loud sounds, moreover, mistakes were painfully evident. Once a mistake was made, there was no way to remedy it. We each had one chance, and one only, to get it right. We knew only too well what fate would befall someone whose chance was wasted.

After the busy round of morning activities—sutra chanting, morning meal, floor cleaning—I headed again for the bell tower. At 10:55, five minutes before noon chanting, the cloud gong by the kitchen was struck three times, followed by three beats of the drum in the Buddha Hall. Then, without any pause, it was my turn. This time the bell was to be tolled nine times at thirty-second intervals, and after each toll instead of prostrating myself I would merely bow from the waist.

By now the rain had let up, and the dark loneliness of the early morning was gone. Now, in place of the dreary rainfall that had blocked out all other sounds, I could hear wind in the treetops and the cries of wild birds near and far. As monks came and went in the covered walkways, the cheerful sound of voices and laughter came intermittently to my ears, creating a mood of unutterable warmth and peace. Once I finished this task, I would be at the halfway mark for the day. The thought lifted my spirits as I executed the final soft-loud sequence.

When the long morning was over and the halfway mark past, time seemed to speed up. My bell-ringing duties resumed in the evening, after the sun had vanished behind the mountain crest and the compound had begun to slip back into bottomless darkness. Tenshin, my assistant for the day, accompanied me to the Buddha Hall, where together we would signal the onset of dusk. The pattern was the same as in the morning, but the bell was rung a single time, while the drum sounded twice, then three times. We swung around to the rear of the Buddha Hall and went in through the back. Then we switched on the light and waited.

Abruptly Tenshin said, "Hey, want to see what I've got?" He held out his hand in the light from the naked bulb. The palm was covered with copious notes in tiny lettering, written with a ballpoint pen.

"Wow. But . . . are you sure it's okay?"

He grinned. "Don't worry. If I'd written it on a piece of paper I might get caught, but this way, who'll ever know? We never have to show our palms."

I conceded his point, but couldn't help adding, "Yeah, but remember what happened the other day when somebody got caught cheating. The poor guy was almost kicked to death. Pretty scary if you did get caught."

"The way I figure it, if I don't cheat, I'll just get kicked anyway for screwing up. Either way, what's the difference?"

Our discussion had led to a strange conclusion. Anyway, it was time to get to work. I beat the drum once, yielded my place to Tenshin, and set off for the bell tower. I needed to begin tolling the great bell exactly as he finished sounding the hour. The covered walkways had begun to fill again with silent darkness as the shades of night closed in fast. The faraway, intermittent tolling of Tenshin's drum reverberating through the dusk produced a deep emotion in me.

I finished tolling the evening bell and hurried toward the Walking Corridor for night sitting, which was already underway. A heavy, stifling silence filled the corridor. I could not go inside the Monks' Hall because I had to return to the bell tower before the end of the session for the final tolling of the great bell. The beginning of sitting was marked by the "stop-and-be-still" bell, the end by the "release-from-sitting" bell. For the space of time between those two sounds, the hall was completely cut off from the rest of the world, with no one permitted to enter or leave. I would participate from a platform in the Outer Hall.

At eight thirty the reading of Dogen's *Universal Recommendation for Sitting* began, and I joined my voice in with the rest. At a fixed place in the reading, I slipped slowly from my platform and stole off to the bell tower. When I got there, I took a little extra time with the triple obeisance, knowing that this was the end of my assignment for the day. In the Monks' Hall the reading would be coming to an end. After that the gong would be struck three times and then, just as that reverberation faded away, I would begin to toll the great bell nine times, at thirty-second intervals.

When I'd completed my obeisance, I checked my watch. I must have walked fast, for I was a little ahead of time. Relieved, I looked up

Alone in the Freezing Dark

casually at the night sky; over the bell tower stretched a shimmering firmament of stars. Then it hit me: was there ever any light so pure? It seemed as if at any moment shards of shattered light might come tumbling down in a soft, jingling rain.

As I gazed at the starry radiance, so beautiful that it blurred the boundary between the real and the unreal, I could scarcely believe that under this same sky shone the lights of the town where I'd so recently lived. That back in the garden of my rental house in Zushi, surrounded by the sea and the peaceful hills I loved, stray cats would be roaming as usual. The streets of Tokyo's Shibuya district, where I'd commuted to work by train, would now be overflowing with young people in a swirl of light and energy. My old friends would be carrying on as usual, laughing out loud at some trifle. And what about my parents? When I'd walked out the front door on my way here, they'd seen me off with smiling faces—yet the secret trepidation I'd glimpsed behind those smiles was something I would never forget. Probably they'd been consumed with worry this whole time. That was the kind of parents they were, as I well knew. What could I possibly do to set their minds at ease?

As I was pondering this, the bell I'd been waiting for began to ring in the distance, and then from the Monks' Hall the wooden gong sounded three times: first medium volume, then softly, then loudly. I gripped the rope firmly, drew the wooden beam toward me with all my strength, and let it hit the great bell straight on. *May this sound carry across the heavens and into my parents' hearts*. That wild, impossible hope filled

Eat Sleep Sit

my mind as I went on tolling the bell for dear life. Under a starry sky so beautiful that it made me want to weep, I could do nothing else.

Self-reflection

Unlike the shrill, insistent ringing of the wake-up bell that rent the darkness every morning, the slow, intermittent reverberations of the evening bell produced a sound that was somehow forlorn. No one could hear that sound without feeling a pang at the waning of another day.

As soon as the evening bell had finished tolling, we gathered for a time of self-reflection. This meant looking back on what we had done that day, stating the mistakes we had made, and getting the slate wiped clean. We did this every night, kneeling formally on the floor, buttocks on heels, with no cushion or mat between us and the floorboards. The average duration of a session was thirty minutes, but sometimes it went on for an hour. We had to maintain our posture on the hard floor the entire time. By learning each other's mistakes, we not only gained practical knowledge of matters not covered in the work ledgers but also were reminded of our proper place in Eiheiji and how to conduct ourselves accordingly.

In the common quarters, whoever was first admitted to Jizo Cloister automatically becomes the group leader. He presides over self-reflection meetings under the supervision of the common quarters' director, who first announces and distributes the following day's tasks before the topic of discussion moves on to that day's errors.

Our discussions focused solely on errors in work performance. We were expected to announce anything that had gone wrong, however minor. It would perhaps be more accurate to say that we were compelled to own up to our errors. All day long, wherever we were, someone was observing us; nine times out of ten, word of our slipups had already reached the ears of the common quarters' director, who would eventually absolve us. Sometimes we were let off with a warning; more often we were yelled at, punched, kicked, and otherwise given hell. Anyone caught covering up his failures was in for an even worse time. No excuses or arguments were tolerated. Each man had to succumb unresistingly to his punishment, and so be absolved.

Eiheiji is a completely hierarchical society. This fact does not derive from any particular era in Chinese or Indian history; it's just the way things have always been at Eiheiji. The hierarchy in batches of newcomers determined on the first day at Jizo Cloister, by the order of admittance, is fixed and immoveable, and it defines one's relation to every other member of the group regardless of age, education, status, or wealth. Herein lies the essence of Eiheiji equality. Among trainees in general, the year of admission is the determining factor; there is little sense of hierarchy between groups admitted at different times in the same year.

The hierarchy of relationships in the monastery can be understood by analogy to the flow of water: just as water flows naturally from a higher vessel to a lower, so Buddhism has always been conveyed from one human vessel to another, drop by precious drop.

In his 1244 text, *Instructions on Revering Monastic Superiors*, Dogen set down the etiquette young monks are to observe in dealing with their seniors:

> When entering the cell of a superior, do so from the edge of the entrance, not the middle.
>
> When facing a superior, always straighten yourself up and hold perfectly still.
>
> Until your superior has sat, do not sit.
>
> Until your superior has stood, do not stand.
>
> Until your superior has eaten, do not eat.
>
> Until your superior has finished eating, do not finish eating.
>
> Until your superior has bathed, do not bathe.
>
> Until your superior has gone to sleep, do not sleep.
>
> In front of your superior, do not scratch yourself or remove fleas or lice.
>
> In front of your superior, do not blow your nose or spit.
>
> In front of your superior, do not rub your face with your hand, scratch your head, or fidget with your arms or legs.
>
> In front of your superior, do not use a toothpick or rinse out your mouth.
>
> In front of your superior, do not shave your head, trim your nails, or change your clothing.
>
> In front of your teacher, do not yawn with your mouth wide open. Cover your mouth with your hand.

In front of those above you, do not suddenly laugh out loud or behave in a disgraceful way.

In front of your superior, do not sigh out loud. Observe the rules of etiquette and approach a superior with respect.

When you are given a lesson or a reprimand, always listen respectfully with your mind open, as when hearing Buddhist truth, and reflect deeply.

Do not forget to maintain an attitude of humility before those above you.

Do not preach to others unless you are instructed to do so by your superior.

When questioned by your superior, answer according to the rules of propriety.

Be aware of your superior's moods, and avoid causing disappointment or anger.

When you are with your superior, willingly take on unpleasant tasks yourself. Leave the pleasant tasks for your superior to do.

When you encounter a superior who is qualified as a teacher, have a mind of respect. Do not show boredom.

When you have a chance to approach a superior who is qualified as a teacher, see that you inquire about the meaning of ceremonies and the thrust of precepts. Do not look down on your seniors or act puffed up around them.

In front of your superior, do not discuss the good and bad points of other eminent priests.

Do not look down on your superior and engage him in nonsensical debates or ask joking questions.

In front of a superior, do not scold another even if he deserves it.

When your superior has forgotten something, inform him politely.

Even if you see that your superior has made a mistake, do not laugh out loud in contempt.

When your superior is preaching to a benefactor, sit up straight and listen attentively. Do not get up abruptly in the middle and walk out.

When your superior is preaching, take a lower seat and do not debate the merits of what he says.

When confronted with the teacher of your superior, be well aware of that fact and accord him full courtesy.

When confronted with the disciple of your superior, treat him with the courtesy due his teacher. There are distinctions of high and low among your superiors. Be aware of them, and do nothing to cause trouble.

Your superiors will be your superiors for all eternity. From the day you first take up a peaceful life they will be there, and when you attain the buddha awakening, they will be there also.

The above instructions for revering your superiors are the very body and mind of all the buddhas and ancestors. If you do not learn them, the way of the ancestors and teachers will be abandoned, and the truth in all its goodness and purity will be destroyed.

From the beginning, self-annihilation has been an important task imposed on Zen monks in everyday discipline. To cast aside the ego means to cast aside your selfhood, determinedly reducing yourself to nothing, all the while revering and obeying your seniors and carrying out your daily chores in perfect silence. Yet mere awareness of this requirement does not enable anyone to easily set aside something so important as himself. Besides, we all had received an education influenced by modern Western thinking, in which all existence is considered from the standpoint of the self.

Those bound up in the self are broken down unrelentingly at Eiheiji through name-calling and thrashing. All the baggage people bring with them—academic achievement, status, honor, possessions, even character—is slashed to bits, leaving them to sink to rock bottom and thus cast everything aside.

Looking back, I remembered that on those first nights in the temporary quarters, sometimes I would fall into a light sleep only to be awakened by a great noise. It was the sound of someone slamming into a glass-paned wooden sliding door, and it was always followed by what sounded, through the intervening walls, like a muffled scream. Every time I heard this, I shuddered involuntarily. Later, the first night that my group held a self-reflection meeting, I understood what lay behind those ominous sounds. But the process of absolution that took place in the nightly meetings was a necessary evil for the purpose of breaking down the ego.

Without going into the history of Zen, let it be said that the relationship between master and disciple has always been fraught with peril.

The hapless disciple is beaten with a stick, kicked, slapped on the head with his teacher's sandal. But to revile all such actions as violence is too hasty a conclusion. Before an act can be labeled violent, its underlying purpose must be ascertained. A little thought will show that in the context of Zen discipline, the fundamental purpose of a beating or thrashing is not to inflict injury or pain. Such acts are rather a means of conveying living truth from body to body and mind to mind, a form of spiritual training and cultivation.

I learned that when one's self-respect and modesty are wiped out and all the things one cannot relinquish are blown to smithereens, life can be apprehended much more calmly. As my days at Eiheiji piled up, I generally cared less and less about all that I'd previously agonized over; I marveled that I'd ever let so many little things cause me mental stress. Problems that had loomed before me as a great wall against which I could only bash my head seemed now, on cooler inspection, so flimsy that I could blow them over with one puff if I chose. Or, if I looked a little to one side, I could spot an easy escape.

Every time I was pummeled, kicked, or otherwise done over, I felt a sense of relief, like an artificial pearl whose false exterior was being scraped away—an exterior that previously I had struggled fiercely to protect, determined not to let it be damaged or broken. Now that it was gone and I had nothing left to cover up or gloss over, I knew that whatever remained, exposed for all to see, was nothing less than my true self. The discovery of my own insignificance brought instant, indescribable relief.

Food Server

When our group was assigned to the common quarters, three other groups were there before us. The eight members of our group brought the total number of residents to thirty-four. Since eleven tasks are allotted to the common quarters, at any given time twenty-three of us were off duty. Those without a special task for the day stayed busy mainly by practicing seated meditation, attending services, and dishing out meals.

The kitchen is located in a splendid edifice with a hip-and-gable roof. Just inside the entryway is a statue of the kitchen deity Idasonten, flanked on the right by Daikokuten, a god of luck, and on the left by Saitokujin, the Year God. Hanging in front of the kitchen is the cloud gong, struck to signal the end of sitting as well as the beginning of meals. The sound of this gong is said to summon rain clouds, and it is hung by the kitchen to ensure a rich harvest.

The job of the food servers begins with transferring prepared food to the appropriate serving containers. Rice porridge, steamed rice, soup, and vegetables are all cooked in huge vats. Servers line up in front of the vats, each with a bucket to fill. The server whose turn it is raises his bucket high, to eye level, and shouts out his assigned number. Then he must position himself just so and receive the food just so. Particular care is taken with the first bucket, food from which will be offered to the image of Manjusri in the Monks' Hall.

While each server shouts his request, the kitchen monks stand motionless, palms pressed together in reverence, before they begin respectfully to transfer food from the vat to the proffered container.

But should a server's voice not be loud enough, or should he make the slightest mistake in the way he positions himself or offers his bucket, he will be instantly yelled at and struck.

Though the task of receiving food is essentially a simple one, doing it just the right way is far from easy. The first time I entered the kitchen as a server, I was intimidated by the darkly gleaming pillars and high ceiling—not to mention the murderous shouts. Before coming to Eiheiji, I envisioned a life so hushed that you could hear ash falling from a stick of burning incense, with endless days of suspended motion and silent introspection. The reality was vastly different. Soon after arriving, I realized that the life of an Eiheiji trainee was a never-ending succession of loud, angry tongue-lashings and beatings—a world away from my fond imaginings. Nowhere was the difference between imagination and reality more striking than in the kitchen.

When everything was ready, the head cook would stand with his back to an image of the deity Idasonten and prostrate himself nine times before the prepared meal. On a table in front of him were the first buckets of food—rice, miso soup, and pickles, if it was the noon meal. The servers would stand facing each other at either end of the table, palms joined, and lower their heads at each of the cook's prostrations. During this ritual, no one was permitted to walk past, so the corridor in front of the kitchen was closed off.

Before coming to Eiheiji, like everyone else in Japan I would say "*Itadakimasu*" (I humbly receive) out loud at the beginning of a meal, but I could never rid myself of a certain embarrassment about, and internal resistance to, saying it with my palms joined. I automatically rejected the gesture as smacking of religiosity. Yet the act of placing the palms together before eating should not be lightly dismissed. At bottom, it is not an acknowledgment of the existence of some superhuman Other whose gift to us is food, but an expression of humble gratitude for what one is about to eat. Such gratitude is an important principle that must be held to if human beings are to coexist peacefully with their neighbors and with nature.

When the cook finishes his prostrations, the meal is borne off to the Monks' Hall by the servers, who then proceed to dish it up. In *Rules for Eating Gruel*, Dogen wrote out the following pointers for servers:

> In serving food, if the pace is too fast, the one receiving will hurry, and be unable to follow the way of Buddha. If the pace is too slow, the one receiving will have time on his hands, and feel tedium. The server should carry out his tasks with due care, making sure never to get broth or gruel on his hands or the rim of the bowl. To prevent this, shake the ladle several times over the bucket, and wait a few seconds before serving. While serving, bend forward; the hand not holding the ladle should be kept folded on the breast.
>
> The amount of food to be served should be left to the discretion of the receiver. The bucket should not be held with the arm hanging straight down. If the need to sneeze or cough arises in the middle of serving, turn away. In carrying the food buckets, always follow the way of Buddha.

Meals in the Monks' Hall cannot take place without the servers. Serving food to others is as important a discipline as the act of eating. In fact, every aspect of life at Eiheiji depends on the close interaction of various people, each diligently performing his allotted task. Not even sitting is a purely individual act, but is made possible by the unseen labors of a great many others. Which actions are central and which subsidiary, moreover, is impossible to say. All are of equal importance, and fundamentally, all are one.

Monks' Food

The *Rules of Purity for Chan Monasteries* says, "One should maintain a way-seeking mind, make adjustments in accord with the occasion, and see to it that the great assembly receives food at ease." In other words, whoever prepares food in a monastery kitchen should do so in a spirit of seeking the way of Buddha; he should use ingredients appropriate to the season and cooking techniques appropriate to the ingredients, in order to give variety to the daily menu and ensure that everyone who partakes can do so with enjoyment.

At Eiheiji, cooking for trainee monks is done not by professional cooks but by trainees themselves, under the supervision of a master whose role is head cook. Cooking, like eating, is considered an important discipline and a form of merit that nurtures goodness within the community. Washing rice, cutting pickles, and cooking radish are not only culinary arts but also forms of ascetic discipline that must be done, as stated in the quotation above, with a profoundly "way-seeking mind."

Utmost care is lavished on the ingredients and menu, taking into consideration the season and events on the monastery calendar. In accordance with the prohibition on taking life, a strict vegetarian regimen is followed—but not all vegetables are permitted. An old saying has it that "garlic and wine may not enter temple gates," and indeed the use of pungent vegetables such as onions, leeks, scallions, pickled ginger shoots, chives, and garlic, is forbidden.

At Eiheiji, the morning meal consists of rice porridge, a sesame and salt mixture, and slices of yellow pickled radish. The porridge is generally made using brown rice, but it is customary to use white rice on the first and fifteenth of the month. On these days, another plate is added containing a dab of two extra foods such as pickled plum, nori or konbu seaweed boiled in soy sauce, butterbur stalks boiled in soy sauce, salted konbu seaweed, miso wrapped in an aromatic shiso leaf, or kichijo shigure—this last a wonder food that looks and tastes exactly like meat or shellfish boiled in soy sauce, but is in fact made of soy protein.

There is also seasonal variety. Some of the various ingredients added to porridge include the seven spring herbs,[1] adzuki beans, tea, soybeans, pickled plum, greens, sweet potato, seaweeds such as konbu or wakame, ginkgo nuts, pounded rice cake, peas, and corn.

The sesame and salt mixture is made by lightly roasting sesame seeds, adding salt while the seeds are still warm, and pounding them roughly with a mortar and pestle. Rather than making large amounts of the mixture at one time and storing it for future use, each day's servings are prepared the same way, day after day.

Pickled radish is made in the kitchen each year in late fall and early winter. An entire year's worth is put up at once, using some eight thousand radishes. Huge vats in the kitchen basement are filled with layers of sliced radish, alternated with layers of bran that has been mixed with salt and cayenne, the level of saltiness varying in different vats. A monk wearing straw sandals tramples this down, and finally a heavy stone is set on top. The vats are opened in order of saltiness beginning in early February.

Lunch consists of rice, miso soup, pickles, and a side dish. The rice is mixed with barley in a six-to-four ratio. Other foods occasionally mixed with the rice include pickled plum, konbu seaweed, ginkgo nuts, vinegared vegetables, shimeji mushrooms, and a mixture of dried shiso leaves, pickled plum, and salt.

Miso soup is usually made with three extra ingredients, typically any of the following: radish, turnip, cabbage, potato, sweet potato, taro potato, eggplant, pumpkin, shimeji mushrooms, nametake mushrooms, Chinese cabbage, parsley, spinach, trefoil, radish leaves, konbu seaweed, dried radish strips, tofu, deep-fried tofu in thin strips or chunks, and wheat gluten. There are no restrictions on miso, and various kinds are used depending on the other ingredients. On occasion a clear soup is served containing strips of tofu, bamboo shoots, or konbu seaweed, and sometimes there is a vegetable chowder.

Pickles for the noon meal are not made from radish as in the morning, but from vegetables such as turnip, eggplant, cucumber, turnip leaves, radish leaves, or Chinese cabbage, which have been packed in salt and left to sit overnight.

The noon meal also includes, in addition to rice and soup, one dish of stir-fried or dressed vegetables. These are among the dishes most commonly served: seasoned vegetables mixed with tofu; green beans with black or white sesame dressing; fermented soybeans and enoki mushrooms mixed with grated radish, soy, and vinegar; tofu lees; blanched spinach; spinach and tofu flavored with ginger and soy sauce; strips of dried radish, deep-fried tofu, and chrysanthemum leaves flavored with sesame and soy sauce; eggplant, green pepper, and corn stir-fried with miso; Chinese cabbage and noodles stir-fried with tofu; stir-fried bean sprouts and wood-ear mushrooms; Chinese cabbage and shiitake mushrooms stir-fried with salted konbu seaweed and wheat gluten; a mixture of cabbage, carrot, green pepper, and corn stir-fried with tomato ketchup; stir-fried burdock root and carrot; stir-fried lotus root and carrot; hijiki seaweed simmered with soybeans; burdock root, parboiled, pounded, and seasoned with sesame and other flavorings; and boiled radish pickle.

The evening meal consists of rice, miso soup, pickles, and two side dishes of vegetables. The rice and pickles are generally the same as for the noon meal, but care is taken not to repeat any soup ingredients twice in the same day. The vegetable dishes are served in a shallow bowl and on a small plate. The shallow bowl generally contains three types of boiled vegetables, including any of the following: radish, turnip, carrot, burdock root, potato, taro potato, sweet potato, mountain yam, pumpkin, eggplant, bamboo shoot, shiitake mushrooms, spinach, flowering ferns, butterbur, green beans, cauliflower, broccoli, konbu seaweed, grilled tofu, freeze-dried tofu, or deep-fried tofu; fried dumplings made of tofu, vegetables, egg white, and sesame; millet gluten; and konnyaku devil's tongue jelly. The cook is not limited to traditional Japanese cooking styles, and may sometimes use cream or margarine. Other foods that make an appearance include chilled sesame tofu, and deep-fried tofu served in a hot, soy-flavored sauce.

The contents of the small plate overlap to an extent with foods served for the morning meal, with the addition of vinegared vegetables, boiled beans, or other foods. The main foods served include a vinegared salad of carrot, konnyaku devil's tongue jelly, and the asparagus-like vegetable known as udo; a vinegared salad of mozuku seaweed and cucumber; rolled wheat gluten with sesame and vinegar; finely chopped bamboo shoots, konbu seaweed, and udo in a dressing of vinegar and miso; cucumber, konbu seaweed, and millet gluten in a mustard miso dressing; macaroni or potato salad; boiled adzuki beans and agar-agar cubes with molasses; peas, black soybeans, or large white kidney beans sweetened with sugar.

Dogen died on September 12, 1253, and on the eleventh of every month the supper menu features tea-flavored porridge and a special soup. First everyone is served a shallow bowl filled with potatoes, carrots and the like, and then miso soup is ladled over the vegetables.

Alone in the Freezing Dark

Although it seems similar to ordinary miso soup, the method of preparation is a little different: the vegetables are first cooked in stock and then removed and arranged in bowls, while the remaining broth is mixed with white miso and then flavored with soy sauce, cooking sake, sugar, and salt.

Although formal meals are eaten in the Monks' Hall as a rule, on occasion they may be eaten in the various residence halls, in an abbreviated style, without using the Buddha bowl. Sometimes—very rarely—foods are served here that never appear in the Monks' Hall. For one, we sometimes ate hot noodles flavored with grated radish, crumbled nori seaweed, and white sesame, topped with three pieces of tempura such as eggplant or sweet potato. We also had curry, and stew with a cream sauce—meatless, of course. The curry sauce is actually referred to as "curry soup," and pouring it on the rice is strictly forbidden. Stew, too, is referred to as "stew soup."

I should mention here that even though the main ingredients are all vegetables, such dishes are not strictly vegan. At Eiheiji, curries and stews are made using standard commercial roux, which does contain meat products. Even so, this does not violate any Buddhist precept.

In Thailand and other countries practicing Hinayana Buddhism, which emphasizes adherence to ancient precepts, monks go begging for their food. They eat whatever is placed in their begging bowl, be it meat or vegetable, without penalty. The *Discipline of the Ten Chants*[2] stipulates three conditions under which it is permissible to eat meat: if you did not see the animal being killed for your consumption; if you did not hear of the animal being killed for your consumption; if it is certain that the animal was not killed for your consumption. As long as these three conditions are satisfied, the meat placed in Thai monks' begging bowls may be eaten with impunity.

What really matters is the determination not to take life. In fact, society is full of people who spend so much energy pursuing the means of doing something that they lose all sight of purpose. Rather than thinking about purpose, people are more attracted by, and more proficient at, having various methods at their disposal. But methods that are devoid of purpose or detached from ultimate meaning will often—like war, and like development in the name of progress—lead only to disaster.

Shaving the Head

Time at Eiheiji is not divided into seven-day weeks, but is marked off by days ending in four and nine. Known as "days of rest," they begin an hour later than usual, at four thirty in the morning. On these days there is no sitting, either in the morning or evening, and no manual labor. Instead, trainees' time is devoted to shaving the head and face, trimming the nails, bathing, mending clothes, and other personal tasks. There is no free time; these are not vacations. At this stage of our training, however, our group was still required to get up two hours before the wake-up bell, and we were not yet permitted to bathe.

Rest days begin with a shorter version of the morning service, followed by the usual morning meal. Afterward, a special bell is rung in the Outer Hall to signify that this is a day off, and special clappers are sounded in the washroom as a signal to begin head shaving. These two instruments, used only on these days, sounded bright and cheerful.

In *Treasury of the True Dharma Eye*, Dogen had this to say about shaving the head and trimming the nails:

> The nails of all ten fingers should be trimmed, as well as the toenails. It is written in the sutras that it is a sin for the length of a fingernail or toenail to exceed the length of a grain of wheat. Therefore, nails should not be allowed to grow long. Growing long fingernails is an abomination. Be sure to cut the nails short.
>
> These days, however, some Chinese monks without correct understanding of the scriptures let their nails grow long—as long as one, two, three, or even four inches. This goes against the teaching of Buddha. It does not represent the mind and body of truth. People do such things because they have failed to learn the way of Buddha. Zen masters with a way-seeking mind do not do them.
>
> Some people also let their hair grow, but this too goes against the teaching of Buddha. Let no one be under the mistaken impression that just because monks on the continent do something, it must be correct. Previous teachers criticized monks with long hair and nails, in these harsh words:

> Those who lack understanding and do not keep their head shaven are neither lay nor monk. They are animals. From of old,

has there ever been any buddha or ancestor who did not shave his head? Those who fail to do so today are indeed nothing but animals.

You should know that long hair is forbidden by the buddhas and ancestors, and long nails are heathen. Those who are heirs to the buddhas and ancestors must not willingly carry out such abominations. Purifying the mind and body means trimming the nails and shaving the head.

On days of rest, floor polishing still had to be carried out as usual, but when it was finished the monk in charge would go to the Outer Hall to fetch the placard that read Head Shaving. These placards are thick wooden boards inscribed with notices such as Sitting or Bathing, one for each of a wide assortment of events in monastic life. Once this placard was hung at the entrance to the common quarters, head shaving could begin.

We residents of the common quarters shaved our heads in the Walking Corridor. Whoever was in charge would spread out a red carpet on the floor and supply each of us with a basin and two buckets, one filled with hot water and one with cold. Those whose heads were to be shaved tied the sleeves of their robe out of the way, and got out a hand towel and razor. After each person filled his basin with comfortably hot water, trainees paired up and took turns shaving each other's heads. At Eiheiji, incidentally, this is done without soap lather, let alone shaving cream;

the head is simply moistened with hot water before applying the razor.

The rite is carried out in an attitude of respectful silence, after mentally reciting the Verse for Shaving the Head:

As I shave the stubble on my face and my head,
I vow with all sentient beings: may all
cut off selfish desires
and enter into the realm of liberation.

Only the scraping of razors across hot, wet scalps echoed faintly in the taut silence in the dim, high-ceilinged space of the Walking Corridor.

The day before I arrived at Eiheiji, I shaved my head for the first time in my life. I did it without any of the glistening array of tools you read about in old tales. I just sat myself down cross-legged in front of a mirror and, after a last look at my face as I might never see it again, snipped off my forelock with a pair of scissors, straight across. In a businesslike way I set about hacking the rest of my hair off, and in no time the newspaper in front of me was heaped with black clippings. Looking in the mirror, I locked eyes with a self whose hair was now grotesquely ill cut. After that I used electric hair clippers, swiping them across my scalp from the forehead to the back of the head, shearing everything off. When I was done, my head felt completely round. Checking the mirror again, my appearance no longer seemed grotesque, yet something about it was vaguely sinister, I thought. Quickly coming to myself, I squeezed out shaving cream and lathered my nearly bald head, then stroked away the white lather with a brand-new safety razor. The sensation of shaving my head for the first time, including the cold feel of the blade on the top of my head, was wonderfully clean and bracing. It was nothing like shaving off the facial hair, which only grows on part of the face. I wielded the razor with caution, trying not to cut myself.

And so, without any dramatic emotional catharsis, having nicked my scalp in only a couple of places, I emerged with a brand-new shaven pate. I sat up then and took a good look at myself in the mirror. I still remember the sensation of that moment. A chill came over me. It felt as if every drop of my blood were being sucked out of my veins; as if second by second my body were turning to ice. The figure in the mirror wasn't me.

"Giving up the hair of one's head means giving up the root of one's desires; when desires are cut off even a little, the true self appears." So goes a line from Dogen's *Abbreviated Etiquette of Becoming a Monk*. Shaving the head is the outward sign of a fierce determination to distance oneself from longings of the heart and eradicate delusion. As I took in my newly shaven-headed appearance in the mirror, I was thunderstruck. It sank in for the first time that I must now and forever cast aside all the human desires that I had until this moment embraced.

Hair that keeps growing as long as we live, shave it as we will, resembles human desires that know no end. In the old days, shaving the pate was done with a blade, and hair clippings were gathered in a board fastened around the head and then burned. Burned hair gives off a foul odor. As they inhaled the stink of their burning hair, monks of old must have reflected deeply on the sad nature of their unquenchable desires.

Daikan

Daikan came to Eiheiji the same day as me, and was the first in our lot to be granted permission to remove his sandals and enter Jizo Cloister. In his midforties, he was among the oldest of the novices that year. His swarthy skin covered a delicate bone structure, and yet—thanks perhaps to the life he'd led before coming here—he gave an impression of toughness.

Daikan had a wife and a teenage son whom he'd previously supported by working as a truck driver for a transport company. Yet now here he was, a shaven-headed monk. His wife was the only daughter of a temple priest, and one day an abrupt change of circumstances in her family had turned Daikan's peaceful existence upside down. He was forced to give up his former livelihood and prepare to spend the rest of his life as head priest of the family temple. Having to go into business might have been one thing; taking the tonsure was quite another.

Becoming a temple priest is not just a matter of shaving the pate, donning a mantle, and chanting sutras. Every head priest of a Soto Zen temple must possess the official rank of "teacher" as determined by the sect's head office. There are various levels within that ranking, and each individual temple has its own traditions and rules; anyone wanting to become a head priest must attain the level stipulated by the rules of his temple.

There is no elitism at Eiheiji; the relative prestige of the temple one is from does not speed up or slow down the course of training. And yet the importance of academic credentials in Japanese society has seeped into the world of Zen as well. It takes less time for a college graduate to complete his training than it does for someone with only a high school education. A college degree counts extra, a degree from a Buddhist university counts still more, and a graduate degree counts most of all. Choshu, who before coming to Eiheiji had only graduated from high school—even though he commuted there from another Zen training monastery—would take far longer to score the necessary points than the rest of us, who had all graduated from college. Yuho's training period would be the shortest, because although he had no prior experience of monastic life, he did have a graduate degree from a Buddhist institution.

Whether monastic training is completed at Eiheiji—one of two head temples of the Soto Zen sect—or at one of the sect's regional branches also figures into how long it will take someone to qualify for the priesthood. Training at Eiheiji takes significantly less time. Daikan, with neither advanced academic credentials nor monastic experience, faced a long haul before he could qualify as a head priest. And so, rather than training at a local temple where discipline would be comparatively light, he had no choice but to endure the grueling regimen at Eiheiji.

He was always up before anyone else, sitting by the hearth with his big, rough hands outstretched over coals just starting to turn red. I liked to sit there beside him and listen to him reminisce about his life as a trucker. My conception of a truck as a mere vehicle for transporting goods was utterly unlike his. He spoke about his truck with the warmth that other men reserve for their family and friends, if not more so.

His face flushed from the fire spreading over the gradually reddening coals, his eyes alight with pleasure, Daikan would talk of how comfortable he felt in the driver's seat of his truck with his hands on the big steering wheel, or describe the lights of unfamiliar cities streaming past his window at night. Little by little, he shared memories of driving all over Japan. "Wish I was in my truck now." How many times I heard him say that, as we sat together by the hearth! He swore that once his training was over and he got back home, he'd buy another truck and take off in it. Picturing him seated in a semi as a shaven-headed priest, it was all I could do to keep from laughing out loud—yet I hoped that somehow his dream could come true. Watching him become more isolated within the group each day, singled out for unpleasant treatment by our instructors, only strengthened the feeling.

Zen discipline is not penance. But for those of relatively advanced years, it exacts a heavy physical toll. Moreover, for Daikan, who lacked any grounding in Buddhism, everything had to be learned from scratch, a monumental task given the mind's decreasing powers of memory in later life. Thanks to a sturdy physique hardened by years of work, he could hold his own physically with the rest of us, but it took him two or three times longer to memorize things. He struggled to master the contents of the work ledgers. His errors meant that whoever was working with him was punished too, so the others gradually began to regard him as a thorn in their side.

Not only did his peers turn cold, but "senior" trainee monks half his age put the screws on him, punching and kicking him daily in what must have been a painful ordeal. But in order to get back to the wife and child anxiously awaiting his return, he had to stick out the full period that would qualify him to be a head priest.

That morning (of course, our "morning" began at one thirty, two hours before the wake-up bell) Daikan was sitting by the hearth as usual, frowning intently at the open ledger before him. I asked how the memorization was coming. His answer was the same as usual: "Terrible. No matter how many times I go over it, I still can't get it in my head." Today, he added glumly, he'd asked a few of the other trainee monks for help with something he didn't understand, and no one would tell him anything.

The tasks were performed as written in the ledgers, but the account there was a bare-bones summary. Usually, whoever did the task first would pass along unwritten practical information to his successor. I went straight to the fellow who had performed that task the day before and asked point-blank why he wouldn't tell Daikan what he needed to know. The reply I got was equally straightforward:

"Because even if I tell him, he won't get it right. It's a waste of time. I'm busy too; I haven't got time to be his nursemaid," he said, contemptuously, without looking up from his work ledger.

I burst out, "Why do you only see the bad in people?" Instantly the mood turned sour. I knew I'd said something stupid, and I regretted it.

As every kind of human craving was methodically stripped from us, a muddle of suppressed desires and emotions, unresolved, built up inside and began to seek some outlet. The lack of any fixed outlet contributed to our precarious mental state. We were all on edge now, testy about the least little thing. Forced to live in close quarters under constant pressure, we were slowly losing sight of normal human pleasures and joys. Scarcely realizing it, we—all of us—had begun taking out our discontent on those weaker than ourselves.

Even I, who had just self-righteously accused someone else of seeing only the bad in others, at times took secret pleasure in hearing of my peers' mistakes or in seeing them physically attacked. Maybe my retort that day had less to do with aiding Daikan than with taking advantage of a needed opportunity to vent my own suppressed anger. In any case, with our backs pressed up against the wall, my fellow trainee monks and I laid bare the ugly side of human nature.

I will never forget how Daikan clenched his fists and said over and over, "I won't give up!"

As his failures piled up, the senior trainees began to keep a weather eye on him. As punishment he was often ordered to kneel formally all alone in the corridor. Sometimes the punishment was excessive; one day he was ordered to go without meals and sit in a corner of the freezing Walking Corridor all by himself. Under ordinary circumstances, a man can forego a meal or two without difficulty, but at Eiheiji, where the food we consumed was the minimum necessary to sustain life, missing a meal was unimaginably painful. That day, Daikan ate nothing in the morning and was kept sitting in the corridor, denied the noon meal as well. Out of pity, even though I knew I shouldn't, while cleaning up in the kitchen I quietly wrapped up some leftover rice and vegetables to sneak to him later.

"Hang in there," I said, slipping the contraband into his kimono sleeve, and he nodded. The clenched, gnarled fists on his skinny thighs shook as he muttered, "I won't give up, I won't!"

And yet before six months went by, he would fall ill and have to be hospitalized.

Hunger

Far away, someone was groaning. I leaped out of bed, only to realize it was a dream. Dismayed at the discovery that someone's stupid dream had interrupted my precious, all-too-short time for sleep, I tried to drowse off again, to no avail. Finally it hit me that the groaning was real. Beside me, Doryu lay curled in anguish, his forehead beaded with sweat. "What's wrong?" I asked, but in answer all he could do was moan, his face screwed in pain. Choshu woke up too, and together we undid his covers. As we suspected, his knees were badly swollen. Since we'd come to the common quarters, he was the third one to come down with this illness.

One morning, I finished shaving my head and set about trimming my nails only to discover with a start that despite the elapsing of many days, they hadn't grown at all. That was when I first began to notice that little by little, our bodies were ceasing to function properly. The rate and degree of this physical breakdown depended on the individual, but the symptoms were all alike.

First, the body would swell. Those who were badly afflicted would find their arms and legs swollen to bursting; the skin lost its elasticity and when pressed with the fingers would not rebound right away, but retained the imprint. Urination increased abnormally in frequency. However often a sufferer went to relieve himself, he would soon feel the urge to go again; some people, unable to make it through long services and ceremonies, wet themselves. Wounds sustained to the knees or the soles of the feet during sitting took forever to heal. The wound would remain gaping, often picking up germs so that the pain and swelling worsened. Some people ended up being rushed to the hospital with a high fever. Doryu, too, was quickly hospitalized.

These symptoms are the result of beriberi, a disease caused by excessive carbohydrate intake and vitamin B_1 deficiency. Among trainee monks at Eiheiji, the cause was clear: eating too much rice. Our seniors had warned us about the risk. Gorging on rice would only make us sick, we knew—and yet we couldn't help ourselves. That's how desperate we were.

At this stage in our training our hunger was at its peak. While sitting or while huddled under the covers at night, we thought of nothing but food, and even suffered from hallucinations. The hunger was indescribable, like nothing I had ever experienced before. Until coming to Eiheiji all of us had lived ordinary lives where any time we were hungry we could eat our fill. But now, from the time we woke up at 1:30 a.m. until we went to bed at 10:00 p.m., apart from the three daily meals we could eat nothing. Moreover, the amount of food served was very small; the vegetable side dishes contained a mere mouthful or two.

The only foods we were allowed second helpings of were miso soup and rice. The soup bowl was small and the soup was mostly liquid anyway, so it did little to assuage our hunger. For those who were famished, that left no alternative but rice. As with miso soup, only one extra helping of rice was allowed, so the maximum anybody could eat was a scant two bowlfuls. That this relatively small amount of rice could lead to an excess of carbohydrate in the diet was a sure indicator of the overall scantiness and poor nutritive value of what we ate.

If we ate rice to satisfy our hunger, we made ourselves sick. If we didn't, we starved. Those were our only choices. Of course, the hunger we felt was not the kind of starvation that leaves you hovering on the brink of death. It was rather a kind of hunger or starvation of the spirit; brought up in an age of plenty, we were easy prey. Our morale plunged, tumbling us into a deep slough that we couldn't climb out of.

It wasn't long before grown men were bickering heatedly over a mouthful of rice, a cup of soup, a slice of pickled radish. Formal meals took place in the Monks' Hall, but anyone whose assigned duties kept him from eating there with the others would eat informally at a low table in the work area. No servers dished out those meals; instead, everyone helped himself straight from the meal buckets. With no one in charge to ensure that there was enough food to go around, it was every man for himself. If you didn't look sharp, the rice paddle would be scraping the bottom of the bucket in no time, and all the vegetables in the soup would disappear, along with the side dishes and pickles.

I was furious with everyone for having no consideration for anyone but themselves. "Think about someone else for a change!" I said self-righteously. I wasn't particularly trying to put on a show of dispassion. The kind of fellow who gorged himself without a qualm just made my blood boil.

Ancient Buddhist regulations treat the act of eating as a kind of defilement. To us at that point, eating did indeed seem like something furtive and dirty. Unable to content ourselves with what we were offered, we were assailed by uncontrollable cravings that deeply wounded our self-respect.

The provision of informal meals is not limited to the common quarters; trainee monks in all the residences take occasional meals in their residences. In the common quarters, informal meals are prepared by the trainee in charge, who also must prepare meals for the two adjacent residences and clean up afterward. This involves bringing in trays of dishes from the neighboring residences to be washed in the sink. Every day, several trainee monks would gather when the trays came in, and proceed to fight over the leftovers. I stood dazedly by, watching others snatch up morsels and cram them into their mouths by the fistful, feeling troubled and guilty for having seen something I should not have. To think that these were human beings—it was all inexpressibly sad.

"Rosan, you think too much," someone said to me. "Lighten up." The next moment, I too had grabbed a fistful of food and was stuffing it into my mouth. A sense of fullness spread inside me, yet at the same time I felt bleak and empty.

Once you get away with something bad, without suffering even a reprimand, it often happens that you develop a new set of values accordingly. In time, I forgot that initial sense of emptiness. Rationality didn't enter into it. When people are locked into a world of unrelenting pressure, their sense of reason, I found, is all too vulnerable. And no amount of reason could fill an empty belly. Everyone was left with that most primitive of instincts fully exposed—the lust for food.

Not long after Doryu went into the hospital, Kijun went in, too. The rest of us kept right on cursing each other in dead earnest over the size of our helpings, and squabbling over others' leftovers. In the end, some people would sneak out in the dead of night to forage in the plastic garbage pails for anything they could find to eat.

At Eiheiji, all leftovers from the formal meals are thrown away, regardless of the amount. When we were assigned to cleanup duty in the kitchen, every day we would throw away huge amounts of leftover food, despite our private struggles with hunger. This practice is hardly commendable, but it was a necessary evil in monastic life. It is a matter of deep regret that food should go to waste; and yet if there were any leftovers, monastic discipline required that they be discarded.

Reason made us obediently throw out leftovers as garbage, and instinct made us treat the garbage as food, pawing through it at the

Alone in the Freezing Dark

mercy of our ravenous appetites. Both actions were inherently and indisputably human in nature. This contradiction is part of the eternal agony and dilemma faced by human beings, who have both a mind and a body. Ascetic discipline at Eiheiji suppressed our raw desires to the point that the divide between body and spirit stood out inescapably, forcing us to face this dilemma head on.

The Passage of Time

Escape

It was shortly after the noon meal when Gikai went missing. We'd barely settled in at the common quarters to study when someone came bursting in and demanded, "Where's Gikai? He wasn't at lunch!" That was the first we knew he was gone. At first we couldn't take in the meaning of this sudden development, but gradually it dawned on us: Gikai had run away.

Gikai, a fellow monk in training, was a member of a group two jumps ahead of ours. Like so many at Eiheiji, he was fresh out of college, the eldest son of a Zen priest. We barely knew him. None of us could remember what he looked like. He'd never done anything in particular to disgrace himself, nor was he an exceptional student. He was a quiet, unassuming fellow—the last person you'd expect to run off.

We were ordered to go look for him. Seeing how distraught our lead instructor was, we realized the seriousness of the situation and fanned out immediately. The number of places to search was limited, though, and we found no sign of him. Eventually the senior trainees in charge of discipline joined in, and the search spread beyond the temple gate.

Every year, Eiheiji accepts new applicants from February through early April. During that time, batches of newcomers arrive every four or five days, adding up to as many as a hundred and fifty freshmen per year.

Of all these recruits, a handful are bound to run away—an undertaking far harder than it sounds, for several reasons. To begin with, Eiheiji is surrounded on three sides by mountains, none of them easy climbing, especially for someone unfamiliar with the local terrain and unequipped for the task. Even if a runaway made it across the first mountain, a number of equally challenging peaks would remain before he came to any village. The only practical avenue of escape is through the town at the temple gate, using some form of public transportation—bus or taxi—to start with. What makes this next to impossible is a huge problem: lack of cash.

Every newcomer is relieved on his first night of any money he may have brought along, except for the one thousand yen reserved for funeral expenses. This is left in the wicker pack he brought with him, which is elaborately bound up in layers of gray cloth and takes considerable time and effort to undo. New trainee monks of course have no free time, and nowhere to be alone except the toilet. Moreover, the wicker packs are never opened in the normal course of things and are of all trainees' possessions held particularly sacred; anyone seen fiddling with them would come under immediate suspicion. Even if someone were to attempt this at night, in the few hours allotted for sleep, it would be risky because of night patrols.

Given all this, the best recourse for anyone bent on leaving is to go into a coffee shop in town, ask to borrow the phone, and call home—or else just hop in a taxi and take off. Even then the temple generally hears about it right away.

Eat Sleep Sit

The relationship between Eiheiji and its monks is different now from what it was in the days of itinerant monks who drifted around the country with their begging bowls. It has become the premier training place for young men who will inherit the leadership of the nation's Zen temples. Eiheiji is responsible for the care of these young men and cannot simply look the other way when someone decides he has had enough and wants out. Those who beg admission to Eiheiji do so knowing full well that the discipline demands do-or-die resolve; Eiheiji must be no less resolved that no one will fail. Upsetting the order and solemnity of this arrangement is unthinkable. Whatever changes may have come about over the course of the centuries, Eiheiji remains the central training site for Zen in Japan. The locals understand this, and so when someone takes off, they quickly notify the temple.

But even if a runaway managed somehow to get hold of some cash and slip aboard a bus or train, he still wouldn't be in the clear. New trainees are expressly forbidden to leave the temple gates on personal business. As one's length of stay extends, this rule is relaxed, but anyone leaving is required to dress in work clothes. Kimonos, rarely seen on the streets of Japan these days in any case, stand out unmistakably, and the sight of a black-robed young man wandering around town would set off instant alarm bells. Without discarding the telltale monk's robe, escape is virtually impossible.

Despite these daunting hurdles, every year several people do make good their escape. Some chance it by breaking into their wicker pack in the dead of night, grabbing what money they can, and making a run for it. Others use bills sewn ahead of time into a kimono collar. Most, however, take flight on the spur of the moment. No doubt an opportunity presents itself out of the blue and they respond reflexively, fleeing barefoot in the dark before there is time to think. By the time they realize what they've done, it's too late to turn around and go back. Regret is not an option.

People run away because they can't take the daily discipline. It's not the ordeal of sleep deprivation or hunger that drives them away. Rather, they run in terror and panic from the constant clashes with senior trainees. For such people, nothing could be more horrifying than the thought of being caught and taken back to face the wrath of their tormenters. And so they run for dear life, trying to get as far as they can, for that is their only hope. They scramble in the mountains in the black of night, tripping on fallen tree branches. Or they steal through the alleyways of the town and hide in shadows, scarcely breathing, fearful that at any moment they may be seized by the scruff of the neck and hauled back.

In the end, Gikai was never found. How he managed to get home I don't know, but a few days later we heard that someone in his family had phoned the temple to apologize.

Registration Ceremony
Gikai was gone. Including the others who had disappeared before him, that made five escapees in all, leaving a total of 111 arrivals who stuck

it out that year. Our registration ceremony was carried out in solemn formality one fine spring day when late plum blossoms and cherry blossoms were both in bloom. The entire Eiheiji community gathered for the occasion. Registration meant that we would lose our provisional status and be recognized, finally, as resident trainee monks of Eiheiji. On the eve of the ceremony, we met in the common quarters workroom and were told to grind ink on our inkstones. Then we were each handed two sheets of blank paper, one for our resume and one for our vow. The director wrote the proper format for each on the blackboard, and we referred to that as we dipped our brushes in the ink and began to write. The vow, in classical Chinese, went as follows:

> I, the undersigned, herewith attach my resume. Now, in view of the enormity of the issue of birth-and-death, I entrust myself to this place. From this time forward I will strictly observe all the rules of this monastery. If I should break any of them, I will accept the punishment. I prostrate myself and hope for compassionate acceptance.

Every character was heavy with solemn implication. As I propelled my brush across the paper, with each dot and stroke I sensed the reality of having come this far. When I was finished, I signed it and affixed my seal, folded the vow together with my resume inside another sheet of paper, wrote "Registration Vow" on the front in big black characters, and handed it in.

On the day of the ceremony we did early-morning cleaning as usual, and then it was time. The director laid our vows on a small red lacquer stand and presented them to the superintendent of monks' training. The superintendent then led us from the Walking Corridor into the Monks' Hall. After one of us offered incense, all of us performed a triple obeisance and then circled around the hall. Next we turned to face the sitting platforms and, at the sound of clappers, did the triple obeisance again, first to the platforms and then to the senior trainees lined up on either side and facing us. The entire ceremony took place in silence. When it was over, we moved in procession to the Founder's Hall, where, as before, incense was offered and we prostrated ourselves. Then in a long line we filed out, past the Dharma Hall and through Heaven's Gateway Corridor until we reached the Patriarch's Interview Hall.

The Patriarch's Interview Hall, where the abbot receives formal visitors, is built entirely of cedar wood in the classic style of the Azuchi-Momoyama period (1568–1600). The enormous main room contains 298 tatami mats, and at one end of the room, in a slightly elevated area behind rolled-up bamboo blinds, were wall paintings—an old pine, a hawk, plum blossoms, and bamboo—by Suiun Komuro, a painter of the literati school of the early twentieth century. The elegant simplicity of the brushwork, in india ink and rich pigments, lent even greater beauty to the formal room. We filed in and stood in rows, facing forward. Since coming to Eiheiji we had not seen colors so sumptuous.

When we were settled, a side door slid noiselessly open and an old priest appeared. This was Master Renpo Niwa, the seventy-seventh abbot of Eiheiji. His eyebrows were as white as crane feathers, and below them his eyes shone with a preternaturally keen light that was discernible even from my far-off vantage point. There was about him an indescribable magnetism; he stirred my innermost being. Few people in the history of the world can have had such powerful magnetism, I thought, imagining that Buddha and Christ must have drawn men to them with this very force.

The holy man seated himself in the center of the elevated area. The member of our group who was acting as representative immediately stepped forward and presented him with the stand bearing our vows. We performed a triple obeisance and then sat down. Three people's names were called, and they went up to the central incense burner. As the very first ones to have arrived at Eiheiji this year, their names headed the roll. They had come in the middle of February, when the snow falls hard and thick. That fact alone spoke volumes about their determination. Each of them picked up his vow and read it aloud with deliberation, then replaced it on the stand and went back to his original place.

The holy man sat on a gold brocade cushion with heavy silk tassels and followed everything with keen attention. Then he began his sermon. Whatever message he may have given us I have since forgotten, but I will never forget the mesmerizing beauty of that voice. For one so old it was amazingly strong, yet it had great dignity and calm, and it pulled on my heartstrings with what seemed to be superhuman power.

Once we had completed all the necessary rites, we trooped back to the garden in front of the Buddha Hall for a commemorative photograph.

Now, studying that photo from that well-remembered day, it strikes me that we all look tense, as if we were in imminent peril. There isn't the slightest trace of relief or jubilation at having passed an important milestone. That stands to reason. Day after day we were being pushed to the breaking point; it was all we could do to grope our way forward, do all that was required of us. Even though our status had altered, we were in no state to know what to think about it. Certainly the registration ceremony was an important rite of passage, but our daily lives were not about to change. That's the nature of Zen discipline. Attaining high office or completing long years of discipline does not alter one's treatment either. Zen discipline is not a staircase or a means of getting somewhere; it is rather about the successive moments of life—of existence itself. It means being fully aware in body and spirit of the fact of your life, and continuing to cultivate and practice the best way to live as a human being. This is the meaning of Dogen's words, "Dignity is itself the Dharma. Propriety is itself the essence of the house."

But the discipline at Eiheiji taught us nothing. All there is at Eiheiji is a string of days with unvarying routine, nothing more. The "why" of that is not something that anyone can teach, but must be grasped with one's own body and spirit in the course of those endlessly repetitive days.

And so a commemorative photo was taken in front of the Buddha Hall, marking an end to festivities, and we embarked on a new succession of days no different from the old.

First Bath

Examinations took place in the interstices between meals and official duties. They took the form of oral questioning by the common quarters' director. We were each examined separately about that day's official assignments, and perfect was the only passing score. After passing the examination for each of the eleven daily assignments separately, we had to take a final comprehensive test covering all of them. Passing this final test would mean we were officially released from this round of assignments, but it was a daunting challenge.

Once the registration ceremony was over, however, the questions quickly grew more lenient, and one after another we passed with flying colors. Evidently it was the custom to subject new arrivals to a raking crossfire of questions in order to provide them with concentrated exposure to monastery regulations. The day all eight of us were finally released came a week or so after the registration ceremony. It was a rest day, and that afternoon we were allowed a hot bath for the first time since coming to Eiheiji. In Zen monasteries, bathing takes places only on rest days (days ending in a four or a nine) and not at all during the initial weeks. Until now we had not had so much as a sponge bath or fresh clothes.

The bathhouse is located in the eastern part of the compound. At Eiheiji, it is divided into a changing room and a room with a bath. In the changing room is a statue of the bodhisattva Bhadrapala, who, it is said, attained enlightenment in the bath. Bathing at Eiheiji, as at all Zen monasteries, is ritualized. The process is overseen by the head of

Buildings and Grounds, known as "the water director," and it begins with the ceremonial bathing of Manjusri. This takes place just after lunch.

To perform the ceremony, the water director dresses in his most formal clothes and then heads to the Monks' Hall, carrying incense. In the hall he sits in front of the statue and lights the incense, prostrating himself three times. Then he goes around behind the altar where a thin white towel hangs from a wooden rack. He takes the towel, rack and all, raises it to eye level, and begins to recite the Heart Sutra as he walks with it to the bathhouse. His recitation is carefully timed to finish just as he arrives at the bathhouse. Then he places the rack in front of the statue of Bhadrapala, lights the incense, and prostrates himself three times. He kneels before a basin filled with hot water, dips the towel into the water, and rinses it out while intoning, *"On shuri shuri maka shuri shu shiri sowaka."* He repeats this incantation, known as The True Word of Cleansing, three times while he rinses the towel in a basin filled with the first hot water dipped from the tub that day. This action represents the ceremonial bathing of Manjusri.

Following this ceremony, the "bath leader" takes his bath. By rights this is the prerogative of the abbot, but generally one of the other masters does the honors. This ceremony is not as complicated as the first. The bath leader enters the bathhouse accompanied by an assistant, lights incense, and performs a triple obeisance before the statue of Bhadrapala, timing his movements to coincide with the beating of a drum in the adjacent drum tower. Then he disrobes and takes his bath, along with the assistant. When he is finished, he bows down three times before Bhadrapala again, while again the drum sounds three times. This is the signal for the other higher ranking monks to come and take their baths. When they in turn finish, the drum is sounded again as a signal that it is finally the trainees' turn.

That day, when bath time came around, we each put a towel and a change of clothes in a cloth wrapper and headed for the bathhouse. On entering, first we stood before Bhadrapala, placed our palms together, and prostrated ourselves three times while silently reciting the following chant:

> Bathing the body,
> I vow with all sentient beings: may all
> be purified in body and mind,
> cleansed without and within.

After that we disrobed in the prescribed manner and proceeded into the next room, towel in hand. The room was spacious, the tub filled to overflowing with clean hot water. We squatted down, rubbed soap on our towels, and proceeded in silence to scrub away the accumulated grime of weeks. Again and again we washed ourselves. Every time I sluiced white soapsuds from my body, I felt exhilarated. When I was finally clean, I submerged myself in the hot water, stretching out my arms and legs luxuriously, feeling the pent-up tension in my muscles loosen and dissolve. I lay back and watched the steam rise through the open skylight to disappear into blue sky ringed with cedars. For a short while, I forgot everything else.

When my bath was finished I left the bathhouse, my steps as light as air. As I hurried to the common quarters, the afternoon breeze felt pleasantly cool against my still-glowing skin. On the way, I looked in at the work area and saw several people whooping it up.

"Choshu, that's a woman's handwriting for sure!" someone was saying. "You sly devil!"

Red faced, Choshu hotly denied the charge. "It's nothing like that!"

"Any mail for me?" I asked. Laughter was bubbling on every face; I'd never seen my fellow trainees in such high spirits.

Someone thrust an envelope at me. "Yeah, there's one for you too, Rosan."

A letter. All this time we'd been forbidden to send or receive mail. Any letters that arrived in the interim had gone into the director's keeping. Now, on receiving these long-awaited letters from home, we were thrilled.

Daikan was there. Our eyes met and he came over, looking cheerful. He'd gotten something from home too. Wordlessly, he held it out for me to see. It was a postcard, something his son had mailed while on a school trip. His face was wreathed in the inimitable smile of a proud father. I'd never seen him look so happy. Shortly after that, however, something inside him seemed to snap. He got sick and went into the hospital, and I never saw him again.

I hurried back to the common quarters and laid down the cloth-wrapped bundle of items I'd needed for the bath, then headed for the privacy of the toilet, the bulky envelope of my letter from home tucked into my kimono sleeve. When I got to the toilet, I went in, shut the door, and took out the letter to read in the dim light from the skylight. The familiar writing on the envelope told me at a glance that it was from my mother.

Trying to steady my racing heart, I opened the envelope and spread out the folded stationery. Instantly, her neat writing leaped to my eyes. The shading of the ink looked fresh, and somehow in each character I could hear the familiar sound of her voice. Before I knew it, the lines of ink took on the shape of her face.

After that I don't remember anything. The next thing I knew, I was crouched in the toilet, weeping, the tears coursing unchecked down my cheeks. There was nothing to be sad about. Yet there I was, a man of thirty, crouched in a dark corner of the toilet with a letter from my mother clenched in my fist, bawling my eyes out. The room began to fill with the night's first quiet shadows, soon to become a blackness that covered everything.

Beginning Intensive Training

Buddhist monks in ancient India used to wander through the country-side on their pilgrimages, but during the three-month monsoon sea-son they would stay in one place for a time of confined training. This is because the monsoon season made their usual wanderings impossible, and, it is said, because there was a fear of inadvertently killing insects that might be hidden in muddy puddles underfoot. The custom made its way to Japan, where it became the rule to set aside two periods a year for such special training, one in summer and one in winter.

Both the winter and summer intensive training periods last three months, the same as in old India. During this time it is forbidden to leave the monastery, and the assembly devotes itself to a number of special practices. The starting day marks a transition to a more rigorous form of discipline, with an intensive schedule of various ceremonies and memorial services. Dogen wrote about the importance of this tradition in *Treasury of the True Dharma Eye*, commenting that anyone who failed to observe it and still considered himself the spiritual heir of the buddhas and ancestors was a laughable fool. Observing these periods of intensified training is in itself the proper transmission of Buddhist truth, and a crucial aspect of Zen training.

The first order of business during this period of intensive training is selecting a head from among the senior trainees. He occupies the leading seat in the Monks' Hall, becoming literally first among trainees. He plays a central role in the various ceremonies performed during this period and must of course be a model trainee. He is chosen, along with two assistants, from trainees with at least two years' experience.

These are the principal ceremonies and services held during the course of the three months of intensive training:

Great Evening Tea Service. A ceremony to announce the assignment of tasks for the periods leading up to, and during, intensive training. While a drum thunders, blazing candles are carried into the Patriarch's Interview Hall, where everyone takes tea.

First Recitation of the Surangama Dharani. Recitation of a dharani is thought to offer protection from calamity. Dharanis are one of five types of texts that it is forbidden to translate; the Chinese characters in which they are written do not convey semantic meaning, but are phonetic representations of the original Sanskrit. This particular dharani signifies that all evildoers will be brought to enlightenment. It tells the story of Buddha's cousin Ananda, who was seduced by the harlot Matangi and seemed about to break the precept against engaging in sex when Buddha ordered Manjusri to intervene. Ananda and Matangi both achieved the state of meditation leading to perfect enlightenment. This dharani is believed to do away with all hindrances, afflictions, and delusions that can arise during discipline. To ensure that all goes smoothly during intensive training, it is recited every morning without fail in the Dharma Hall.

Opening Day Invocations. Invocations to the protective deity of the monastery and to Daigen Shuri, a bodhisattva who is the guardian of truth. They are enshrined next to the Buddha Hall along with other protective deities.

Special Tea Service. In honor of the opening of intensive training, the masters treat the trainees to ceremonial tea. Incense burners are placed in the four corners of the Monks' Hall, filling the room with the aroma of fine incense. The silent ritual involves a staggeringly large number of prostrations. Of all the tea services at Eiheiji, this ranks with Tea Service by Attendants as the most impressive.

Opening Formal Salutations. Formal congratulations and thanks are exchanged by monastic officers and ordinary monks-in-training assigned to offer incense or worship. The salutations are given ceremoniously in a number of locations in the monastery.

Inspection Tour. The abbot makes the rounds of the residences, inspecting for proper attire and maintenance of standards, and urging the Eiheiji community to prepare for the coming period of intensive training.

Honoring the Lineage. In the Outer Hall is an oblong lacquer board on which the names of all who have taken monastic vows at Eiheiji are inscribed in white pigment, in order of seniority. The list is headed by the bodhisattva Manjusri, followed by the various masters and then the monks-in-training. The board is venerated with incense.

Tea Service by Attendants. On behalf of the abbot, attendants treat the trainees to ceremonial tea in the Monks' Hall.

Lecture and Tea Service. The day before the head trainee expounds on basic Zen tenets, the abbot delivers a lecture on those tenets and offers tea to all in the Patriarch's Interview Hall.

Celebratory Tea. To celebrate his appointment, the head trainee treats his fellow trainees to tea. This ceremony takes place in the Patriarch's Interview Hall.

Student Lecture. The head trainee expounds on basic Zen tenets in place of the abbot and engages in a question-and-answer colloquy with his peers. This practice is based on the ancient tradition that Sakyamuni, the historical Buddha, shared his seat with Mahakasyapa, the disciple who would transmit his teachings faithfully to later generations, and had him preach in his stead. A particularly important occasion, marking the climax of the period of intensive training.

Confession Service. A service setting forth Buddhist principles in literary style, using melodic chanting of classical texts, and based on an important monastic rite of soul-searching and confession dating back to the time of Buddha. The principle of confession and purification is set forth in this service, which takes place in the Dharma Hall.

Final Recitation of the Surangama Dharani. The daily recitals of this dharani are brought to a conclusion.

Closing Day Invocations. Final invocations to the protective deities.

Closing Formal Salutations. An exchange of congratulations and thanks on the last day of intensive training.

The ceremonies and services listed above are a small fraction of all that goes on during this time. Naturally, regular services, manual labor, and sitting continue as well. Each ceremony and service is carried out with deep solemnity and attention to detail and has the mysterious power of imparting a feeling of reverence to anyone who happens to be in the same room.

There is a Buddhist term "fragrance learning," which means a kind of unintentional absorption. Just as passing by an incense burner can imbue clothing with fragrance, so we are affected unconsciously by the atmosphere of a place, just by happening to be there. One effect of these ceremonies and services is precisely this effortless absorption, which partly explains why such religious observances are firmly established. During the three months of intensive training, we would take part in these kinds of events every day, following our schedule to the letter—becoming the schedule. It was a time, in other words, of following the Dharma and becoming the Dharma.

Manual Labor

An integral part of Zen life, no less important than sitting itself, is manual labor. This refers to the physical labor done in a Zen monastery. In ancient India, monks were detached from all physical labor and devoted themselves only to spiritual labors. All their material needs were met by believers who provided alms and did any necessary work. In China, high esteem for physical work was tied to a practical turn of mind that resulted in the establishment of labor as a form of discipline.

Life in a Christian monastery is also based on prayer and work, as in a Zen monastery, but the two religious traditions have a fundamentally different approach to work. In the Christian monastic tradition, work is a means of supporting the life of prayer. Continued prayer is the goal, work the means. But for Zen practitioners, work has inherent spiritual value and is integral to the life of discipline.

At Eiheiji, along with sitting, which is done morning and night, collective manual labor is done twice daily. There are two basic types of manual labor. One is done by the members of individual residences, the other by all the trainees together. The former includes manual labor related to the official tasks of each residence, as well as cleaning of the residence and its surroundings.

In our residence, the common quarters, our main tasks consisted of cleaning and bell ringing, and our manual labor, too, was cleaning. The areas we were responsible for included the Monks' Hall, the washroom, the Walking Corridor, the common quarters, the common quarters work area, and its washroom and toilet. These places weren't just cleaned as part of manual labor; they were also cleaned daily as part of the regular round of cleaning tasks. That's the great thing about cleaning at Eiheiji: it isn't done on special days or in special places, but takes place energetically every single day, whether or not there's any dirt to speak of.

Manual labor done by the entire body of trainees is greater in scale and varies according to the season. In spring, there is raking to be done. Because the temple is surrounded by huge cedars, after the spring thaw sets in, the ground is littered with dead leaves and branches brought down by the snow. Everyone would spread out to rake them up and dispose of them. We also did "river labor," wading out into the stream where dead leaves and branches swept along by the current would catch between rocks and pile up. Attired in rubber boots and raincoats, we removed every bit of detritus. Fed by melting snow, the water was ice cold, and our hands and feet turned numb as we mutely picked the river clean, leaf by leaf and twig by twig.

In summer, we focused on one chore: weeding. The least letup on our part and weeds spread everywhere, relentlessly. The compound is huge, the weeds persistent—even with a hundred-odd trainees laboring day after day. Human beings are no match for the laws of nature, nor should they be. Weeding at Eiheiji is not done in a frenzied attempt to get rid of all the weeds. It's natural that weeds grow and people pull them; it's equally natural that the weeds grow back. The point is not to get rid of weeds once and for all, but to carry out the simple repetitive action of pulling them up.

Eat Sleep Sit

In summer, the scope of communal weeding extends beyond the monastery grounds to the surrounding hillsides. This is called "mountain labor." We would go out on the steep hillsides and take a scythe to waist-high vegetation. For days on end we would swing our scythes vigorously under a cloudless azure sky, breathing in the heavy scent of cut grass while we listened to the distant cries of the Himalayan cuckoo.

In autumn we raked again. Mixed in with the cedars on the monastery grounds are maples and a variety of other deciduous trees that constantly scatter their leaves. Just as the weeds of summer would zealously proliferate, the fallen leaves of autumn went on piling up no matter how hard we raked. Leaves fall and people rake them, people rake them and more leaves fall. Until winter came, we devoted many a long autumn day to this task.

Eiheiji is famous for the heavy snows that blanket it in winter. Before winter set in, we would set up shelters around compound buildings to protect them from colossal snowfalls; this is called "snow-shelter labor." First we would build a frame with stout wooden poles, and then fasten on a screen made of woven split bamboo. The complex is huge, the buildings high. Erecting snow shelters around each of the buildings in the complex takes an enormous number of woven screens and many, many days. Once this task is completed, Eiheiji is ready for the quiet of winter.

When winter gets underway in earnest and snow starts to pile up, next is "snow-clearing labor." We cleared it away one shovelful at a time, not only from the ground but from the rooftops as well. No sooner would we finish than—without the least regard for our labors—another snowfall would begin, turning the world white again in the blink of an eye. Once again we felt the power and grandeur of nature.

Other forms of collective manual labor are not seasonal, such as changing the paper screens in all the sliding doors and windows. First the door or window is removed from its tracks and then, to loosen the old paper, it is moistened by spraying with water or immersing it in a pond. Working in teams of two, we would strip the wooden frame clean and then apply new paper. The number of doors and windows to be repapered was truly daunting. Most of us had never done such work before, and not all of us were good with our hands. All too often a pair would finish repapering a door only to see they had made a mess of it, and at inspection they would be ordered to do it over.

There were many other kinds of collective labor as well: washing all the glass windows in the complex; carrying in the sawdust charcoal briquettes left by the deliverymen; distributing the Eiheiji news bulletin.

Of all the forms of monastic discipline at Eiheiji, manual labor is the only one in which one's actions produce a tangible, visible result. I would work alongside the others in silence and feel a rush of elation as we finished. After spending most of our time in the dim interiors of the complex, it was refreshing to be out in the sun, getting covered in dirt and grass. During this three-month period of intensive training, manual labor was also done more intensively; we were outdoors every day, working up a sweat.

One day during intensive training I was assigned to weeding again. Hard pressed as I was to keep up with the round of special observances, when it was time to go I quickly changed into work clothes, wound a white towel around my head, and headed for the Main Gate, our meeting place. After roll call, led by a senior trainee, we set off at a double trot for the place we were assigned to that day. We jogged from the Main Gate, past the Gate of Unimpeded Truth and the Imperial Gate, until we came to the Dragon Gate.

The Dragon Gate. Here it was, the boundary between the worlds of the sacred and the profane, a boundary I had crossed on that first day in the predawn quiet, weighed down not only by my wicker packs, front and back, but by a myriad of anxieties and forlorn hopes. How long ago that was, I thought. On finding myself back in this place where everything had begun, I pondered the lapse of time—and realized that the stream of days at Eiheiji was working a transformation of some sort in me.

Just then the signal was given to begin work. Plastic bag in hand, I began the familiar task, pulling up the weeds in front of me blade by blade until there were no more, and then moving on to a new spot. I thought of nothing at all as I continued working in silence. After a while I casually looked up and saw that I had come to the edge of the road by the Dragon Gate. This was my first glimpse of the world I had been completely cut off from since coming to Eiheiji. A world that was now so close I might have reached out and touched it. I stared transfixed, clutching a fistful of half-pulled weeds.

The Passage of Time

Before my eyes, time moved in a way I used to know well. In a scene that might have played out anywhere, people were freely crossing the street or lingering to chat and exchange a laugh. All around them time flowed, so clear and transparent that its very existence was forgotten, just as it had once flowed around me. Like air, it had been pervasive and invisible, so natural a part of life that I never gave it a thought. But now from the time I got up till the time I went to bed—no, even while I was in bed—I had not a moment to call my own. All of my time was subject to the dictates of Buddhist law.

The asphalt road in front of the monastery seemed like a mountain watershed, separating the current of time into two completely different streams. I felt a sudden urge to jump up and dart across to the other side. Ten strides would do it. If I ran straight over, the moment I passed through the invisible membrane separating here from there I would return instantly to reality, awakening from a long dream. This world where I was now could not by any stretch of the imagination be considered reality. Now was the time to wake myself up.

And yet I did not run off. Yes, it would be good to wake all at once from the dream of life at Eiheiji, I thought, and yet I was also inclined to stay and dream a little longer. Besides, looking down at my feet, I saw plenty of weeds that still needed pulling. In that moment, the boundary between the sacred and the profane disappeared. I went back to pulling up weeds and stuffing them in my plastic bag.

Penance

"Ah!"

Enkai quickly leaned forward, but he was too late. His chopsticks tumbled off the edge of the platform and fell to the concrete floor with a clatter that resounded through the hall. The rest of us froze, all eyes on him.

Now you've gone and done it, I thought, looking at Enkai's face beside me. He looked back at me with a pitifully helpless expression. Then I saw the server standing waiting in front of me and quickly thrust out my bowl to be filled, failing to notice in my haste that the saucer was stuck to the bottom. It followed Enkai's chopsticks down onto the floor with a noise that drew everyone's gaze in my direction. *Damn it*, I thought, and looked at Enkai again. This time he was smiling in relief.

As we returned to our quarters after the meal, Enkai came up to me and said, "Boy, I'm sure glad I'm not the only one. Just knowing you're in this with me helps, Rosan." I for my part was less than thrilled to have been caught up by chain reaction in his blunder.

Enkai, a priest's son, was extraordinarily plump, as though the love of his doting, well-off parents had settled on him in layers of fat. He claimed that since coming to Eiheiji he'd slimmed down and toned up considerably, but the rest of us saw little if any change. Because he and I had dropped sacred utensils during a formal meal, we would now have to make a votive offering in atonement. In *Treasury of the True Dharma Eye*, Dogen wrote, "Anyone who drops a utensil on the floor during the morning or noon meal must keep the oil lamp in front of Manjusri burning for twenty-four hours." This meant that the butterfingered monk was responsible for providing enough oil (or the necessary funds) for the lamp to burn for that long. The requirement applies only to the two formal meals; at the informal evening meal, anything can be dropped with impunity.

First we were required to fold a sheet of paper to make a special kind of envelope on which we had to write the words "Oil Offering" in large characters, using a prescribed style of calligraphy, followed by our name and the characters for "Nine Prostrations." Then we would slip money inside.

But we'd been relieved of our cash that first night in Jizo Cloister, so how was this possible, you ask? Simple. After the registration ceremony, everyone's money was returned in full. We even began to receive a modest monthly payment called "material for robes." After all, while it's true that people come to Eiheiji for rigorous Zen training, they also form the organizational backbone of the place. Rather than a true salary in the sense of the wherewithal to pay for food and housing, however, the payment is really just a small bonus. As the monastery paid our living expenses, we had little use for money in daily life.

Enkai and I each slipped a five-hundred yen coin into the envelope we'd made. The amount of money to be offered is not fixed, but is decided by one of the senior trainees in charge of discipline. Our offerings would go straight into the coffers of the common quarters and so be returned to us in various ways. When we'd finished preparing the offering, we changed into our most formal clothes and headed for the

Monks' Hall carrying incense and the envelopes. We lit the incense, prostrated ourselves reverently three times, laid our offerings at Manjusri's feet, and left.

"What a pain in the neck," grumbled Enkai. "Why all this hassle just for dropping a couple of chopsticks on the floor?"

"Hold on," I said. "We're not done yet." Our process of atonement had barely begun.

We armed ourselves with more incense and set off for the bell-ringers' quarters, where the senior trainees in charge of discipline lived. Absolute, unquestionable authority was theirs. If they should declare that crows were white, then at Eiheiji, white they would be. Going to their quarters, a place that strikes fear into every junior trainee's heart, took considerable resolve. We would have to perform a rite of penance: more prostrations, confession, and apology.

When we came to the door, Enkai blurted out, "You first, Rosan." By rights, the usual rule of seniority should have applied, as it did whenever two or more trainees from the same group did anything together. Based on that, it was Enkai's place to go in first, as he had been admitted to Jizo Cloister before me, but I wasn't going to stand there all day arguing the point. With resignation I went in, knelt down in the prescribed place, and apprehensively called out a greeting.

From behind the sliding door, a laconic voice said, "Just do your penance and go."

What a relief! Not all senior trainees were vindictive tyrants; some were surprisingly mild tempered and grew weary on occasion with their role as censorious scold. Having escaped a tongue-lashing or worse, we quickly performed the ritual and left before someone less forgiving came along.

"We lucked out, didn't we?" said Enkai, grinning from ear to ear.

But that wasn't all. We also had to do penance before the trainee monk who was head of intensive training, and as such outranked even the high and mighty senior trainees from the bell-ringers' quarters. We replenished our incense and set off for his room.

Keikou, the current head, was a second-year trainee who'd decided to become a monk while in college, his interest stirred by a course on Zen. After graduation his intention held firm, and eventually he'd taken the plunge and come to Eiheiji. *Shukke*, the traditional word for taking Buddhist vows, means literally "leaving home." In common usage it applies to all Buddhist clergy, but at Eiheiji, trainees fall into two categories: *shukke*, "those who have left home," and *zaike*, "those who are at home." Keikou, whose father was an ordinary salaryman, was one of the former. The latter category includes all sons of priests, based on the reasoning that anyone who grew up in a Zen temple has not actually "left home."

I have to say that while the above explanation made sense to me at first, later on I became confused, unsure what the real significance of home leaving might be. At Eiheiji, there were generally three kinds of home leavers. Some, like Keikou, came because they were interested in Zen. Others, like Daikan, had been adopted by marriage into a family responsible for running a Zen temple. Still others were propelled by doubts or disillusionment about the meaning of their lives.

Many Japanese unconsciously regard the renunciation of the world to take Buddhist vows as inherently tragic. I myself had largely subscribed to this view. But after coming to Eiheiji, it struck me that there wasn't necessarily anything tragic about it at all. People like Keikou, who'd chosen the monastic life for positive reasons, altered my thinking and inspired me. A serious, sober young man who devoted himself quietly to Zen practice, he had fully earned the honor and responsibility of being named head monk, and all of us held him in high regard.

When we stood in front of Keikou's door, once again Enkai nudged me forward, and again I nervously announced our presence. The door slid open and Keikou appeared. "Oh, it's you two. Come in and do your penance." We entered in trepidation and began kowtowing while Keikou looked on with his arms crossed.

Then, just as we stood up for the last time, it happened. In his nervousness, Enkai trampled the hem of his robe and stumbled forward, almost falling. The robe, unable to support his weight, tore with a loud *rrrip!* Keikou nearly burst out laughing, but managed to recover his composure. To preserve the spiritually charged atmosphere of the intensive training period, he was required to maintain his dignity at all times.

"All right," he said, "now sit facing the wall." We obediently seated ourselves side by side, and without warning the stick came down hard on our shoulders. "Now go clean the toilets."

We said goodbye and left.

At Eiheiji, punishments differ according to the nature of the offense. The two most common forms of punishment are sitting and floor cleaning. Sitting, commonly assigned for misdemeanors like dozing off during morning service, means spending hours on the corridor floor in formal sitting posture, back erect and heels under buttocks. Floor cleaning means cleaning the same wooden passageway endlessly, tearing back and forth at breakneck speed.

Toilet cleaning usually is done in the evening, and is followed by a strict inspection to make sure not a speck of dust or dirt remains. Failure to pass inspection means the piling on of yet more punishments. During intensive training the inspections are even more sharp eyed, the punishments for failing to pass muster even more severe.

Enkai and I began by setting brooms, dustpans, buckets, and washrags in front of the lavatory building. Working barefoot, dressed in work clothes and a headband, we began by rolling up the bamboo blinds at the entrance and in the passageway and sweeping every inch of the floor. Then we scrubbed the walls, doors, and windows, including window frames, thresholds, everything. Finally, using clean washrags, we scoured the floors and toilets.

Washing the inside of a toilet by hand with a cloth may sound like an unbearably filthy job, but once you get started, it's nothing. Even if some waste should get on your hand, wash it off and your hand is as good as new. There is no filth in a toilet that can pierce the skin and infiltrate the body.

And so we worked hard to make the place sparkle.

Enkai was grumbling again as he scrubbed the inside of a toilet. "Man, this is too much! Making a guy go through this every time he drops his chopsticks . . . Agh! I got some on me."

All of these punishments were one more way in which the importance of the sacred eating utensils was impressed on us—that and the quirkiness of religion.

Main Lecture

Once the cherry blossoms had fallen, the trees began bursting into leaf, their vibrant green an early promise of summer. The vague shimmer of new leaves transfigured the valley, and a moist, sweet breeze, fragrant with the scent of new grass, swept through the covered walkways from end to end. Seasons all come in their turn; here in our mountain valley, spring was drawing to an end, and summer was on its way.

The shift in seasons affects not only all of nature, but the lives of trainees as well. First comes the changing of the curtains at the front and back entrances to the Monks' Hall. The winter ones, made of heavy woven cloth, are replaced with ones made of woven split bamboo.

As another sign of the approach of summer, cold tea is served at formal meals—not iced tea, of course, just tea that has been chilled with spring water. Still, our first taste of it in the Monks' Hall was exciting. After a lifetime of habitual, year-round access to drinks cooled by refrigeration or ice, it was the first refreshingly cold drink we'd had in months.

As the mercury climbed higher, baths were allowed on other days besides rest days. These extra baths were not treated as formally as the others, and much of the preliminary ritual was dispensed with: instead of a triple obeisance, for example, we prostrated ourselves just once.

Summers at Eiheiji are oppressively hot. People imagine that summer in a deep mountain valley must be delightfully cool, but they are wrong. The humidity would sometimes soar so high that the concrete floor of the Monks' Hall would be covered with moisture, as if it had been sprayed with water. Dim interiors where the sun never shone grew hot and stuffy. As we continued our arduous training in the midsummer heat, extra baths were a small boon, something to look forward to.

Seasonal change also affected the various bells, drums, and gongs that sounded in the course of the day. Until now, the great bell in the bell tower had been tolled noon, evening, and night, but from this juncture on it was replaced by a smaller bell next to the Founder's Hall. Unlike the deep, billowing waves of sound that emanated from the great bell, this one produced delicate, cool vibrations that spread mysteriously through the compound without impeding any other sound in creation. And so June came on, bringing these unmistakable signs of summer to our seemingly uneventful lives.

June was the month for a lecture series on Dogen's *Treasury of the True Dharma Eye*. Life at Eiheiji is filled not only with sitting, sutra reading, and manual labor, but also with lectures on various Buddhist texts and rituals. These take place at odd intervals and are called "internal lectures" to distinguish them from the June lecture series, known as *Genzo-e*, or simply "the main lecture." The hour-long internal lectures are usually held in place of evening sitting, and are given by someone of the rank of lecturer or master. The trainees sit formally in a great hall and listen in respectful silence. Additionally, sometimes there are videos on human rights or welfare, which are referred to as "audiovisual studies."

The main lecture is held in great solemnity over a period of several days. It starts off with sutra chanting in the Founder's Hall, after which wooden gongs around the compound are struck in order: first the one by the Monks' Hall, then the one in the Founder's Hall, followed in turn by those in the Dharma Hall, the Patriarch's Interview Hall, and the Memorial Hall, each with its own distinctive timbre and pitch. The progression of sounds brings home the majestic scale of the monastery grounds. The echoes roll far and wide, resonating among the ancient cedars and dying away across the distant reaches of the surrounding mountains. As the rains of early summer set in, of all the seasonal adornments to life at Eiheiji, this musical introduction to the main lecture is the most beautiful.

The lecture is given by a learned master in the huge, 150-mat Seat of Enlightenment Hall. Listeners wearing their mantles sit in the full lotus position to show respect for the teachings of Dogen. The ninety-five essays in *Treasury of the True Dharma Eye* begin with "A Talk on the Search for Truth," which Dogen wrote when he was thirty-two, and end with "On the Eight Realizations of a Great One," the last thing he ever wrote, completed at the age of fifty-four. The title *Treasury of the*

True Dharma Eye signifies that the writings contained in the book point the way to the essential truth of Buddhist teaching.

Each year the master who is appointed lecturer selects one of the essays and devotes himself to explaining all the ramifications of Dogen's thought contained therein. And yet *Treasury* is notoriously challenging; explaining any part of it in detail—not to mention absorbing a learned explanation—is no easy task. Perhaps not surprisingly, then, the event is known for putting listeners to sleep—so much so that monks-in-training refer to it irreverently as *Minzo-e*, instead of *Genzo-e*, where *min* means "sleep." By this time, we first-year trainees were all chronically hungry and sleepy. The drone of the lecture, along with sounds that drifted in through the open windows—the beat of raindrops on the branches of ancient trees, cuckoo songs echoing in the sky, anything and everything—was powerfully soporific. Whenever someone yielded to sleepiness and their head hit the desk in front of them, the master would let out a roar of disapproval. That would wake everyone up for the moment, but in no time we'd be drowsy again, until someone else succumbed.

And yet even though it made us so sleepy and the voice of the master passed in one ear and out the other, sweeping over us like the breeze on the meadow, when the event was over we felt strangely blessed. Whether this was because Dogen's teachings worked on us without our knowing it, even in our sleep, or whether it was all in our imagination, I don't know. In any case, the end of the main lecture meant that summer had arrived.

Eat Sleep Sit

Transfer

As the early summer rains ended and a clear blue sky spread over the compound, the current of time, at first so sluggish that every moment seemed an eternity, returned to its usual flow. Little by little, like the water of a stream washing stones clean, time's passage wrought a change in us. The once-unfamiliar monk's robe, at first so unaccommodating, had started to fray and come apart at the seams; as stains accumulated from spilled porridge, or soup, or tears, it had adapted to the contours of our bodies. The ritualized movements of our hands at mealtimes and at face washing were now automatic and unthinking. It was at this time that we heard the rumor: a round of transfers was imminent.

Moving to new quarters would of course mean taking on a new set of duties. Who would be transferred where was largely up to the superintendent of monks, and became official when approved by the temple director. Trainees are transferred in order of seniority; most of those ahead of our group had already left the common quarters. There was never any advance warning; preparations were made in secrecy, and the announcement came all of a sudden. We eight would be dispersed among the residences or "quarters" that accept novices, of which there are fourteen. Their names and principal duties are as follows:

Common Quarters. Sounding bells, drums, and gongs that mark the flow of daily life; cleaning floors; overseeing sitting and formal meals in the Monks' Hall. All new trainees are assigned here first. Life in the common quarters forms the backbone of Zen monastic training.

Accounts. Selling and distributing various items used in daily life; seeing to scriptures, altar fittings, and other items used in rituals and services; hosting special visitors.

Kitchen. Preparation of meals for trainees and special visitors, and preparation of food offerings to be placed before statuary.

Lesser Kitchen. Preparation of meals for people on lay retreats.

Buildings and Grounds. Inspection of compound cleaning and security; also overseeing lighting, heating, fuel, and everything to do with the bath.

Reception Hall. Hosting people on lay retreats.

Office. Clerical work in the general office.

Memorial Hall. Carrying out memorial services that are held in perpetuity for lay parishioners on death anniversaries and at the equinoxes; looking after the adjacent Charnel Hall, where parishioners' bones and ashes are laid to rest.

Perpetuity. Managing data related to the above memorial services.

Missions. Guiding visitors around the compound.

Sansho Staff. Editing the Eiheiji newspaper *Sansho* and overseeing the repository and exhibition hall for temple treasures.

International. Propagating Zen overseas, handling media relations, and providing interpreting services as needed.

Computer Room. Computer storage of all Eiheiji data.

Human Rights Protection and Promotion Room. Coordinating responses to various human rights and social welfare issues.

There are nine quarters where only senior trainees are assigned, and they are the following:

Abbot's Quarters. Secretary and personal attendants to the abbot.

Administration. Secretary and personal attendants to the director.

Head of Training and Training Director's Quarters. Secretaries and personal attendants to the head of training and the training director.

Superintendent's Quarters. Secretary and personal attendants to the superintendent of monks.

Attendants' Quarters. Management of the Founder's Hall.

Dharma Hall. Management of the Dharma Hall.

Bell-ringers' Quarters. Supervision of trainees; ringing bells at ceremonies and memorial services.

Lay Practice Staff. Reception and instruction of lay practitioners.

Instructors' Quarters. Instruction of novices in the common quarters.

Once the rumor about transfers got started, we talked of nothing else. Chubby Enkai ventured the opinion that Missions was the most desirable destination. "It'd be cool," he said. Everyone jumped on this.

"Enkai, they'd never pick you as guide," said one. "Take a look in the mirror. If tourists saw you coming, they'd run!"

"That's for sure," agreed someone else. "I'll bet you're headed for Buildings and Grounds. They'll whip you into shape in no time."

"What about you guys, then?" said Enkai, miffed.

"Kitchen for me, probably, since I've got a cook's license," someone piped up. "Wish I hadn't been so darned honest when I filled out that form."

Before coming to Eiheiji, we'd each submitted a form containing a simple resume. The transfers, we were told, were decided on the basis of that, as well as our overall performance. "Rosan will probably be put on the newspaper staff," someone predicted. But on my form I'd written that my college major was fine arts, my occupation was designer, my favorite sport was swimming, and my special talent was performing ancient court music. In short, my background was nothing more than a hodgepodge.

The transfers are a big deal, partly because they offer a change of scenery and the possibility of pleasant perks. If you landed in Missions you could talk to cute girls who came as tourists, for example, and if you went to the computer room you could spend all day at the keyboard, which sounded pretty painless. By contrast, people who worked in the kitchen or the Reception Hall spent all day rushing around with barely time for sleep. The most physically exhausting assignment was Buildings and Grounds, which entailed considerable heavy labor.

Individual preferences played no part in the transfers. For some, their destination meant heaven, while for others it was sheer hell. Either way, you went where you were told to go, period. The announcement came without warning and landed like a ton of bricks. In the meantime, the air prickled with uncertainty.

If I could have had my druthers, I'd have picked the kitchen. That's because in college I read Dogen's *Instructions for the Cook*, and the idea of a monastery kitchen had appealed to me ever since. On the other hand, I had no kitchen experience to speak of and, considering what I'd written on my resume, I doubted I stood a chance.

The announcement would come during the morning meal, just before the final chant. It was supposed to be top secret, but somehow word got out that today was the day. It was my luck to be stuck in the common quarters office that day, so I couldn't be present when the assignments were read out. When I judged it was time, I slipped out and went around to the back of the Monks' Hall to listen in.

They had just finished chanting the Verse for Rinsing Bowls. *Here it comes*, I thought. I pricked up my ears nervously as the superintendent began to read the list, but to my dismay many of the words were unfamiliar and incomprehensible, made even more so by the echo in the hall. I edged closer to the curtain, focusing hard on the superintendent's voice.

"*Fu-nan-ken-zui-un-kaku-setsu-ju*, Sozen. Also Rosan."

There it was! At last, my name had been called. Sozen and I were assigned to the same place, and it wasn't the kitchen—that much I could tell. But the long, complicated name made no sense to me. As I stood there stupefied, suddenly the final chant started up, and I hurried back to my post.

The Source of the Warmth of Life

New Job

Eventually I discovered that I'd been assigned to Accounts. The transfers had been announced not by the quarters we were assigned to, but
by the work we would do. *Fu-nan* turned out to be an abbreviation for
fusu anja. The fusu, or treasurer, is responsible for overseeing temple
financial affairs—Eiheiji's minister of finance, as it were—and anja are
his assistants. The rest of the job title meant I would also be looking
after special visitors in the Guest Pavilion.

The transfer announcements brought everyone a rush of emotion,
glad or sad. Of our group, Tenshin was assigned to the Reception Hall,
Yuho and Enkai to the Memorial Hall, Choshu to Buildings and Grounds.
The remaining three—Daikan, Kijun, and Doryu—were still laid up in
the hospital. Until now the eight of us had functioned as a unit, always
lined up in our original order during every activity from sitting to communal labor to meals. Over the past months we'd become fast friends,
encouraging each other when the going was tough and exchanging
covert smiles when something struck us as funny. The thought of split-
ting up was sad, but our orders were irrevocable and immediate. We
must pack and move out at once; no trace would remain in the common
quarters of our shared stay, nor was there time for goodbyes.

Sozen and I quickly packed our few things and left. He was from the
group just before mine. In the common quarters he'd been top-notch,

able to carry off every task with aplomb. It was reassuring to know he'd be at my side in this next phase of life at Eiheiji.

Our new headquarters were in a three-story wooden building shared by two other residences. Buildings and Grounds was in the basement, the kitchen was on the main floor, and Accounts was on the second floor. On the third floor was the huge Seat of Enlightenment Hall where we had attended lectures on *Treasury of the True Dharma Eye*, and above that was a spacious attic for storage. There was also a rickety old elevator with a door of steel grating, first installed in 1930— a surprisingly early bit of modernization.

When we arrived, we put our things in the washrag room, a place that lives fully up to its name as it contains built-in shelves jammed floor to ceiling with cardboard boxes full of hand-stitched washrags. Altogether there were some ten people in Accounts, again in a hierarchy based on order of admittance to the temple. Those with seniority had better rooms. Though now Sozen and I were at the bottom of the totem pole and had to sleep in the washrag room, later, as new transferees came in, we in our turn would be promoted to a nicer room.

When we had laid our things down, the residence head appeared; as in the common quarters, here too the trainee who had been here longest was appointed head. We followed his instructions and set off in formal attire to announce our arrival in a ritual that involved lighting incense, prostrating ourselves, and reciting a set greeting. The first person we saluted in this way was of course the treasurer himself, whom we would now assist. My first impression was of a man of robust build who also conveyed an air of elegance; later I learned that he was a virtuoso accordion player. We did our prostrations before him with particular care, and moved on.

Next came our new colleagues and the senior trainee in charge of them and us. I was startled to see that it was our old instructor back in the common quarters, who had been transferred here along with us. His name was Jigen. When we'd finished our salutations, he came up to me and said, "Hey there, Rosan. Back together again, huh? Kuk-kuk-kuk." He walked out of the room with one hand over his mouth, chuckling in his peculiar way.

I was taken back to be addressed in this way by Jigen, who had always been a stern-eyed disciplinarian, but I was to find that one of the biggest differences between the common quarters and elsewhere was a lessening of the distance between senior and junior trainees. There were still clearly defined distinctions, but now we were in no danger of being clobbered just because we happened to look a senior trainee in the eye.

When we had finished these in-house salutations, we made the rounds of the various other places where our work would take us on occasion: the kitchen, the Memorial Hall, the Reception Hall, the general office. All told, this involved a prodigious number of prostrations. The importance of these ritualized greetings goes beyond self-introduction: by lowering our heads to the floor at every juncture, we were also reinforcing the rigid social hierarchy that governs all relationships in a Zen training monastery.

The Source of the Warmth of Life

All new transferees had to undergo a period of initiation. This time round it was shorter, however—generally about a week, with an examination on the last day. Initiation duties varied, but almost always involved copying out ledgers, memorizing the contents, and going into a frenzy of cleaning.

Once the business of greetings was out of the way, Sozen and I set to work. The number of places we had to clean was mind-boggling. First, the Guest Pavilion: every guest room as well as the reception room, bath, toilet, linen storeroom, lacquerware storeroom, and the kitchen with its enormous sink. There was also the Seat of Enlightenment Hall with its 150 tatami mats. All this the two of us had to clean, working like madmen. Even if we had somehow managed to get through it all in two or three days, we wouldn't be done; we'd simply have to start over again from the beginning. Being on cleaning duty meant a week of nonstop cleaning. Just like before, we got up two hours before the wake-up bell. And every day for a week, from one thirty in the morning till almost nine the next night, we cleaned.

The first few days went well enough, but midway through the week we became impossibly sleepy. Looking after the bedding was accordingly fraught with danger. Quilts and mattresses were stored by the hundreds on great shelves in the high-ceilinged attic storage room, which had a mezzanine floor and was air-conditioned to protect the bedding from humidity. Human beings are conditioned to become sleepy on sight of soft bedding in snowy, starched sheets—and on top of that, the attic was the one cool, dry place in the sweltering summer heat, a true world apart. It was our lot to sit in that pleasant milieu, achingly short on sleep, and refold hundreds upon hundreds of mattresses and quilts.

Once, as I was plugging away, I suddenly realized that I could no longer hear Sozen working at a different set of shelves farther in. *That bum, he went and dozed off!* I thought indignantly—and then my head jerked forward, abruptly waking me up.

Sales

Our week of marathon cleaning was soon over. On the last day, we were tested as scheduled on the contents of the work ledgers. This test was not as rigorous as the one in the common quarters, however, and Sozen and I both passed easily. Elsewhere the test was similarly lenient. In a sense it is the common quarters that preserves the traditional lifestyle of Buddhist monks in its purest form—ringing bells, sweeping and cleaning, attending services—and therefore does the greatest credit to Eiheiji as a Zen community. The other residences are more like practical mechanisms for keeping the huge organization running smoothly. If transferees failed their tests and were forced to continue cleaning morning, noon, and night, essential work would not get done. And so the examination is a mere formality, so that people can make an immediate contribution.

My first assignment after passing the test was to spend all day on duty in the office. The night before, I lugged my bedding to the

Accounts office and slept there. The Accounts office may be the financial nerve center of Eiheiji, and the place where the treasurer works, but it bears little resemblance to our image of a modern office. Workers kneel at low desks set side by side on tatami mats in a traditional Japanese-style room with an alcove where a Buddhist painting is displayed. The reason for sleeping there overnight, I was told, is that the safe is full of cash and important documents—but having never seen the inside of the safe, I wouldn't know. Anyway, I spread out my bedding in the middle of the room and went to sleep.

At two thirty in the morning, one hour before the wake-up bell, I got up and boiled water in a big kettle in the Guest Pavilion kitchen, then filled five thermoses with hot water. After that I roasted tea leaves in an earthen pan, and filled two more thermoses with tea. I was a bit anxious about whether the leaves were properly roasted, but eventually I finished and carried the thermoses back to the office. By then it was almost time for the bell.

Quickly I switched on the light in the corridor, stepped out, and positioned myself in front of the office. Soon, from the recesses of the third floor came the footfalls of the ringer of the wake-up bell, flying in my direction at top speed, while ringing the bell for all he was worth. He tore past the Seat of Enlightenment Hall, raced down the stairs, and charged past Accounts, where I was required to stand with my palms pressed together in reverence and shout out words of encouragement as he sped by: *"Gokurosama deshita!"* Thank you! Looking back, I had a dim memory that when it was my turn to ring the wake-up bell, right around this point on the course someone had yelled out something, but I'd always been so intent on running that I'd never known who it was or what they were saying.

Today's runner was Kosu, from the group just after ours. Seeing the dead-serious look on his face as he dashed by, I felt a touch of nostalgia. The trainees in the common quarters must have gotten up at one thirty this morning and studied in that old familiar room with the hearth cut in the floor. Meanwhile, with no notion that I was standing there cheering him on, Kosu bounded down the stairs to the kitchen and disappeared. Hoping that he would finish the course safely and arrive at the Monks' Hall without taking a tumble on the way, I set about my next task—cleaning the office.

Unlike the office in the common quarters, the Accounts office was full of furnishings that had to be moved during cleaning, so the task took a surprisingly long time. Nevertheless, I managed to finish more or less on schedule and was just catching my breath when the phone rang.

Here goes, I thought.

This was the dreaded call from Administration giving the schedule for the day. Some of the most intimidating senior trainees in the monastery were posted there; if you couldn't catch everything they said the first time and had to ask them to repeat it, I'd heard they would summon you and rake you over the coals. I didn't want to pick up the phone, but I had little choice.

"Hello, this is Accounts."

"Here's the schedule: *samu-kouhou-kujihan-sanmon-tou-shuugou-*

kusatori-zamu-nitchuu-kouhou-nitchuu-nyojou-handai-nyojou-samu-
kouhou-ichijihan-sanmon-tou-shuugou . . . That's it." Click.

My anxiety had been justified. It was like hearing someone rattle off a long tongue twister and then abruptly hang up. Still, somehow I'd managed to get it down on paper. Just as I was congratulating myself, the phone rang. Gingerly I picked up the receiver again, fearing the worst.

"Hello, this is Accounts."

"This is Daimei in the kitchen. Um, is that you, Rosan? Oh, good!"

Daimei and I had been in the common quarters together. Of all the trainees who were sons of priests he in particular seemed to have grown up sheltered and cosseted in the confines of a great temple, innocent of the world at large. He may have been ignorant of the ways of the world, but I liked his simple, unquestioning honesty. His transfer had landed him in the kitchen.

"What's up?" I said.

"Rosan, did you get the schedule just now? I couldn't make head or tail of it. I was scared to call back and ask for it again, so I called you instead."

For a moment there, I'd had a real fright, thinking it was Administration on the phone again. Though indignant, I relayed the information I'd jotted down.

Once the busy morning was over, I spent the rest of the day in the office, handling sales. Besides handling Eiheiji's finances, Accounts also sold trainees various daily necessities. The office was furnished with an old cash register and had old-fashioned drawers and shelves filled with goods. The would-be buyer could not rummage through these directly, however. First he had to kneel in a set place in the corridor and announce himself, then slide open the large window and tell the person on duty what he wished to purchase. The person (me) would stroll over to the proper drawer or shelf, take out the item, and hand it over in exchange for cash.

There were lots of different things for sale. And yet, because this was Eiheiji, there were limits on what was available. Reading material consisted mostly of *Treasury of the True Dharma Eye* and other writings by Dogen and other Zen masters. There was also a magazine—not a weekly gossip rag, of course, but a quarterly called *Zen Friends*. There was a generous assortment of writing materials: pens, pencils, notebooks, stationery, office supplies—pretty much what you'd find in any ordinary stationer's. There were split-toe socks, underwear, and other items of clothing; towels for mealtime, face washing, and the bath; toothbrushes and toothpaste; nail clippers, ear picks, safety razors for shaving the head, packets of razor blades.

The kinds of medical supplies on sale, meanwhile, aptly reflected the rigors of Zen training. Trainees go barefoot most of the time, year round, so the skin on the feet gets hard and tough and can split wide open like a pomegranate. As a result, there was a particularly wide assortment of medicinal ointments and creams. For those suffering pain after long hours of sitting, there was a truly rich array of poultices,

The Source of the Warmth of Life

plasters, and compresses, including pads, ointments, and sprays. There were also headache and cold remedies, digestive medicine, eye drops, Band-Aids, and bandages.

More surprising, perhaps, were little containers of mint-flavored and blueberry-flavored spray to eliminate mouth odor. This may seem an odd item to sell to monks-in-training, but I see it as a reflection of our times. The young men at Eiheiji had all grown up during the affluent postwar era, when living standards rose dramatically, and they were a fastidious bunch. Many people visualize Zen trainees as ascetics with only the clothes on their backs, devoting themselves to sitting without regard for anything else, including personal cleanliness; but this is certainly not the case at Eiheiji. The quickest way for a trainee to be disliked or bullied would be for him to neglect his appearance or hygiene. Everyone washed their clothes diligently, stayed neat and clean, and lavished attention on their skin—partly, no doubt, to make up for the absence of hair to fuss over. Eiheiji is not immune to such signs of the times. Owning stuff is a kind of aesthetic imperative in our age, and the repeated act of throwing things away keeps the economy going while also spurring on the fever of fashion. True children of their age, the trainees took delight in any purchase, however small, and found a respite from the heavy demands of training in these little shopping trips. They snatched brief moments as they could, and came all the way to the store clutching their small savings, just to buy a single eraser or ear cleaner. Then, tucking the precious item in a sleeve, they would straighten themselves and go back to wherever they belonged.

Distribution of Goods

The day after being cooped up all day in the office, I was given a job that involved stepping outside to do various chores around the monastery. I began by cleaning corridors in the Visitors' Meditation Hall and outside the Seat of Enlightenment Hall. Then I went to fetch the newspaper, which was delivered every morning to a special shelf on the first floor of the Visitors' Meditation Hall. Only masters and senior trainees were allowed to read the paper; we novices were cut off from world events.

In summertime, once the eastern sky grew faintly light, the dimensions of the world around transformed with dizzying speed until the sun came up, waking all nature from its dream. Before that transformation had yet begun, while the covered walkways were still enveloped in blue-black night, I headed out to fetch the morning paper.

This was my first taste of the outdoors since transferring to Accounts. I took in a bracing lungful of the clean air that came rolling down from the hills and then, just as I crossed in front of the bathhouse, I happened to glance up at the shrine on a nearby peak. I could make out the figure of a trainee, rubber boots on his feet and a cotton band tied around his head, diligently scrubbing the long stone stairs. I squinted harder and saw to my surprise that it was Choshu. That's right, I reflected, he'd been sent to Buildings and Grounds. The sight of him working up a sweat in the predawn stillness made me appreciate anew the relative ease of my situation.

The Source of the Warmth of Life

The Visitors' Meditation Hall, a modern ferroconcrete building with four stories and a basement, is where lay worshippers come for study and retreats. It has guest rooms, a lecture hall, a meditation hall, and a room for copying sutras. Next to the shop on the first floor is a cupboard where newspapers for each monastery residence are deposited in labeled slots. One morning, as I drew out the newspaper for Accounts and turned to leave, someone called my name.

I looked around and did a double take. It was Tenshin, who'd been transferred to the Reception Hall. I could hardly believe the difference in him. Back in the common quarters, he used to stuff himself with so much rice that his body swelled up like Kintaro, the strong boy of legend; now his cheeks were sunken and he looked emaciated. Trainees spoke matter-of-factly of "Reception Hall hell," but I'd never imagined anything this dire.

"Rosan," he said plaintively, "I want to go home."

"You've lost a lot of weight," I said. "But hang in there, buddy. You've come this far. Time will take care of everything."

He responded to this pat advice with an uncertain smile, picked up his newspaper, and left. As I watched his forlorn figure walk off, I cursed myself for having given such a glib and self-righteous answer. Who was I to say such things to him, when I'd experienced no suffering like his?

When I got back, Jigen told me to get ready for distribution of goods, and strode off with his usual briskness. I dropped off the newspaper and hurried after him.

The distribution of various monastic articles used in daily life takes place on days ending in a three or an eight. Jigen and I got in the ancient elevator and rode up to the attic storeroom. Besides bedding, the large space was crammed with sundries galore: sutras and ritual implements, incense and candles, books and writing utensils. Jigen and I loaded cardboard boxes with items likely to be needed that day, carried them back down to the office on the second floor, and then went to a different storeroom on the same floor for everyday items like laundry soap, bath soap, and toilet paper. Again we loaded items into cardboard boxes and schlepped them to the office.

Buildings and Grounds was responsible for heat, lighting, and maintenance, so a few items—things like trash bags, light bulbs, and charcoal—were stored and distributed there. The main items we distributed were incense, candles, writing implements, tea, medicinal supplies, soap, and cleaning supplies. One of the more unusual things we always kept in stock was baby powder, which went to trainees in the Dharma Hall and attendants' quarters.

What use could Zen monks-in-training have for baby powder? Certainly there were no infants in need of powdering, nor do monks need to powder their skin for any special reason. In fact, the powder went to make ashes for incense burners. Every year at the height of summer, some of the trainees venture out into the surrounding hills to collect fallen leaves, enough to fill upward of a hundred jumbo trash bags. The leaves are spread out and sun-dried to a crisp, then burned to a fine white ash. The amount of ash produced from this enormous supply of leaves is, however, startlingly small. The pure white ash used in incense burners is made by straining the leaf ashes and mixing them with one part lime, six parts baby powder.

Distribution of goods started after morning cleaning was finished. Every residence sent a list of items requested. I would show the lists to Jigen for his approval before handing over the items to the waiting trainee.

Jigen could be curtly dismissive. "What's this? What do you people need boxes of tissues for? No. Permission denied." He'd served a long time in the strict Dharma Hall residence, and was one of the most revered and feared of all senior trainees. None of the trainees who came for supplies ever dared to stand up to him.

When everything had been distributed, each trainee would wrap up his haul and carry it away. If the load was extra heavy, he would fasten it to an old-fashioned wooden frame worn on his back. There was something pathetic and deeply moving about the sight of trainees staggering off under these punishing loads.

Modern civilization has continually sought to eliminate hard labor from people's lives through economic advances. Work that people used to do on their own is now done quickly and efficiently by gas and electricity, with a minimum of human effort. But at Eiheiji, the point is not to avoid work but to embrace it and do it all on one's own. In a sense it is a life of true independence and self-reliance—a style of life that establishes confidence in one's strengths and abilities, mental and physical alike.

Guest Pavilion

One evening, as the sun that had been scorching roof tiles all day long finally began to sink in the west, I stood and waited for a woman. It was my job that day to look after special visitors in the Guest Pavilion.

There are two main places in Eiheiji where visitors are received, the Visitors' Meditation Hall and the Guest Pavilion. The former is mainly for ordinary lay visitors, and the latter for distinguished visitors or those granted special permission to come. In addition to its many guest rooms, the pavilion has a reception room, a communal bath and toilet, and a kitchen. The guest rooms are mostly two-room suites. Guests are shown first to an outer room opening onto the corridor, where they are served tea; the adjoining inner room is where they take their meals and sleep.

Every guest room has an alcove, where incense is lit just before the guest is scheduled to arrive. This is called "welcome incense." The custom is followed elsewhere as well; when trainees finish a memorial service and return to the Monks' Hall, for example, welcome incense is waiting for them. Incense is lit again when trainees leave the hall, and this is called "sending-off incense."

To ready a guest suite for its occupants, a low table and cushions are set in the middle of the outer room, and a tea service and kettle filled with hot water are laid out on top of the table. The placement of the table is carefully calculated by counting off rows of woven straw in the tatami mats, and must be done just so. The cushions must face a certain direction with their tassels attractively arranged in a precise way.

Green tea and rice crackers are served to all guests. Guests who are Buddhist clergy are first offered a hot drink called "plum water," which is made by pouring hot water over sugar, covering the teacup with a lid, and setting it on a red-lacquered saucer along with a pair of cedar chopsticks bearing a seedless pickled plum at the tips. The recipient stirs the hot water with the chopsticks and pickled plum, then drinks the beverage down.

Meals in the inner room are also served on red lacquerware. It was my job to sit across from the guests and offer assistance, serving second helpings of rice, pouring tea, and so forth. If the guests stayed the night, they would sleep in this inner room as well. At Eiheiji it is the rule for sexes always to sleep in separate rooms, even if they are family.

I finished readying the room and went out to the pavilion entrance to see what was happening. The woman's arrival had been scheduled for four thirty, but the hands of the clock had long since moved beyond that time. I began to wonder if there'd been an accident of some sort, but then the office phoned to announce that she was here. Quickly I lit the welcome incense, looked out the window, and waited for her to arrive.

Eventually, in the glow of the setting sun I caught sight of a tiny figure approaching, accompanied by a trainee. Eiheiji's covered walkways and sloping corridors may be picturesque, but they can also be arduous to navigate. It took the old woman some time to climb up.

"I've been expecting you," I said. "You must be tired from your long journey."

She had apparently had difficulty making a series of train connections, and that was what had delayed her. She bowed and apologized over and over. I took her bags from the receptionist who'd brought her this far, and led her to her room.

When she went in, before sitting at the table she knelt facing the alcove with her palms joined in reverence. From then on, whatever I did, she bowed her head in silent thanks.

Even in the summer, night comes on early in a mountain valley. The song of the evening cicada eased the lassitude instilled by the heat of the day, giving way imperceptibly to the chirping of crickets. I switched on the lamp, and the old woman sat with her back to the alcove for her evening meal. In front of her I laid an array of bowls containing simple, graceful arrangements of foods that the kitchen staff had prepared with infinite care.

As she ate her meal in the evening quiet, gradually she relaxed, and we began to chat. After a bit she laid her chopsticks down on the table and said, "You know, no matter how many times I come here, Eiheiji is always the same. The first time I came was so long ago, I don't even remember when it was. I've gotten so old . . . before I knew it, I turned into an old lady." She glanced around the room before continuing.

"I lost my little brother in the war. His death was sudden, such a shock. My mother and father cried and cried—he was their only son, you see. Not that any amount of crying could ever bring him back from the dead. They must have felt that was all they could do for their poor little boy who died without ever becoming a man—just cry. They bore no one any rancor, though. Hatred wouldn't have done any good, and there was nobody to hate, anyway. It was the times, that's all. So they just kept crying until they couldn't cry anymore.

"I can still remember that sad and lonely house. In time we moved my brother's bones here, and from then on my parents used to bring me here every year for his memorial service. That's my connection with Eiheiji." She picked up her chopsticks again and held them in her hand on her lap, staring fixedly at them as she went on.

"Eventually my father died, and then last fall my mother went, too. They both lived long lives, as if to make up for his short one. I'd like to think they're with him now in heaven, having a joyous reunion. And here I am, all alone now on this earth . . ."

She abruptly raised her eyes, and as she did so tears spilled out and streamed down her deeply wrinkled cheeks. Catching herself, she hastily wiped them away and smiled. "You must forgive me. The older I get, the easier it is to weep. And somehow, sitting here talking with you like this, it almost feels as though I'm having a conversation with my dead brother . . ."

I bitterly regretted that although my head was shaved and I was wearing the robe of a monk, I could do nothing for this old woman but nod dumbly.

Later, when I left her room, I knew from the slight coolness of the breeze against my skin—the same breeze that carried the chirping of night insects in the grasses—that autumn was not far off.

In the morning, she and I walked together along the covered walkways, where traces of the cool night still lingered. Bright shafts of morning sun stabbed through the surrounding trees, portending another hot day. Moment by moment, the hum of cicadas waking from their slumbers swelled louder in our ears. The corridors were mostly empty—it was too early for the day's visitors—but we passed several monks. As they went by, the old woman held her hands together, palm to palm, and bowed her head. Then she said this:

"The monks here all have such good faces. The polished floors are nice to see, but really it's the faces of the monks that shine the brightest. I come here every year, and every time I see their faces, my heart is washed clean."

I mulled over her words. In all the times I'd looked at the faces of my fellow monks, I'd never felt any such thing.

When we came to the front entrance, I thanked her sincerely for coming and told her to have a safe journey home. She smiled sweetly at me.

"Thank you for everything," she said. "Now this year's service for my brother is over, and that's a load off my mind. Thank you for listening to my foolish ramblings yesterday. I feel much better now. Meeting you has made this year special. I'm an old lady, and I don't know how much longer I can keep on coming back, but I'll do it as long as I can. I'll be here next year. You take care of yourself, now, and do your best. Goodbye." She took my hand in her two wrinkled ones and clasped it tight, again and again.

I watched as her small figure wove in and out of sight in the crowd of morning visitors, growing tinier and tinier before disappearing from view. Before I knew it, my palms came together in a silent entreaty that she might return in good health next year, the year after, and forever.

Inspection

There was a new candle in the lantern, and the flashlight and wooden clappers were ready. All I needed to do now was wait till it was time to summon Jigen and the treasurer, whose turn it was to make the late-night rounds of the monastery. The various masters took turns performing this nightly inspection, accompanied by their personal assistants. As Eiheiji has burned down many times in the past, the main purpose of the inspection is fire prevention, but at the same time it is a way to check whether trainees are properly in bed: failure to retire before rounds is considered a grave offense.

There are two inspections, one at ten thirty and the other at midnight. I glanced at the clock and, seeing it was getting toward ten thirty, quickly gave Jigen a shout before heading off to the treasurer's residence.

When I got there, I heard an unusual sound coming from inside: the treasurer was playing the accordion. Musically gifted, he could play anything on that instrument and also sang with impeccable phrasing. Daily sutra recitation naturally improves the voice, and apparently it also hones musical sense. The treasurer's musical accomplishments were highly thought of; at one internal lecture he'd taught us all to sing

Buddhist hymns, consisting of Buddhist-themed verses set to Western-style music. As he'd stood before us in his monk's robe with the accordion slung over his shoulder, singing away, he'd been truly marvelous to behold.

By the time the treasurer was ready to go, Jigen had made his appearance, too. The three of us set off, the treasurer carrying a lantern with the characters for "Inspection" brushed on it in black ink, followed by Jigen with the flashlight and me with the wooden clappers hanging around my neck. We stopped at every residence, opening doors and checking interiors with the flashlight beam to make sure everyone was in bed. Wherever there was a gas outlet, we checked to make sure it was closed. Because of the constant need to make ashes for incense burners, some of the hearths were kept burning even in the middle of summer, and we looked carefully to make sure each one was out.

Novice trainees have limited access to the different areas of the monastery, and tagging along on inspection offers a rare chance to see other work and living quarters. In general, novices are housed in large communal rooms, senior trainees in doubles or triples. Though different in design, the various quarters all are traditional in style. Each trainee is given a low desk with drawers: his only inviolable space. Sleeping space in the quarters is assigned based on the usual hierarchy; in general, the more recent your arrival, the closer you are to the door.

Jigen and the treasurer proceeded swiftly and carefully with their inspection. Then we came to the common quarters, a place of some nostalgia for me—and as the door slid open, a half-forgotten memory

The Source of the Warmth of Life

came flooding vividly back. It happened just after I'd first been sent there. It was the day before I had been assigned to perform miscellaneous tasks in and around the premises, which meant I had to drag my bedding to the common quarters office and sleep there, just as I'd done recently in the Accounts office. The common quarters office has no safe or anything of monetary value to be guarded; what needed protection was rather the live coals buried in the ashes of the brazier. In winter, every office in Eiheiji has a charcoal brazier, as do the quarters of every master, and tending to them is one of the trainees' most important tasks. It had been my job to blow on the live coals first thing in the morning to start the day's fire.

That night I'd gone to bed only to toss and turn, wide awake. I yearned for sleep in the blessed night that had finally arrived, yet at the same time I was unwilling to sink into oblivion. Once I fell asleep, I knew that a moment later it would be time to get up and face another day. If only tomorrow would never come . . . I lay with my mind full of dismal thoughts, surrounded by darkness. Eventually, however, fatigue won out, and I drifted off to sleep.

The next thing I knew, thinking that someone had yelled at me, I was on my feet, shouting out a reply. The door slid open and the beam of a flashlight swept over me. "You idiot!" barked a shadowy figure in the doorway. "What'd you get up for? Go back to bed!" The door banged shut, and he was gone.

At the time I'd had no idea there was such a thing as a midnight inspection tour. While asleep, I must have dimly heard an outer door being opened and assumed someone had come to bawl me out—so I automatically sprang to attention, shouting a response. Imagining it now was comical; but in those early days we'd been unable to relax for a second, even in our sleep.

That was six months ago. With the passage of time, things that had once lain hidden in darkness had started to come clear, little by little, but I'd lost sight of other things. As the painfully strained nerves of those early days flashed across my memory, I mourned the ineffable things I'd left behind.

When the hands of the clock pointed to twelve, we set out on the second inspection. This time there was no probing of the inner recesses of the various buildings. Instead we did a perfunctory tour of the covered walkways and checked everything from the outside.

The walkways were lit at night by the faintest light possible, which only increased the depth of the surrounding blackness. The night is the night because it is dark. If night were as bright as day, a great portion of the world's beauty would surely vanish. The monastery complex deep in the heart of the mountains was full of beautiful pools and shallows of darkness unknown to a city at night.

When we finished our round, I sounded the wooden clappers with all my strength, marking the end of that evening's inspection. The hard, clear sound echoed far into the darkness of night that enfolded the trainees, and then it disappeared.

Washrags

One day this letter came to Accounts.

To the Eiheiji Monks

This summer it is surprisingly hot up here in Hokkaido. That is usually a sign that the coming winter will be bitterly cold, that we are in for a time of it. I am sure that you all must be busy with your many activities, and I hope that this letter finds you well.

Recently, when I sent some washrags I had sewn, you were kind enough to send me various items in return, for which I heartily thank you. Also, after I asked that a sutra be said and incense lit on behalf of my only son, who was killed in action at a young age in Siberia, you sent word that a proper memorial service had been carried out. Again, all I can do is express deepest heartfelt gratitude.

I lost my husband when my son was still little, and from then on it was always just the two of us. Then the war came along and tore us apart. Even now, when I think of my son breathing his last on that frozen battleground, I can't help crying. Knowing that Eiheiji has performed a memorial service for him as I'd always hoped means everything to me. I thank you from the bottom of my heart.

If you can make use of the washrags I make, I will be happy to keep on sending them. Now that I am in my eighties, there isn't much else that I can do. I will devote myself to making them with all my heart.

I know your lives must be busy, but do take good care of your-selves and continue your Zen training in good health. With all my thanks.

Yours sincerely.

Eiheiji receives packages from all over Japan containing a plethora of items—rice, vegetables, fruit, tea, towels, and straw sandals, to name a few—but by far the most common item that people send in is hand-sewn washrags. Perhaps it is a sign that the image of monks silently polishing Eiheiji's many long corridors has permeated the public con-sciousness; in any case, the number donated is truly staggering. And in fact, the washrags are an essential tool in Zen training. In this sense, our daily lives were directly supported by the benevolence of people all across the country.

Food donations go straight to the kitchen, but everything else is sent to Accounts where there is the special room just for washrags. In token of appreciation for this outpouring of goodwill, Eiheiji sends a small gift in return for each donation, another important job managed by Accounts. Inevitably, we would get back a polite letter of thanks in which every word revealed the life and circumstances of its author. I found such letters very moving, and this one from the old woman in Hokkaido is still imprinted on my memory.

Since I belong to a generation with no direct experience of the hor-rors of World War Two, I'd always thought of the war carelessly as a page of history, nothing more. But that day, when I finished reading the old woman's letter about her son, it hit me for the first time that there were people who had lived through that era whose hearts were still racked with pain, and that for them the war would never be over. The thought of that woman in her eighties living day after day with the photograph of her dead son made me ashamed of myself—ashamed of having mouthed words like "peace" and "freedom" without a thought for such still-raw wounds. As I pictured that solitary old woman mutely stitching cloths on behalf of myself and the other monks, I could only bow my head in respect.

Among all the washrags that we received, there was one delivery that to this day I cannot forget. Word came one day that a number of packages had arrived for Accounts, and I went to pick them up. One was shabby-looking, tied with fraying string. I loaded all the packages onto a wooden frame and carried it on my back to the office, where I turned my attention first to the shabby one. My usual practice was to snip off the string and toss it in the trash, but as I held the scissors to that fraying old string, something made me hesitate. I took a closer look and saw that it was fashioned from strips of an old cotton kimono. On top of the package, the string had been considerately wound around with more string to make a soft handle that wouldn't dig into the hand of whoever picked it up. In the end, I laid the scissors aside and painstakingly undid the tight knots until finally I could open the box and look inside.

What I saw amazed me. The box was full of washrags that were made from worn and faded scraps: bits of old flannel nightgowns, cotton kimonos, and thin hand towels, stitched together in multiple layers with stout thread. I'd opened many boxes of washrags sent here before, but mostly they were made of brand-new materials. I think what surprised me most, to begin with, was how very old the material all was. And yet it wasn't dirty in the least; everything had been washed clean, and gave off a pleasant soapy fragrance.

I picked up one of the cloths and asked myself if I had ever put anything to such long use. After a lifetime of throwing things away one after another without a second thought, the sight of so many carefully saved rags was like a dash of cold water in the face.

There was a letter in the box. On the front of the envelope, written in large letters with a ballpoint pen, were the simple words "To the Monks." I opened the carefully sealed envelope and drew out a sheet of stationery. Here again were words written painstakingly with a ballpoint pen, the size of the writing rather larger than usual for an adult.

It is now mid-August, and the cries of the cicadas in the surrounding hills have gradually faded away. At Eiheiji, today must have been another day of hard practice. I wish you well.

At this old people's home, every morning fifty people or so gather in the chapel for Buddhist services. The priest here always tells us about Eiheiji. I've never had the chance to go there, but I feel close to the temple in my heart.

These washrags are something we all worked hard to make. As we sewed, we prayed we might have a chance to visit Eiheiji before we die. There must be many visitors there. We would be thrilled if you used these to help with the cleaning.

When winter comes, mornings at Eiheiji will no doubt be bitterly cold. Our thoughts are with you as you undergo your ascetic practice. Good luck and best wishes.

I finished reading the letter with a mix of emotions that found expression in a sigh. I looked closely at the cloth in my hand. The rows of uneven, awkward stitches in the faded rags brought tears to my eyes. Without knowing why, I felt overpoweringly lonely and sad.

That night, as I pulled up the covers and closed my eyes, I thought again of those washrags. I could vividly imagine the residents of the old people's home in thick-lens spectacles, sitting hunched over as they intently stitched scraps of cloth together with gnarled and wrinkled hands. They each had survived perilous struggles and adventures on life's troubled sea, only to end their days in an old people's home. But just as we all have our own life to lead, so happiness, I thought, must mean different things to different people. Some residents of the facility must be truly happy and relieved to be there—some, but not all. I felt as guilty about the others as if I personally had abandoned them. I must do something, I thought. What that might be I had no idea, but I felt strongly compelled to do something for them in return.

Every single person on this earth has to live out their allotted years one by one, as they come. Young and old alike need to live with the dignity appropriate to their age, and society must ensure that this is possible.

From that day on I kept one of the washrags from the old people's home in my desk drawer, and sometimes, when I was feeling down, I would slip it out and look at it. Every stitch was replete with the burning spirit of someone whose faith had stayed strong over a lifetime. In the warmth and solidity of that person's handiwork, I could laugh away the frailty of my heart.

What is religion, and what is faith? I found my answer in the careful stitching of that cloth. It became a constant inspiration.

Ending Intensive Training

"At ten o'clock the great bell, at ten thirty the gongs, followed immediately by the Dharma Hall bell and the final recitation of the Surangama Dharani." This message, in a phone call from Administration, signaled the end of the three months of intensive training, three months when each morning without fail we had recited the Surangama Dharani as a prayer for the successful conclusion of the event. Now the final recitation was at hand.

That morning when we entered the Dharma Hall, we went straight into morning service, without reciting the dharani first as usual. The great bell began to toll at ten o'clock and went on for half an hour, stopping precisely at ten thirty. The gong outside the Monks' Hall was immediately struck three times, followed by three more wooden gongs in successively higher locations in the complex. On the heels of the last gong came the ringing of the bell outside the Dharma Hall, signaling the start of the final dharani recitation. Unlike the predawn darkness of previous recitations, now bright sunshine poured into the hall, quickening our pulses.

Three months had gone by. The thought of all that had gone into each one of those days, and of the swiftly approaching conclusion, filled our voices with strength. The rich music of over one hundred male voices chanting in unison swirled around the hall, spilled outside, and rose above the treetops to heaven's highest reaches to disperse in a burst of light.

Then came a rush of closing invocations and salutations, and the three months were finally at an end. It was over. Everyone's face was full of the satisfaction of having brought the intensive training period to a successful conclusion. As I walked back to my quarters, I felt lighter in body and spirit.

"Hey, Rosan," I heard, just as I was starting up the stairs. I turned around and saw my friend Daimei from the kitchen. "It's finally over— what a relief! But I've got my work cut out for me now. My folks are coming, and they'll be staying in the Guest Pavilion. They'll eat food I prepare—I've got to study hard so I'll be ready. You'll take care of them, won't you, Rosan?"

All smiles, Daimei went in the kitchen. I thought about what he'd said, and felt with renewed conviction how good this life at Eiheiji was. When he first arrived, like the other sons of Zen priests, he'd had mixed feelings about these circumstances he'd found himself in, but little by little those feelings had changed. It seemed to me that during the past months he had stopped seeing himself as someone making a sacrifice for the sake of his family, that his heart had softened. Part of it might have been the relief of being surrounded by people in the same situation as himself, but in any case he seemed to have come to terms with the life he was destined to lead. Nor was he glumly resigned; rather, he had gained a firm footing, and was building confidence to face the future fearlessly.

I went upstairs and was arranging my things when Jigen called: "Rosan, it's time to collect the offerings, so get ready."

"Collecting the offerings" meant going around and emptying every offering box in the compound. Managing the funds from offerings was, naturally, the responsibility of the treasurer. Jigen led the way, bunch of keys in hand, and I followed him with a wooden box the size of an apple crate fastened to a strap around my neck and clearly labeled Offerings. There were offering boxes in the Dharma Hall, the Founder's Hall, the Buddha Hall, the kitchen, and the Memorial Hall. The amount collected naturally varied from day to day; in the past, I'd heard, the collection had sometimes weighed so much that the bottom of the collection box fell right out.

But even on days when the offerings were slight, the collection box was good and heavy, and at every stop on the route it grew heavier still. For some reason it had to be carried at chest height, suspended from a strap around the neck. Carrying it on my back would have been far easier on me—but would not have demonstrated proper respect for the precious offerings.

Jigen strode ahead without a backward glance, as always. By the time we got to the kitchen my neck was wobbly, my knees shaking. Just then a serious-looking woman came up to Jigen and asked him a question about the enormous pestle in front of the kitchen. Back when the Buddha Hall was built, the tool known as a "ground-piercing stick" was made in the shape of a pestle and later set in front of the kitchen. In time a tradition grew up that touching it would improve one's cooking skills; the story is very popular with visitors.

The woman listened attentively to Jigen's explanation and then asked in all seriousness if there was a mortar somewhere to go with the pestle. Jigen's answer did not disappoint her.

"Yes, of course. It's in the kitchen—let's see, it must be a good sixteen feet across. Unfortunately, it's not shown to the public."

She'd picked the wrong person to ask. I marveled that anyone could tell such a bald-faced lie so smoothly. Never suspecting she'd been deceived, the good woman thanked Jigen politely and walked off toward the Buddha Hall, while he strode off in the opposite direction, chuckling with that peculiar "kuk-kuk-kuk" of his and leaving me to totter after him as best I could.

PART SIX

The Colors of the Peak, the Echo in the Valley

Attendant to the Director

With every rain cloud that passed high over the treetops, summer faded further away until the feel of it on the skin was a dim memory. One by one, people above us were transferred out of Accounts, and eventually the day came when Sozen and I moved into a room for high-ranking trainees. He was promoted to residence head, and I was next in line below him. The head has the difficult responsibility of leading the other residents—a job that Sozen, who could handle almost any situation with aplomb, was perfectly suited for.

The first time I'd ever spoken to Sozen was back in the common quarters, when he was going over some of my new duties: "Put the charcoal in the incense burner and smooth out the ash," he'd said, "then put in new candles and set up the incense. You're a monk, so you know how to do it, right?" His words caught me by surprise. Did others come here already knowing this stuff, having mastered the basics ahead of time? I remember feeling added respect for my peers. Since I was ignorant, Sozen had gone on to demonstrate exactly what to do.

Now, as residence head, Sozen was in the unenviable position of having to take responsibility for the acts of every trainee in Accounts. When a problem arose, he was always the first to be summoned. Every time this happened to him I sympathized, but I couldn't help feeling glad that I'd entered Eiheiji after him, and not the other way around.

One day a rumor started to circulate that a new set of transfers was pending, and that this time just one person would be leaving Accounts. Who starts such rumors I don't know, but the moment I heard this, my heart sank. Now it would be my turn to be residence head. Sozen was all smiles, visibly relieved at the prospect of being released from his burden. He began to say things like, "Well, pretty soon it'll all be in your hands, Rosan. Good luck!" I only felt glummer. But there was no point in objecting. Whatever orders we received, all any of us could do was silently comply. I would just have to make the best of it. Once again I began learning from Sozen the ins and outs of my upcoming responsibilities.

The fateful day soon came around. (Again, how did we know? Who spilled the beans?) We grabbed our bowls and headed to the Monks' Hall for the morning meal. The latest transfers would be announced just before the end of the meal, as usual.

Everything proceeded normally, but the air in the hall was restive; we were fidgety, and with good reason. The announcement would determine our fates, some of us to experience heaven in the days ahead, others hell. The meaning of the moment was just that dramatic. Yet I found a keen pleasure in the tension that preceded the reading of the list. The thundering heartbeats of all the trainees in the great hall seemed to come rushing in my ears.

"Announcement of transfers."

Finally the superintendent began to read from a scroll. We listened, hushed, with faces of constrained seriousness. With every announcement someone's expression changed slightly, softening in relief or betraying mixed emotions. As the reading of the list went on, a variety of facial expressions flickered around the hall. I glanced at Sozen, who was listening impatiently in stern silence. I thought that I'd never seen him so on edge. That's when it happened.

"Attendant to the director, Rosan."

"Huh?"

The news was so unexpected that I couldn't help letting out a squawk of surprise. This couldn't be happening. That was the only thought in my head.

So in the end it was Sozen who stayed put and I, though with less seniority than him, who was transferred out. My new destination was Administration, which was the director's residence and a place we all held in fear. Responsibility there was heavy; the junior trainees were constantly on edge and the senior trainees looked sinister. There was nothing cheerful about the place. I was despondent. Why *there*, of all places?

"Well, well, Rosan. Coming up in the world, aren't we?" When I went back to the office, Jigen greeted me with this unfeeling comment, chuckling in that odd way of his. "Never mind," he said. "Resign yourself. Who knows, once you're there, you may find it's heaven."

I knew this was no time for whining, yet my shoulders slumped and my spirits sagged. Then the residence head from Administration came looking for me. "Where's Rosan?" he roared. "You still here? What's the holdup? Get a move on!"

This is the end, I thought. Then I threw my things together and rushed off without time for a backward glance.

Conference Room

The residence head led the way and I followed, toting all of my belongings. He took me first to the room where I would now sleep. I changed clothes as instructed, and off we went on a quick round of ceremonial greetings. We were to start with the director himself.

We stepped out into the corridor and climbed the stairs, coming out by the Seat of Enlightenment Hall. Administration headquarters was between there and the Patriarch's Interview Hall, reached by a shallow staircase with a pair of sandals neatly arranged on each step.

"Take off your sandals here," said my guide. "They go in order of seniority, so yours will be at the very bottom. Okay?" He took his off and set them on the third step from the top before going on in.

I saw that as the staircase rose, the sandals became progressively more worn looking. There was something vaguely disconcerting about the extreme age of those at the top. I slipped my sandals off and aligned them on the lowest step before following him up.

The entrance opened on a corridor fitted with tatami mats. On the right was the Administration office, to the right of that was a conference room, and all the way at the end of the corridor were the director's private quarters. I stepped timidly into the conference room, where important discussions and meetings took place, and seated myself near the door. Hanging in the alcove was a scroll painting of birds and flowers by the seventeenth-century painter Kano Tan'yu, and on the wooden transom was a row of photographs of successive abbots. I studied them in order and located the face of the current abbot at the far end. Then I heard the door of the inner quarters slide open, and prepared to meet the great master.

The Eiheiji director is the equivalent of prime minister, with ultimate responsibility for all that goes on. Nothing can happen without his say-so. He has to be familiar with all the workings of the monastery, and hand down appropriate decisions as needed. His attendants must likewise deal swiftly with situations as they arise. Mistakes, I realized, would not be tolerated.

There soon appeared before me an elderly man of delicate build and an air of regal dignity. I respectfully performed the ceremonial greeting and then reseated myself formally in front of him, as instructed. He began to speak.

"Your name is Rosan? A remarkable bond with our founder has brought you to this place. You must give up all thought of self and devote yourself single-mindedly to the pursuit of truth. The work is demanding, but again, you are here because of a deep karmic bond. 'Do all for the Dharma, nothing for the self.' Impress these words on your heart and, I repeat, devote yourself to the pursuit of truth."

From the first words out of his mouth, I marveled that a voice of such resonance and strength could emerge from a body that looked so frail. Nearly overwhelmed by his power, my body went rigid and my palms grew sweaty. Every joint in my body seemed locked in place. As I sat there frozen, he sprang to his feet and returned to the inner quarters.

Next I greeted the seven other residents in turn, including the director's personal advisor and the steward. None of them looked like people you could warm up to. The future seemed dark. How I missed Jigen and his comfortable, foolish laugh.

When all the greetings had been properly done, the residence head next took me out to the vice-director's quarters, at the far end of the great hall. I drew myself up before going in nervously. But the moment I saw the vice-director's face, relief flooded through me. I felt as though I had encountered the proverbial buddha in hell.

Back in Accounts I often used to run into him. Sozen and I would regularly carry red lacquerware from the Guest Pavilion up to the third-floor hall and polish bowls by the dozen for hours on end. Each evening we used to see a master dressed in brown work clothes with a towel around his head and a pedometer at his waist, his forehead beaded with sweat, going around and around the hall at an indeterminate pace, too fast for a walk and too slow for a trot. When he saw us silently polishing, he would raise a hand and call out a word of friendly encouragement. That had been the vice-director.

From the beginning, I always thought he looked like Santa Claus. I used to think I wanted to be like him when I got older—someone who offered sincere encouragement to others. Now, as I finished the ceremonial greeting, he beamed at me with his jolly-old-elf smile and said, "Rosan, isn't it? Welcome." For the first time since the news of this transfer, I felt saved. Thanks to that cheery smile, my spirits were high as I tagged along after the residence head, back out the door.

In Attendance

Once the greetings were over, as usual there followed a period of initiation. In Administration, however, initiation was handled differently from everywhere else. First of all, there was no need to get up two hours before the wake-up bell. Second, it lasted only three days. Third, once you had cleaned the designated places, you were done. The hard part was undergoing a thorough drilling in the new protocol, starting on day one.

The first thing I needed to learn was the most important of all: how to see properly to the personal needs of the director. Whether arrangements were in exact accordance with his wishes, however, was in many cases hard for me to judge.

Just before the wake-up bell, I had to set out his sandals and wait for him at the entrance. When he set off for early morning sitting I would follow behind him, but I was cautioned that I must walk in perfect silence, without letting my footsteps be heard. The director himself possessed the rare ability to walk anywhere with inaudible footsteps. Eiheiji corridors were sprinkled with signs reminding people to walk quietly on the left and greet superiors respectfully, signed "Director of the Monastery" in big letters. As his signature was on these orders, he above all had to walk noiselessly, and he succeeded brilliantly.

In a Zen training monastery where silence is the rule, walking noise-lessly is an important element of life. Dogen set down the correct way of walking in his early text *A Talk on Cultivating the Way*:

> The leg alone should extend in front; do not lean forward as you walk. Move body and feet forward together. Keep your eyes fixed at a point on the ground approximately six feet ahead. One pace should be about the length of your foot. You must walk slowly and quietly. Walk as if you were standing still.

Hoping to avoid a scolding, I walked fearfully with extreme care, but I couldn't manage it very well. I concentrated so hard on the mechanics of walking that I took too much time, and before I knew it the director had disappeared around a corner ahead.

In the Monks' Hall, every time the director mounted or dismounted the sitting platform, I had to go up to him, kneel, and put away or bring out his sandals. The director was accompanied not just to early morning sitting but everywhere he went. Whenever he stepped out, an attendant went with him. We opened and closed all doors for him and saw to his sandals. While he was conducting business, one of us always waited for him and then accompanied him on his return.

There were also various rules about his meals. At Eiheiji, while masters generally eat the same foods as trainees, at suppertime they receive an extra dish—any of a variety of elaborate dishes prepared in accordance with monastery rules. All of the director's food was served in special lacquerware bowls reserved for his exclusive use. Careful attention had to be paid to the timing of his meals: interrupting his work was forbidden, as was letting his rice and soup grow cold. His meals had to be served at just the right time, in just the right condition.

We also drew his bath. The director has a private bath where the tub is filled every evening, not just on days of the month ending in a four or a nine. The water had to rise to the level of a certain row of tiles, counting down from the top—neither above nor below this line. We used a thermometer kept on a shelf in the anteroom to check the water temperature, which also had to be just so. When all was ready, we stole away and never, under any circumstances, informed the director that his bath was ready, as it was forbidden to bother him with such minor details. Instead, it was up to us to predict when he would wish to bathe, gauging it so that the water would be the right temperature at the right time and lighting incense in the anteroom just before he went in. All of this necessitated repeated trips to check on the temperature of the bathwater or replace incense with a fresh stick on evenings when our timing was off. Presiding over the bath was a nerve-racking experience.

While the director bathed and soaked in the hot tub, we whipped around and straightened up his private rooms: put fresh water in the kettle, washed out his tea things, emptied the trash, and did a thorough cleaning, ending by folding a moist hand towel in a prescribed way and leaving it on the table for him. After that one of us would slip out to wait for him to emerge from his bath.

The Colors of the Peak, the Echo in the Valley

Other duties of personal attendants include relaying telephone calls, looking after guests, and doing a mountain of miscellaneous chores. Because the job of director is pivotal to the workings of the temple, and because the director was extremely demanding of himself and others, we were kept so busy that we rarely had a moment to relax.

Besides the director and the vice-director, we also saw to the needs of the steward, a taciturn monk with a voice normally so soft that it was like listening to the muffled bleating of a goat. He was also a little on the quirky side.

When first assigned to the steward, I received a strict warning: "When you clear away his dishes, if there's a plate of coriander on the floor by the brazier, whatever you do, don't touch it—just leave it alone!" Once before, when the steward lived in a different residence, some dried bits of coriander in his room had been carried off by a zealous new transfer. The steward had immediately phoned to demand that the coriander be returned, only to be told that it was already in the garbage. He thundered, "Didn't you hear me? I want it back now! On the double!" In a panic, the trainee overturned the trashcan and pawed through the garbage until he finally came across the by-then bedraggled coriander, put it back on the original plate, and apprehensively returned it. "Pay more attention to what you're doing," the steward had grumbled, and resumed his work as if nothing had happened.

On hearing this story, I warmed to the man. The exchange had the flavor of a traditional Zen question-and-answer session between master and acolyte, for one thing, and for another I was pleased to think we had a true eccentric at Eiheiji. Whenever I went to his room I would glance out of the corner of my eye at the dried-up coriander next to the brazier and go about my duties cautiously, to avoid incurring his wrath. I was intrigued: why coriander, and why only dried-up pieces of it? Why lay it out and protect it with such fierce urgency, as if his salvation depended on it? What would happen to it in the end? I never found an answer to any of these questions.

Morning Session

On the second day of my initiation period, morning session was held in the conference room. Attended by all the masters in the temple, morning session is held on the first and the fifteenth of every month. We rushed around getting ready by spreading a carpet in the room, laying out cushions, and preparing tea and refreshments.

The Eiheiji administrative bureaucracy is a pyramid. On the bottom are novice trainees and the senior trainees who instruct them. All alike are assigned to residences overseen by masters. At the apex of the pyramid is the director, who has jurisdiction over everyone. Poised above the pyramid is the symbolic figure of the abbot.

The masters at Eiheiji are responsible for running temple business and guiding trainee monks. Apart from those who hold posts in Administration, the other principal masters and their main responsibilities are as follows:

Head of Training. Has supreme responsibility for and command over all aspects of trainees' lives.

Training Director. Ranks just below the head of training; guides and oversees trainees directly.

Treasurer. Handles monastery finances; has charge of all utensils and furnishings.

Superintendent. Oversees trainees' Zen practice; presides at ceremonies and memorial services; serves as cantor.

Head Cook. Has charge of all meals served at the monastery.

Labor Steward. Has charge of repairs and maintenance, construction, and manual labor.

Guest Manager. Has charge of greeting, entertaining, and seeing off all visitors to the monastery.

In addition, every housing and work unit has a master in charge. Also, one master is appointed to give periodic lectures to the assembly.

Morning session took place right after morning sutra reading. As soon as the service ended, all of the masters went straight to the conference room. Among them was of course the treasurer, who greeted me courteously by name as he went in, joining his palms in that way he had that made it look as if he were rubbing them together. Then came the vice-director with his bright, friendly smile and greeting. Behind him came the shrine keeper, whose job it is to serve in the Founder's Hall and the shrine dedicated to Dogen.

I had a painful memory of the shrine keeper from my days in Accounts, when he was first appointed to that post and it fell to me to prepare for his welcome. I had readied the quietest guest room, inspecting it with care to make sure all was in order. When he arrived, I took one look at him and cringed. The expression "sourpuss" must have been invented to describe someone with a face like his. He didn't appear just ill-natured but positively dangerous, as if he might bite my head off if I didn't look sharp. Of the gamut of human emotions, he seemed oblivious to all but one: anger. Tensely, I made his green tea and plum-water tea with extra care.

After serving the tea I made a quick exit and was congratulating myself on having gotten by without mishap when Jigen came looking for me, visibly upset. "Rosan," he said, "you screwed up big time. The shrine keeper's calling for you, so get your ass over there."

What could it be? Wondering, I went back to the room, and there he was, sitting in glowering silence, true to form. The monk at his side was livid with rage. "You drink this," he rasped, holding out the plum-water tea I'd served moments before. Obediently I took a sip—and felt a chill down my spine. It tasted salty. I'd meant to put in sugar, and somehow had used salt instead. Moreover, thinking that perhaps my usual way of making the drink might not be sweet enough, I had thoughtfully heaped in more than usual. The monk at the shrine keeper's side was furious, and he bawled me out. I prostrated myself and begged forgiveness.

Finally the shrine keeper, who had been observing our exchange in silence, interrupted. "That's enough," he said. "Salt is used to purify, after all—let's just say I got a little extra purification this time." To my amazement, on his face was a crooked grin.

Once again, I was thoroughly chastened. I learned the hard way that appearances truly are deceiving. I never quite recovered from that experience, either. Whenever I saw him I shivered involuntarily, my mouth burning with salt again and my spine feeling the trickle of cold sweat.

"Ah, there you are, Rosan," he said at that day's morning session, smiling when he saw me. "How are you?" With that he joined the others.

There were no tables or chairs in the conference room; instead, people sat on cushions on the carpeted floor. The rigid hierarchy among masters was reflected in where they sat, with the director seated closest to the alcove. When everyone was seated, he called for tea and sweets. We served them and then seated ourselves at the back of the room by the door.

Announcements were made, followed by topics for discussion, but very little actual debate took place at morning session. Generally it would be agreed to keep an eye on a particular situation for a while longer, and the session would be adjourned. Important issues tended to be resolved in one-on-one discussions or private conferences.

That day the head of training picked up his sweet and remarked: "That's funny. In all my years I've never seen *monaka*[1] served cut in half this way." The attendant on duty today had apparently sought to make an aesthetically pleasing presentation by cutting each sweet in two.

"Neither have I," someone else chimed in. "And you know, what I like most about monaka is biting down into the wafer circle. That first bite is the best."

"There's something nice about not being able to see the filling right away, too," said another. "The way you're kept in suspense."

At that particular morning session, more time was devoted to discussing the refreshments than anything else. But that only went to show how peaceful things were at Eiheiji that day, so it was fortunate. Session wasn't always so relaxed, by any means. There were times when everyone wore a frown and looked extremely concerned.

When morning session was over, I picked up one of the leftover monaka halves, studied it, then suddenly sank my teeth into it—and laughed out loud, feeling like a fool.

Incense Bearer

In the great Dharma Hall, brilliant with candles, someone grabbed me by the collar and dragged me back. For an instant my mind went blank.

Of the many duties in Administration, there is one that trainees often look forward to with pleasure: that of assisting the leader of ceremonies and memorial services as incense bearer. Once his period of initiation has ended, a newly transferred attendant is always assigned this role in the various services for the dead that may be held during morning service at the request of the chief mourner. These include memorial services, offerings to spirits of ancestors and others, and sutra recitations.

Usually the chief mourner stays at Eiheiji the night before and attends morning service in the Dharma Hall. On these occasions, the director presides as leader. If he is away, the vice-director does the honors, and if the vice-director too is unavailable then another replacement fills in, and so on, in a carefully prescribed order. On rare occasions the abbot himself may preside by special request. When the director performs the ceremony, his personal assistant serves as ceremonial attendant and his attendant serves as incense bearer.

The incense bearer, as his title would indicate, follows the leader into the hall carrying a stand on which sits a round, metallic incense holder containing a cylindrical charcoal briquette covered in snow white ash. While in tea ceremony and *kodo* (the classical art of incense appreciation), ashes are arranged in patterns, here they are smoothed as flat as paper.

Unlike the memorial services held routinely every day, these occasional services are performed with visual flair and drama. The leader's mantle, for example, is made of gold brocade or some other gorgeous fabric, and his robe is a conspicuous yellow or crimson. Trainees, normally barefoot, wear white socks. One notable moment comes when the assembled monks parade around the great hall chanting a sutra. In the dim, predawn interior of the hall, the reddish luster of candlelight from the gold canopy overhead falls on a moving sea of black robes, flecked with white socks, gliding across the tatami mats. This spectacle, accompanied by resonant waves of chanting and the sweet fragrance of smoke rising from the incense burner, can impart an almost hallucinatory sense of exaltation.

Just before the chanting begins, sutras are distributed, so that each monk has a copy of the sacred text. Several altar attendants come out, each holding a wooden box full of books, and flow between the rows of sitting monks in an unswerving line, as if gliding across thin silk. When at a designated place the altar attendants make a designated gesture, the sutras slide against the side of the box with a little click. This clicking sound is an important acoustical element of the service, heightening the atmosphere and the showiness of the occasion. The most beautiful part of the service is this distribution of sutras.

The altar attendants who play this central role are exquisitely graceful in their gestures, ways of walking and standing, and overall demeanor. This seemingly effortless beauty of movement is achieved as a result of excruciatingly difficult daily training.

Back when I first transferred to Accounts, every evening I was mystified by the sound of loud drumbeats coming from the Dharma Hall, accompanied by cries and moans. I soon learned that this was the

The Colors of the Peak, the Echo in the Valley

sound of altar attendants undergoing training. They did so on an empty stomach, I was surprised to hear, as the routine was so punishing that they could not have kept their supper down in any case. No one was allowed to watch the training in progress. Behind the elegant, flowing grace of altar attendants' movements in the Dharma Hall lay this harsh and unforgiving regimen of practice.

When it came time for my debut as incense bearer, I was unnecessarily nervous. I personally felt no elation at the chance to do this job, which meant staging a show in the vast Dharma Hall without benefit of rehearsal, watched by an assembly of nearly one hundred monks and the chief mourner.

Everything is choreographed in detail, from the route the incense bearer takes to his bodily gestures. The incense bearer does not act alone but in concert with the others, in such a way that the event unfolds smoothly from beginning to end without pause. For example, while walking along reading the sutra, at one point he folds his sutra book and tucks it into the folds of his kimono, then turns around to see the attendant behind him holding out another one. He immediately takes this sutra book, opens it, and begins reading aloud without breaking step. This sequence of movements must be executed with instantaneous precision.

A similar maneuver must be carried out with an altar attendant as well. Midway through the service, one of the altar attendants presents the cantor with a small wooden stand bearing a book of readings. The cantor takes this and simultaneously lays down the text he has until then been reading from, which the incense bearer must later receive from the altar attendant.

Of course, the role of the incense bearer is not limited to such exchanges, which form only a fleeting part of the service overall. All of his movements must be perfectly synchronized with those of the leader and the other assistant, in split-second timing. If, in my debut performance, I were to make even a slight mistake, I would disrupt the flow of the entire memorial service and be left stranded in the middle of that enormous hall, a laughingstock.

While my first performance as incense bearer may not have approached the grace and beauty of the altar attendants, my worst mistake was to stand not on the second tatami mat from the altar but the third, and thus I found myself unceremoniously jerked back by the collar. So my debut in the Dharma Hall went off without a major hitch.

Preparations for Winter

In the corridor
the higher I mount
the redder the leaves.

I was summoned by the director and then hurried to the Visitors' Meditation Hall to deliver a missive. My errand done, I turned around and headed back up to Administration.

Overhead the cloudless sky was a brilliant blue, and here and there in the dim covered walkways lay pools of dazzling sunlight. The fierce summer heat now a distant memory, I climbed up through warm sunshine puddles. Near the top of the compound, I glanced outside the latticed corridor, and it was then that the words of the haiku by the early twentieth-century poet Kyoshi Takahama flashed into my memory. Up here by the Dharma Hall, the leaves were deep red. I had just climbed up from the bottom of the compound to the top, and it was true—the higher I climbed, the richer the color of the autumn foliage. Had I not known Kyoshi's haiku, written about Eiheiji, I might never have noticed the subtle variation in the color of the leaves as the mountain sloped higher. The sharpness of his perception was surprising.

And so, scarcely before we knew it, the red and gold autumn of Eiheiji was upon us.

One chilly afternoon when the hills were ablaze with color, all the hearths were ceremoniously lit for winter and charcoal braziers were taken out of storage. One large one was set at the back of the Monks' Hall, and two smaller ones were set at either end of the Outer Hall. Keeping hearths and braziers going is the duty of junior trainees in the common quarters. I could well remember when it had been my turn to sit by the common quarters' hearth and tend to the embers all day long, starting at one thirty in the morning, with scarcely a moment's rest.

The temple uses an enormous amount of live coals—so many that those on duty are occasionally known to collapse from mild exposure to carbon monoxide. The trainees assigned to the common quarters are responsible not just for the brazier in the Monks' Hall and the ones in the Outer Hall but also for those in the formidable bell-ringers' quarters. They would be kept busy tending the braziers every day from now until spring, when it would be time to put them away again.

While the details of the task differ according to the residence, it involves more than simply adding coals to the ashes. While certainly not as exacting as the rules for shaping ashes in the tea ceremony, there are carefully prescribed ways of setting the coals, leveling the ashes, and so on. In the bell-ringers' quarters, for example, a set number of coals have to be set in a square in the center of the brazier, and the ashes arranged in a corresponding square.

Besides being fitted with a brazier, the Monks' Hall is prepared for winter by replacing the reed curtains with heavy woven curtains. The hall is high ceilinged and cavernous, with a cement floor that turns ice-cold in winter. The walls are nothing but thin wood, the windows paper and wood. The heavier curtains surely have negligible powers of heat retention and yet, strangely enough, just a single brazier is sufficient to warm the hall. The warmth it gives off is of course different from that of an electric, kerosene, or gas stove; it is perceptible only to those who have become accustomed to the natural fluctuations of heat and cold.

The spirit of Zen is one with nature, never seeking to conquer it or rise above it. The Zen practitioner sits face to face with nature, striving to take in its many revelations and call to mind its many truths. In "The

Sound of the Valley Stream, the Colors of the Mountain," an essay in *Treasury of the True Dharma Eye*, Dogen wrote this:

> The sound of the valley stream, the colors of the valley stream, the sound of the mountain, and the colors of the mountain all reveal truth unstintingly. If you do not prize honor and gain, then the valley stream and the mountain will expound truth to you without stint. But even then, unless you undergo the discipline necessary to perceive that the stream and the mountain are in fact the stream and the mountain, you will not be able to see or hear their truth.

The rapprochement with nature that Dogen described consists in recalling nature internally and searching out how to live the way we were meant to live, as beings in and of the natural world. The Zen precept to "live as you are" means not to live as you wish but to follow the laws of nature. Embrace those laws with body and soul, Dogen is saying.

Life at Eiheiji is miles removed from modern life. It is a life of turning increasingly toward nature, of opening oneself to it. As I grew physically closer to nature, I became more and more sensitized to it, more easily wonderstruck. Inevitably, the things that surprised me most—though often so slight that anyone might easily overlook them—told of the ephemeral passing of the seasons. Nature speaks eloquently to those who listen; to others, she barely shows herself.

We have to become better acquainted with nature. At the same time, we have to realize that we ourselves are intrinsically part of nature. It has to sink in that the environment we live in on this earth is not our creation, but a gift. All beings whose life has arisen from nature, including us, can only survive in and with nature. This awareness needs to underlie all our progress and development.

Intensive Sitting

The heavy front doors of the Monks' Hall slid shut. Just as a small bell finished ringing, it was officially declared that the period of intensive sitting was underway, and we finally embarked on this week-long sitting marathon. I say "finally" because for each of us it was a weighty, long-anticipated moment.

Long ago Buddha attained enlightenment under the bodhi tree on December 8, and *rohatsu sesshin* is held to commemorate the occasion and follow his lead. *Rohatsu* means December 8 and *sesshin*—which literally means "collecting the mind"—is a period of intensive sitting. Every year, the first week of December is devoted exclusively to sitting. Beginning December 1, trainee monks rise at three in the morning, half an hour earlier than usual, and spend all day sitting facing the wall, until nine at night. This continues for seven full days—no small feat.

In the old days, it was customary to continue sitting all through the night. In a tradition that harks back to those days, the usual wake-up and lights-out bells are replaced with bells that normally mark off sessions of meditation. Thus time spent sleeping consists technically of one sitting session. In a sense, therefore, we did continue meditating around the clock, even at night while asleep in our beds.

For seven days, from three in the morning onward, we alternated forty-minute periods of sitting with ten-minute periods of slow walking. Not only is it painful to sit for long periods of time with the legs folded, but sleepiness interferes with concentration as well. Between periods of sitting, therefore, we would step down from our platforms and shuffle around at a fixed pace, moving so slowly that in the time it took for one complete breath, in and out, we took just half a step. Slow walking is not considered a break from sitting, but must be undertaken with the same meditative frame of mind.

During intensive sitting, participants remain seated in the Monks' Hall not only for meals, but also for morning, midday, and evening services, which are held between sitting sessions. For seven days we practically never left our platforms.

In the second part of his essay "On Ceaseless Practice" in *Treasury of the True Dharma Eye*, Dogen mentioned intensive sitting with reference to the Chinese master Dayi Daoxin (580–651), as follows:

> From the time he inherited the teachings of the buddhas and ancestors, he devoted himself to intensive sitting without sleeping, and for sixty years he never lay down to rest.

As this passage shows, focusing the mind and continuing to sit for extended periods of time was a practice of utmost importance to revered masters of long ago. It remains a sine qua non of Zen monastic discipline.

I had read of intensive sitting before coming to Eiheiji, and ever since it had held a peculiar fascination for me, lingering in my mind as the one practice above all others that seemed to embody the deepest, most sublime aspects of life in a Zen monastery. At the same time, I was anxious to know if I had it in me to carry off such a feat.

The seven days of sitting were beyond anything I could have imagined. Any feelings of fascination and curiosity I had at the start were quickly demolished. There is no way for me to convey the magnitude of the experience. With each passing day, the pain in my legs grew more agonizing; worse yet, fatigue built up in every corner of my being until my consciousness began to flicker and dissolve. After a while I was no longer capable of the slightest thought or emotion, not even of wondering why in the world I was sitting like that. Everything ceased to exist except for the simple fact of me sitting facing the wall.

Time drifted by like incense smoke, and in the incense burner, the wreckage of elapsed time stacked up quietly in the form of white ash.

Intensive sitting certainly transcends the mere act of sitting. The final day, when everything comes to a climax, is called "all-night sitting." On that day, we remained sitting from 3 a.m. until 1 a.m. the following day—in other words, the morning of December 8, the day of Buddha's enlightenment.

As the hour of our liberation approached, we were gripped by an intense excitement that wrecked the stillness in the hall and made breathing difficult. Eventually the wall clock finished striking twelve; at long last it was December 8. *One more session and it will be over.* The thought made time drag all the more. My body was covered in sweat, my arms and legs shook. I held my breath, squeezed my eyes shut, and gritted my teeth.

And then it happened. The cloud gong broke the silence, proclaiming the end of intensive sitting. With the first reverberation, I felt sound transform to light and wash over me. The solemn tones inundated me in billows of radiance, flooding the darkest recesses of my mind with blinding light. While the gong continued to resound, the great doors clattered open and the pent-up, feverish excitement that had made breathing difficult gave way to a silent influx of cold, wintry night air. I let out the tension inside me with a sigh, and in that instant all the hardship of the past seven days disappeared without a trace.

When the gong had sounded for the last time, the bell in the Buddha Hall immediately began to ring. We clambered stiffly down from our sitting platforms, lined up, and walked in single file to the Buddha Hall to perform a ceremony celebrating Buddha's spiritual awakening. In the center of the hall hung a scroll painting titled *Sakyamuni Buddha Leaving the Mountain*, and before it was a bowl of five-flavored porridge made with adzuki beans and other special ingredients. The ceremony was carried out with due formality, accompanied by numerous prostrations and sutra readings. When it was over, the sound of the big drum began to roll through the hall, marking the beginning of a question-and-answer session.

The master sat in front of us in the center of the platform, an incense burner before him. Each questioner in turn would perform an obeisance, walk closer while shouting his question out, and then drop to his knees. The master would deliver an instant reply, upon which the questioner would say, "*Sonto, jashite tatematsuru*" (I humbly appreciate your august reply) while backing up, and then return to his place.

Having just completed a week of sitting, experiencing physically what Buddha had also experienced, we dredged up every question and doubt that had arisen in us during that time and poured them out at his feet. Singly and in pairs, we stood up one after another and shouted questions in voices loud enough to crack the walls. The hall shook with excitement. The enforced silence of the past seven days was blown to smithereens.

Finally, the last question was asked and answered. We knelt on the stone floor of the Buddha Hall and began a slow choral intonation of the sacred name: "*No-hon-su-shi-kya-mu-ni-ra.*" Hail to Sakyamuni Buddha the True Master. As the bell ringer struck a large, bowl-shaped gong, we slowly chanted the phrase over and over, drawing out each syllable to the maximum length. Late at night in the dim and shadowy Buddha Hall, our voices echoed off the walls and high ceiling with soul-stirring beauty.

As the invocation continued to resound without pause, an attendant appeared with a Buddha bowl containing five-flavored porridge. He went around spooning a drop on each of our palms as we continued to kneel and chant the holy name. A drop fell on my palm in turn.

When we all had received our drop, the chanting ceased and the bell ringer rang a small handbell. This was the signal for each of us to lick our palm in unison. I licked the drop on my palm. It had no discernible flavor. But in that moment I exulted, *It's over! It's all over*. My heart was full, and I felt like shouting.

When we filed out of the Buddha Hall, it was still too early to see the morning star that Buddha saw when he attained enlightenment, but my eyes were greeted by a host of winter stars like sparkling chips of ice.

Year-end Cleaning

On December 23, the first snow fell. As our daily routine returned to normal, the falling snow deepened the hush. In perfect silence the snow piled up until in no time our world was white.

Snow becomes Eiheiji. I wonder if it is the unstained purity of new snow that makes me think so. Certainly, Eiheiji is similarly pristine. In a sense the temple is extremely inorganic, like the Buddha bowl. Food never seeps into the bowl and alters it, nor does the bowl dissolve into its contents. Whatever is put into it, the bowl remains itself, inviolate. To some it manifests the essence of living Buddhist truth; to others it is nothing but a utensil to be filled with grub. It has its own unswerving existence, whose meaning the one who holds it in his hands is free to interpret as he will. That, in essence, is Eiheiji: depending on his frame of mind, the monk in training can see it as a holy place imparting sermons without words, or as mere shelter from the elements. There is no compulsion to take one view or the other. Eiheiji is simply itself, and what each one makes of it is up to him. This is the nature of Eiheiji freedom.

The snow fell and melted and fell again, piling up steadily until the valley was inundated with winter. Finally, one day, when yet again a new layer of snow covered everything, we did the year-end sweeping. Typically, this was done in the old-fashioned, traditional way: our tool for the job was a long pole of green bamboo tipped with leaves of bamboo grass. I put on my work clothes, wrapped a towel around my head, and covered my face and mouth with another cloth. Then I was ready to go about the compound with the others, sweeping away the year's accumulation of dust and cobwebs.

But as I set to work, I soon discovered how inefficient the bamboo tool was. The pole was heavy, and the leaves did an imperfect job of cleaning, as far as I could see. Yet to my surprise, after we had finished going over the ceilings and walls they looked clean and fresh. Perhaps it had something to do with the aura of the bamboo leaves, which were an invigorating green.

As I was taking clumsy swipes at cobwebs in the corridor by the Patriarch's Interview Hall, one of the bamboo leaves on the end of my pole got stuck between two ceiling boards. I did my best to dislodge it, without success. Finally I grabbed hold and pulled—and a piece broke off in my hand. There between the boards remained a bright green bamboo leaf, clearly visible. It was hopeless. There was no way to get

The Colors of the Peak, the Echo in the Valley

it out, so I decided not to mention it to anyone, and just forget about it. But from then on, every time I walked down that corridor I always thought about that leaf. I would resolve not to look at it—but couldn't help sneaking a peek before guiltily averting my eyes and hurrying on.

With the cleaning done and everything back to normal, we were busy with preparations for New Year's Eve. Of particular importance was the rice-cake-pounding ritual that took place in the basement kitchen of the Visitors' Meditation Hall. First, a special service was held, and then with every trainee pitching in we spent the whole day pounding rice in wooden mortars. The total number of rice cakes was staggering. Many of them, of course, were placed before the Buddhist statuary enshrined throughout the temple; others went to alcoves in the various residences, and still others were distributed to each of the monks-in-training.

Eiheiji has a special style of New Year's decorations. Each trainee hangs in his alcove the scroll he brought with him when he first arrived at Eiheiji and beneath it sets his bound wicker packs, along with an origami feudal samurai helmet that is folded from heavy, fine-quality handmade paper and red sutra-copying paper and topped with a decorative cord. Finally, in front of this he reverently sets a mound of two round rice cakes made from rice he has pounded himself.

It is also the custom for trainees to present fresh rice cakes to those who have been their special teachers. The first step is to write out a suitable greeting in classical Chinese, using a particular calligraphic style. Then the rice cakes have to be cut into thin diamond shapes about three-quarters of an inch across, refiguring the upper angles so that from the side the cakes make a trapezoid shape. Next, each rice cake is wrapped by placing it on a small square of paper, folding the paper around it in a special way, and fastening it with a small red paper seal on which is written a character meaning "long life." This packet goes inside another container, also made by folding paper in an elaborate way, and is sent off with wishes for longevity.

I performed this complicated task between my other rush of duties, managing to make three rice-cake gifts. Two were for my parents; the other one I sent to the old woman I had looked after in the Guest Pavilion, with whom I'd been corresponding ever since.

And so, embraced by the clean, cold air of the valley, Eiheiji was finally ready for a quiet New Year's Eve. Starting at midnight, the great bell would be tolled 108 times, once for each earthly passion that afflicts mankind.

New Year's Day

New Year's Day began like any other day, with the clamor of the wake-up bell whizzing by in pitch dark. After it was gone, I stepped out into the covered walkway and looked down at the compound spread out below me. Under the high, clear night sky, frost on the tiles of the over-lapping rooftops shone palely in the starlight.

New Year's at last. This time a year ago, could I have imagined myself as I was now, standing looking out on this tranquil scene? Even had

I tried to peer into the future, back then all that lay before me was a stretch of emptiness with no end in sight. I'd had no desire to look at it squarely, had preferred that time bear me blindly on into the unknown.

Yet life's very unpredictability is what makes it interesting. Though I had no way of knowing where I might be or what I might be doing the following New Year's, either, I was heartened by the thought that uncertainty can be a dynamic, life-giving force. Whether such a thing as destiny might exist, I couldn't say. Rather than worry about it, I wanted only to go on believing in the reality of my own existence, day by day. In the sacred stillness of early New Year's morning, these were my thoughts.

The usual wake-up bell was followed by the usual early morning sitting. Then we proceeded to the Dharma Hall for sutra chanting and morning service. After that the great drum sounded, marking the start of another question-and-answer session. Today our questions must include no inauspicious words, and instead of replying with the former expression of humble thanks, we were to say: *"Kichijo, kichijo, daikichijo."* Good fortune, good fortune, great good fortune.

After these words had been said for the last time, there was a period during which everyone visited each other's quarters and exchanged formal congratulations and thanks. Then we paid our respects to Dogen in the Founder's Hall, and to the abbot in the Patriarch's Interview Hall. We prostrated ourselves before the abbot, who received rice cakes on a small stand. After graciously accepting this New Year's gift, he seated himself and made a propitious statement:

On this day when monastic life shines with fresh radiance, I turn eighty-eight as abbot of Eiheiji: this is truly a spring of good fortune in a temple of good fortune.

So this year marked his eighty-eighth birthday;[2] the occasion and the remarks could not have been more felicitous.

Once all these observances were finished, the trainees gathered in the Seat of Enlightenment Hall for a traditional meal of soup containing grilled rice cakes and assorted New Year's delicacies. We assistants to the director, however, had no time to eat. Once the ceremony in the Patriarch's Interview Hall was finished, all the masters would be served tea in the abbot's quarters and then repair to the conference room for their soup. As soon as we got back to Administration, we set to work grilling rice cakes and serving soup. When that was finished, there was still no time to rest, for a vast number of lay patrons rushed in to offer New Year's greetings to the director. One after another they came and went in a never-ending procession. Each one had to be announced, ushered into the conference room, and served tea. As soon as the visit was over, the sliding door had to be opened and the visitor politely seen off. This continued all day long without letup.

Just as we were nearing the point of mental and physical exhaustion, along came Tsubota-san, owner of a bookstore in Fukui. She always dropped by on rest days with a delivery of books. Anyone who'd been at Eiheiji past a certain length of time was allowed to read freely, as long as it didn't interfere with his work. Nothing was off limits; we could read

The Colors of the Peak, the Echo in the Valley

whatever we pleased. But because leaving the precincts was still forbidden to us at this stage in our training, we couldn't go out to buy books; instead we told Tsubota-san what we wanted, and she delivered it. She wasn't the only one who did business at Eiheiji, either; dry cleaners, Buddhist altar suppliers, and other tradespeople also freely came and went.

Men, it seems, are always seeking a mother figure, and all of us adored Tsubota-san. I was no different; no matter what unpleasantness or difficulty I might be experiencing, the sight of her cheery smile banished it from my mind. I always looked forward to the next rest day, when I knew I would see her again.

But for Tsubota-san, accommodating the reading tastes of a temple full of monks involved hard physical labor. She would hoist a bagful of books onto her back and trudge up the long corridors, climbing stair after stair to hand deliver each order. Administration was at the very top, and although I breathed a sigh of relief when I saw her face, I also felt guilty for making her lug such a heavy load.

On New Year's morning she came dressed in her best and offered me the traditional greeting with her usual cheer: "Happy New Year, Rosan. Let's have another good year together."

And so the hectic day passed quietly into night.

New Arrivals

Around January 20, after "Great Cold"—the coldest time of year according to the traditional calendar—the weather underwent a change. In the blink of an eye the compound, and indeed the entire valley, was buried under a heavy blanket of snow. Encased by sturdy wooden boards that provided protection from the snow, the covered walkways were dim even in the daytime and profoundly hushed, as the snow piled high on either side erased all sound. Sometimes as I walked along I would look up at the sky through a gap between boards and see a dizzying amount of snow falling thickly down, as if the sky itself had broken into a million pieces and was tumbling down on our heads.

It was on just such a snowy morning that I heard the news: the year's first applicants had arrived. For Eiheiji, this was the season of new beginnings. There were ten of them, petitioners who this very moment would be standing dismally on the icy pavement, shivering in the snow. The thought roused mixed feelings as I reflected back on all that we eight had suffered through, trials that lay in wait for this new group as well. They too would have to deal with all that came their way—hope and disappointment, rage and tears—breaking it down into manageable size and swallowing it all.

After the first bunch, new trainees came nearly every day. Once again the compound was filled with an atmosphere of painful nervous tension that we had all but forgotten. There was such eager beauty in these novices that instinctively I stood straighter in their presence. I remembered what the old woman I had looked after in the Guest Pavilion had said—that the sight of Eiheiji monks "washed her heart clean." That figure of speech now made a kind of sense to me. The fiery hearts of these new trainees made me realize just how long it had been since my own arrival. One year ago, had I shone as brightly as they did now? A full year had gone by. A year of clumsily feeling my way, of ceaseless groping in the dark. What had I gained in the past year, I wondered, and what had I lost?

I was on my way back from supper one evening when it happened. The cold, clear darkness of a snowy winter night had already settled in, and the lone bulb in the corridor glowed like an ember, a strangely warming sight. As I left the Monks' Hall, I met a group of fresh trainees coming from the opposite direction. As soon as they caught sight of me, they pressed themselves against the side of the corridor to let me by and stood with heads bowed low, palms reverently joined. I found the sight somehow sad. Was it pity for their stiffness and trepidation that I felt, or distress at finding myself the object of it?

Unable to endure their presence a moment longer, I prepared to slip on by—but then happened to cross gazes with one of them. And felt a rush of panic. By rights, I should have cuffed him on the spot for daring to look me, his senior, in the eye, just as I had been cuffed for that same breach of etiquette in my time. But I couldn't bring myself to do it. Now a senior trainee, I was supposed to relate to these novices in a way appropriate to my elevated status. That the rigid social hierarchy in a training monastery helps maintain balance and order, and that immersing oneself in that system is a key part of Zen discipline, I understood perfectly. But on that day I was the one who averted my eyes first, abashed.

After that blunder, I grew to dread the sight of new arrivals. Every time I heard a senior trainee deliver a loud scolding, I was ashamed of myself all over again. The senior trainees assigned to instruct these newcomers were all from last year's crop of arrivals, like me. Rumor had it that only the fiercest-looking were chosen as instructors, but that proved untrue. In any case, they threw themselves into their job with a will. One of them was an amiable fellow who I doubted had ever so much as interrupted anyone in his life; seeing the way he lit into his charges was a revelation.

Day by day, as the number of new arrivals increased, the newly assigned instructors began to show obvious signs of fatigue. In order to maintain the proper level of tension, they couldn't relax their guard for a second, but had to keep after their charges with great strictness. Needless to say, not all newcomers are quick learners, either. Some have trouble learning, no matter how many times they are shown. Extreme dullness can be exasperating. And yet the instructors were responsible for shaping all comers into monks worthy of Eiheiji. Giving up on someone was not an option.

Now that we were in the position of the instructors who had slapped us around and yelled at us when we first came, it was easy to see the strain they must have been under. It's always easier to be a nice guy, someone with a perpetual smile on his face. Reflecting back on the events of the last year, I felt renewed respect for the senior trainees who had been so uncompromisingly hard on us, and inwardly I bowed my head to them.

The atmosphere in the compound grew thicker with tension by the day, as the snow piled ever higher. So began my second year at Eiheiji.

Just Sit

Rain began to fall on the snowbound valley, bringing an end to the long, quiet winter. Snowmelt ran down the mountainsides in rivulets that joined in small crisscrossing streams before flowing into the river that ran alongside Eiheiji. The river took on the light and color of budding life as, little by little, signs of spring appeared in pools of sunshine along its banks.

The tension that had reigned in the monastery seemed gradually to ease as the piles of lingering snow under the eaves slowly shrank. Even so, there was still a kind of electricity in the air. The uneasy atmosphere in which these conflicting elements intermingled was one more sign of spring at Eiheiji.

One evening after supper I picked up my cushion as usual and headed for the Monks' Hall. Supper was over by six, and the hour from then till seven o'clock, when night sitting began, was a rare period of freedom in the busy day. I always spent it in the Monks' Hall, sitting by myself in the deep quiet dark where only a tiny bulb shone. At some point I had come to love being alone in the all-embracing dark and stillness.

Idly I wondered how much time I had spent sitting there all told. Life as an Eiheiji monk in training swung between times of frenetic energy with no time to think and times of tranquility when one could do nothing else. The tranquility came from sitting like this.

My first long-ago night of sitting was unforgettable. As I folded my legs in the heavy, hot silence and faced the wall, I'd felt with a tremor that I would now be peering into unfathomable Zen depths. My blood had rushed faster through my veins. Back then I'd thrown myself headlong into sitting without having the least idea what it was all about. I simply sat. Now I reconsidered the matter: what, indeed, was the point of all this sitting?

Dogen instructed, *"Shikan taza."* Just sit.

At Eiheiji, sitting is neither a purpose nor a means to an end. One doesn't sit in order to gain enlightenment; one just sits. But what does "just sitting" mean? The act of folding the legs and sitting transcends everyday acts of sitting, standing, and walking. When sitting, the sitter assumes a certain form. To assume this form is to become perfectly one with it, removing all fetters and ego—to be unselfconsciously present in the moment, like air.

The question naturally arises: why, in order to remove the ego, is it necessary to sit with legs folded, facing the wall? Why this form and no other? I doubt whether anyone could put the answer into words. Only in sitting for oneself, and persisting in sitting to the very end, does the answer come welling up in one's blood and bones. This, I believe, is the essence of religion, which of course is something different from mere membership in a religious body. Religion isn't something to explicate, but something to believe in; something that stands apart from all our probing. Some find their inspiration in the laws of nature, others in the lives of great predecessors. What I believed in was the successive moments of my life at Eiheiji.

Whenever I sat with my legs folded, quietly facing the wall, various physical sensations became paramount in turn. My eardrums registered delicate vibrations from the currents of air and the flux of nature all around. True, the longer I sat, the more my legs hurt, but in time I came to grasp the importance of this and of all else that happens in the course of sitting. Devoting oneself to sitting, getting used to sitting, and conquering the pain of sitting are all equally pointless. The only point of sitting is to accept unconditionally each moment as it occurs. This is the lesson of "just sitting" that I had absorbed after one year.

I found great freedom in this way. Freedom in Zen means liberation from self-interest, from the insistent voice that says "I, me, my." Liberation not from any external circumstance but from a host of internal mental or psychological states, including desire: herein lies genuine, untrammeled freedom. This insight is nothing I stumbled on myself, but a truth that has been transmitted ceaselessly down the ages from ancient India, the cradle of Buddhism.

Days at Eiheiji are relentless in their sameness. For a while in the beginning, the monotony was upsetting and bewildering to me. Day after day, from the moment we got up until the moment we went to bed our time was strictly regimented, without variation. Over and over we

Eat Sleep Sit

repeated the same routines, without end and without question. What was that monotony about, I used to wonder.

But now I realize that apart from a few special days now and then, life mostly does consist of one dull, insignificant day after another. Human beings are attracted to drama and variety. The humdrum we hold in disdain. Wrapped up in the routines of our daily lives, we let them slide by unnoticed. But I believe that hidden in these ordinary, unremarkable routines of life is a great truth that requires our attention.

The business of living is not in the least special. In a sense it all comes down to two things: eating and excreting. These activities are common to all life forms. Every creature on earth is born, through eating and excreting helps maintain the balance of the great chain of being, and dies. In the realm of nature, these activities are essential to the continuity of life, and they give value to each being's life. People are no different. If human life has meaning, it lies above all in the essential fact of our physical existence in this world. This is what I strongly believe.

By contemplating life as it is, stripped of all extraneous added value, I found I could let go of a myriad of things that had been gnawing at my mind. Through the prosaic repetition of Eiheiji's exacting daily routines for washing the face, eating, defecating, and sleeping, this is the answer that I felt in my bones: accept unconditionally the fact of your life and treasure each moment of each day.

Departure Survey

When I went to the Visitors' Meditation Hall one evening to see a movie, Choshu was there ahead of time, sitting alone. When he saw me, he blurted out, "I've decided to leave Eiheiji and go to college."

Evening sitting had been canceled, and we were scheduled to have a "lecture" instead. Normally lectures were held in a room in the Missions residence, and they tended to be learned discourses on Buddhist texts or services, but tonight a video would be shown here instead: Hayao Miyazaki's 1988 animated film *My Neighbor Totoro*.

"What made you decide to do that?" I asked, surprised.

"Well, for one thing, I've only graduated from high school, and it would be better to have a college education. Besides, I went into a Zen temple right after graduating from junior high. I haven't known any life but this for years, and I want to experience something different for a while."

"That's great, Choshu!" It struck me as a brave decision.

"Not really," he demurred, and then asked if I'd ever seen *My Neighbor Totoro*.

"No," I said.

"I saw it on my way home from school once, secretly. Not much of a secret, though, huh—I guess my bald head must have stood out a mile. I was worried the whole time that somebody would catch me in there."

In high school not only does the body mature, but the urge to define oneself becomes paramount, driving teens to wear "cool" clothes and experiment with hairstyles. I'd been no different. At a time of life when most people try in various ways to test their limits and learn who they are, Choshu been a baldheaded monk. He seemed far more mature than I'd been at his age, yet he cut an oddly pitiful figure, too; it was too bad that he'd had to become an adult so early in life.

"What about you, Rosan, what are you going to do?" he asked.

"What do you mean?"

"Are you going to stay on at Eiheiji another year?"

"Well . . ."

Just then the lights went out, and *My Neighbor Totoro* started up.

Spring at Eiheiji is the season for admitting novices and also a time when those who have reached a certain level in their training may leave. After my conversation with Choshu, I realized for the first time that people in our group might be ready to move on.

Every spring, a monk is assigned to ask each trainee whether he intends to stay or go. Most do in fact leave after a single year.

A few days later, after the morning meal, I happened to walk alongside Doryu, who had recently returned to Eiheiji after a bout in the hospital. I asked him what he intended to do.

"Why?" he asked.

"No reason. Tenshin and Yuho are leaving, I heard. Yuho's been to graduate school, so he's got extra qualifications—he was even talking about leaving here after six months."

"Huh."

"And Tenshin is the second son in his family, which means he isn't likely to become a priest. He probably figures, what's the point in suffering through another year?"

At that point, Daimei caught up with us from behind and jumped into the conversation: "I'm staying."

"Nobody's asking you," retorted Doryu. Still, the declaration was a surprise coming from Daimei, with his pampered and mollycoddled upbringing. "Why not stay?" he said breezily. "I'm going to hang in there. Let's both hang in there, Rosan."

Full of confidence, he bounded on ahead of us. He was from a fairly large and formal temple, which might have had something to do with his decision to stay on. In any case, I was amazed by his cheery exuberance.

Kijun, who had followed Doryu into the hospital, also came back after a short time and announced his intention to stay on another year: "Yeah, I'm staying. I always wanted to be an altar attendant, before I ever got here." (At a certain point, second-year trainees were allowed to assist in the Dharma Hall or the Founder's Hall.) In contrast to the miseries of "Reception Hall hell," achieving "altar attendant glory" was every trainee's dream. "Besides," he went on, "seeing as I'm here, I want to keep going till I make bell-ringers' quarters. Spending just one year at Eiheiji is nothing to brag about. My family temple is small, anyway, and there aren't many parishioners, so I can't make a living as a priest. If I went back home now, I'd be stuck."

After completing their second-year service in the Dharma Hall and the Founder's Hall, trainees who stay for a third year are assigned to the bell-ringers' quarters—the final and most prestigious destination for monks-in-training at Eiheiji—where they acquire authority over the first- and second-year trainees. A very few remain on after that for yet another year.

Japanese people imagine that temple priests rake in tons of money while sitting around enjoying a life of leisure, but this is seldom the case. Many temples, like Kijun's, are so small that they don't provide a living, and the priest is forced to keep his own struggling temple going while hiring himself out elsewhere—no easy task.

After I left Accounts, Sozen had eventually been transferred to the lesser kitchen. I asked him what his plans were.

"I'm staying," he said. "I'm the second son, so my brother will take over the family temple when the time comes. There's nothing for me there."

"What'll you do, then?" I asked.

"Stay here as long as I feel like it, then marry into another temple when I get the chance."

This was actually a fairly common career path. Someone not in line to take over his own family temple would marry the daughter of a priest lacking an heir and be adopted into the family; that way, he could one day take over as head priest.

Wearing the white robe of the lesser kitchen, Sozen looked and sounded more mature than ever to me.

The longer a person has been at Eiheiji, the more things he is permitted to do. After a while he can skip morning cleaning, and attendance at the various services and ceremonies, too, ceases to be mandatory. He can leave the monastery grounds, coming and going as he pleases, and is assured much more private time.

Who knows—perhaps real Zen discipline begins only when all restrictions have been taken away. Then the trainee faces a clear choice: whether to stretch out comfortably in his newfound freedom and idle around, or brace his spirits and stay committed to his initial purpose. How each one responds is up to him, and the nature of his response changes the meaning of the remainder of his stay.

After my talk with Choshu, I wavered. It was tempting to stay on and see if I could indeed stay true to my purpose. But the more I thought about it, the more inclined I was to return to life in society, which I had fled without a backward glance, and test myself in those waters. It had already been a year. Only a year, and yet I felt that little by little I had changed. When it came to me that I was no longer the tragic hero of a year ago, I made up my mind.

"Rosan, are you really leaving?" said Enkai.

"Yeah, I am."

"That's a surprise. Knowing you, I figured you'd be here a good ten years."

In ten years I would be forty. Where would I be then, what would I be doing? Those ten years would no doubt pass in the blink of an eye.

"What about you, Enkai? What are you doing again?"

"Leaving. But I decided that when I go, I'll walk home."

"Really? But you're from Shizuoka, aren't you?"

"Yup."

Like Enkai, many of the trainees choose to walk home from Eiheiji. In the spirit of wandering monks of old, they don a deep-brimmed hat, tie on straw sandals and set out, remembering with each step along the way all that they had learned at Eiheiji.

Enkai's rotund body would definitely be leaner after the long walk home, I thought.

Once I had decided to leave, my presence in Eiheiji seemed all the more precious, and I felt a growing desire to use my remaining time to focus simply on being there. From then on, I devoted every possible moment to sitting in the Monks' Hall. The darkness, the silence, the air—I wanted to store as much of it as I could somewhere inside me.

So much had happened during the past year that it seemed as if the events of five or six years had been compressed into one. My fellow trainees and I had been at loggerheads and had hurt each other; had laughed and wept more times than I could count. As I sat in the Monks' Hall with my eyes shut, I could summon up all their faces. Time would dim my memories of them, one by one. But never in my life would I forget that together we had shared profound emotions, laughing through our tears and weeping in the midst of laughter, and all the while feeling intensely alive.

Leaving

After the morning meal, I began packing my bags alone in Administration. The time of departure had come. No less than induction, the rite of leave-taking is an important turning point in the life of a trainee, carried out with full pomp and courtesy.

The first step is to compose a petition to leave the monastery. Once this is written out in proper calligraphic style, it is taken around to the various monastic officers in all the residences, beginning with one's own, to receive their seals. Finally the seal of the director, Eiheiji's highest authority, is affixed, and the petition is submitted to the Administration office.

Since I was assigned to that residence, I received this seal first. While he pressed it on the appropriate place on top of the document, the director told me, "Rosan, it's my opinion that you should stay here longer, but if your mind is made up, so be it. Here is a parting gift. Take it with you when you go." He thrust a paulownia box toward me, inside which I found a tea bowl.

One time I had gone to his private room to deliver a package. Several guests had just left, and still out on the table were the tea bowls they had used: black Raku ware, Oribe ware, white porcelain, an "oil-drop" bowl. One tea bowl in particular caught my eye. It was clearly the work of a modern potter, with a large lip and beautifully shaped body rising from a low foot in perfect form and balance. But what gave it exceptional beauty was the flowing glaze, the result of a chance combination of variables in the kiln.

I couldn't keep back an admiring exclamation. After that, every so often the director would call me to his room and make tea for me in what he jestingly called "Rosan's bowl." I appreciated his generosity but was often taken aback by the accompanying sweets, which tended to be moldy.

The director was a severe man. He would become wrathful over transgressions, no matter who the offender, and brooked no compromise in either himself or others. For that reason he gave me the impression of being rather isolated among the masters. When he was making tea for me in the inner quarters, though, he was just an ordinary, kindly old man. The time the spring orchid I'd been watering for him put out pale green flowers, his face had worn a broad smile.

As I thanked him sincerely and was preparing to leave, boxed tea bowl in my hand, he declared, "Solely pursue the truth by practicing Zen. Don't forget that commitment is for a lifetime."

After getting his seal, I went next to the vice-director. "You're leaving, are you, Rosan?" he said. "The place won't be the same." His trademark Santa smile was missing as he opened his drawer, took out his seal, and pressed it beneath the director's. The man was goodness itself. People like him who are truly good show it naturally, without even trying. Their warmth reaches out imperceptibly and embraces all those around them. His smile and his warmth had helped me more than I could say.

"Come back and see us any time," he said. "I mean it." Feeling his smile on my back, I dragged myself out the door.

After that I went round to each of the others in turn, starting with the treasurer, and had them all stamp my paper. The steward did it next to his scattering of dried-up coriander, the shrine keeper with his usual scowl. When I was finished, I took my petition back to Administration, filed it myself, and signed the ledger. That was that.

When the final day came, just as I had done a year before, I went to the morning meal wearing my formal socks and carrying my bowing cloth folded over my wrist. When the meal was over, I reentered the Monks' Hall with incense to perform the ceremony of leave-taking. This was my final time in the Monks' Hall, I told myself; this triple prostration would mark the end of everything. As I looked around, the moment didn't seem real. Even so, I was rather nervous as I did my prostrations. Then, just as I had done a year before, I circumambulated the hall, bent over at the waist with my hands palm to palm and my head lowered. The other trainees stood with their hands pressed reverently together but as I passed by, each one picked up his cushion and gave me a swat. This custom is of course not part of any etiquette that Dogen laid down, but an unrestrained expression of free spirits, tacitly allowed on the final day. We were comrades who had gritted our teeth and practiced sitting here together. Now as I passed among them with my head bowed and my palms held together at my chest, getting smacked by their cushions, which of course didn't hurt, I couldn't keep tears from starting in my eyes.

Packing was easy. I'd come here with nothing, and after one year, my belongings had scarcely increased. I set about wrapping the wicker packs. When packing to come to Eiheiji, the cloths were overlapped to form the character for "enter" (入), but on leaving they were reversed to form the character for "person" (人). As I wrapped the packs I wondered: had I at last become a person?

When my packing was done, it was time to go. The usual practice when departing Eiheiji was to have some of your closest friends assemble at the Main Gate to see you off. I had participated in several such farewells myself, and they were invariably moving. People would recall a year of shared pain and pleasure, and pat each other on the shoulders before reluctantly parting. But from the time I made up my mind to leave, I had been determined to do it alone. For that reason I had chosen midday service as the time of my departure.

The cloud gong sounded three times, followed by three beatings of the big drum in the Buddha Hall and one tolling of the great bell. Then the bell that signals the start of midday sutra chanting started up. Every one of those sounds was now part of me. At different times I had stood, trembling in fear and uncertainty, and struck each of those instruments with my own hands. Last year, and today, and from now on, they would go on being struck by other hands, indefinitely.

As these thoughts passed through my mind, I quickly shouldered the wicker packs, picked up my straw hat and sandals, and left Administration. I decided then to take a last look at the monastery grounds, knowing I would likely never see them again. Every inch was associated vividly in my mind with scenes from the past year. Day after day I had scrubbed and polished here with a vengeance. Quietly I laid my hand on a black pillar, the wood darkened with age; it felt slightly warm to my touch, as if conveying the living pulse of other days, other times.

When I started down the corridor beside the Patriarch's Interview Hall, I looked up from habit at the ceiling. The bamboo leaf that had gotten stuck between two planks was still there, now brown and dry. Once I left these grounds, all trace of my presence would vanish; it was oddly cheering to think that the leaf might linger there forever.

"Goodbye. Take care."

At the Main Gate, I heard the distant sound of sutra chanting from the Buddha Hall behind me. I set my wicker packs down, turned toward the hall and prostrated myself three times in farewell. With every prostration, as my forehead touched the ground I thought of the twin inscriptions that the lead instructor of the temporary quarters had explained to us a year ago, the morning I'd first set foot here:

> The tradition here is strict: no one, however wealthy, important, or wise, may enter through this gate who is not wholehearted in the pursuit of truth.

> The gate has no door or chain, but is always open; any person of true faith can walk through it at any time.

The tradition here is strict. That was certainly true. Never in my life had I encountered a world of such severity. My lack of ability had been impressed on me to a painful extent, and I had witnessed the worst of human nature. It was demoralizing.

The gate has no door or chain. What was the source of this great spirit of generosity? A spirit that silently accepted everything, embraced it, imparted courage to live. Humanity was not so bad after all. I felt encouraged to live as a human being, with other human beings.

I wanted nothing more than to give a shout of thanks for my year at Eiheiji. As I completed my last prostration, from my tightly shut eyes a single hot tear squeezed out and spilled on the ground. Just then I heard the sound of the gong that signified the end of sutra chanting in the Buddha Hall. There was no time to waste. Unless I hurried, the mid-day service would be over.

I slipped my feet into the straw sandals, put on the wicker packs, and rushed out the gate. After this I could not, would not look back. But then, I didn't need to. To walk looking determinedly ahead: that was what I had learned here, and that was what I would now do. I felt that if I turned now and looked back, the year would vanish like a soap bubble.

I passed under the giant cedars, my eyes focused on the path ahead. Scenery from a year ago unreeled backward before my eyes. I went past the ageless trees, around the Gate of Unimpeded Truth and past the buildings where temple construction workers once lived, past the Imperial Gate, and came finally to the Dragon Gate.

The Dragon Gate. This was where it had all begun. I remembered everything as if it had been yesterday. But the Dragon Gate itself had gotten smaller—or could it be that I'd gotten bigger? No, it had loomed big in my eyes that morning because it *had* been big, that morning. There was no other explanation.

I crossed the shrunken Dragon Gate just as I had done a year before, and thereby entered the outside world. As I did so I remembered the story of the fish who'd become a dragon. *Back to being a fish*, I thought, and laughed out loud.

But the sensation of venturing into the world again after a year in the sacred precincts of Eiheiji was truly strange. As I stood there with my two feet planted on the ground and looked around, a thought came to my mind: zero. I had nothing. But it was a wonderfully refreshing feeling. This was a zero that would turn into a one, then a two. Beyond that, I could see it turning into a three, a four, a five, even a six. I embraced the sensation of zero and took a deep breath, rejoicing physically in the liberation of being stone broke.

I hailed a passing taxi. The hike to Fukui Station would have been okay, too, but I suddenly felt like riding in a taxi again. With a sense of returning to a deeply familiar place, I climbed into the back seat and told the driver my destination. The taxi slowly began to move. And then, though I had sworn I wouldn't, I turned and looked back. The Dragon Gate that had seemed so small became smaller and smaller as the taxi sped farther away.

Eiheiji is receding into the distance. At the thought, I felt a strangling sensation in my chest, and had trouble breathing. The days I had spent at Eiheiji over the course of this year flashed before my eyes. The ice-cold stone paving where I'd been hurled down before the Main Gate. Sitting in the frigid temporary quarters, my teeth chattering and my body shivering from cold and loneliness. The flavor of miso soup gulped down in fear, coughing. Cleaning the corridors at such breakneck speed that my heart nearly burst. The jarring blackness of the Monks' Hall when I awoke there, rubbing my eyes. Tolling the great bell under a starry sky while praying that the sound would carry to my parents. Self-reflection meetings when I was thrashed till I was nearly in tatters, body and soul. Hunger and the emptiness of fighting over scraps of leftovers. The night I wept, clutching the letter from my mother . . .

As these images came and went, Eiheiji kept getting farther away. The Eiheiji I knew. The Monks' Hall. The dark and the quiet, the atmosphere. All of it slipping away by the moment as I watched. When the tips of the last cedar vanished from the back window, scalding tears overflowed like memories and ran down my cheeks.

"Goodbye, Eiheiji . . ."

As the taxi drove on, my tears dried, and in the back mirror I happened to meet the gaze of the driver, who was, somewhat to my surprise, a woman. Amid deep creases on her face, her little black eyes were smiling. She asked me if I was leaving Eiheiji today. Embarrassed at having been caught in tears, without trusting my voice I gave a sheepish smile and nodded.

"Well, now. Bless your heart. You know, I was born right here in town, so all the young men at Eiheiji are just like sons to me."

The Colors of the Peak, the Echo in the Valley

I still said nothing, just smiled, but she obligingly kept up a one-sided flow of conversation, chatting about this and that. All the while, in my mind's eye images of Eiheiji rose and fell.

"Tell you what," she said. "How about if I take you someplace real nice?"

"Uh, sure. Yes, please." The words came out before I knew it. I had no reason to hurry away.

The cab sped up a wooded mountain road. On either side were huge fallen branches that had come crashing down under the weight of snow; beneath them, the spring grasses that would in time cover up the broken branches were putting out new shoots. The cab crossed over a ridge, went through a small village and along a narrow lane lined with low houses. Then all at once the view opened up.

We had come out by the Asuwa River, a twisting stream that meanders slowly through the prefecture. Stretching as far as I could see on both sides of the sparkling river were cherry blossoms in full bloom, basking in the soft spring sunshine. The radiance of the scene left me speechless.

"Go on, go for a little walk on the bank," she urged.

I got out of the cab and walked along the bank. A warm, slightly moist breeze gradually unwound the tension that had lain tightly coiled inside me for so long. I looked up. Over my head, a canopy of branches festooned with pink blossoms shut out the sky; along with a shower of petals, dazzling spring sunlight filtered through the branches, spilling down on me.

This is it—this is spring.

At that moment I understood the meaning of spring for the very first time. I had been alive for thirty years, and all that time I'd been caught up in an urgent search for meaning. Now, here, finally, I knew the meaning of spring. That was enough. I didn't need anything else.

Pink petals detached themselves from the branches and drifted on the breeze to land on the surface of the water. Then, slipping in and out of view in the gleams of sunlight reflected on the moving water, they gave themselves over to the lazy flow, moving now to the right and now to the left, floating on and on wherever the river might take them.

AFTERWORD TO THE JAPANESE FIRST EDITION

Looking back, I wonder what it was that led me to turn my back on
the world in the first place. If pressed, I would have to say that it was
everything about myself then, and perhaps everything about the world
around me as well. For a long time, a breathtakingly long time, I walked
aimlessly and alone through a season that was neither spring nor summer nor fall nor winter, an interstitial season. When I was a college student, like my peers everywhere I was stirred by youthful cravings and
frustrations, felt a fragile sense of accomplishment, suffered my share
of sweet injuries. But all that might as well have happened to someone on TV: the season I lived in was cold, and empty, and frighteningly
unreal. I lived through that season in a state of uncertainty, unable to
say if my life was agreeable or not.

During my senior year in college, just as the competition to find a
job after graduation was heating up, I came to a dead stop, brought face
to face with the reality of society. In that moment, I lost sight of myself.

I wanted a firm reason to go on living, and then desire slowly changed to need. A way of life in which I could find no meaning was a threat to the value of my own existence.

The weight of this enormous idealism sometimes felt crushing. Everything about myself would then seem bothersome. And yet my refusal to give up an ideal I could not really understand was the sole value of my existence. Since I could not for the life of me see the shape of my future, I might just as well have followed societal conventions and continued groping for answers in the very heart of society, swallowed up in it. But without reaching some conclusion about life that made sense to me, I couldn't bring myself to carve out a comfortable niche for myself.

In the end I stopped looking for a job, graduated without self-insight of any kind, and set out on a journey through Asia. My first destination was Bangkok.

In the course of my travels, the sun darkened my skin and asphalt wore out the soles of my shoes. Eventually, without the dramatic discovery I had vaguely hoped for when I set out, my long travels came to an end. But I felt invigorated. When I came back to Japan, before that pleasant excitement could dissipate, I quickly found a job and took my delayed first steps as a full-fledged member of society.

The old idealistic longing was still there and would occasionally cross my mind. Unable as ever to find meaning, slowly, amid the pressures of everyday busyness, I began to suffer from smoldering discontent. I was nagged by a sense of emptiness, as if the cogwheels of my life were spinning idly, broken-toothed. At high-pressure moments on the job I would be assailed by sudden, indefinable anxiety. If I kept on this way, my life would pass by uneventfully, I knew, wrapped in society's protective cocoon. But by the time I was forty, I felt sure, my heart would be shriveled and dry. Without a plan to restart my life, I felt trapped, cornered. As I neared thirty my mind began to fill with a dead weight that no comfort could relieve, and every aspect of society around me became increasingly irksome and repugnant.

It was around then that the word *shukke* ("leaving home": renunciation of the world to take Buddhist vows) first crossed my mind. Why it did, I had no idea. It was like tripping on a stone and then, instead of continuing on one's way, stopping to pick it up. For me that stone was shukke. In retrospect, I think that all the traveling I did in my twenties—Thailand, China, Tibet, Burma, Laos, Vietnam, Cambodia—was a journey whose destination was always, from the start, Eiheiji.

Five years have gone by since I left Eiheiji. My life picked up again exactly where it had left off. I ride crowded trains to work and stop off on the way home at the municipal swimming pool to swim twenty laps. I eat supper alone, and when it gets later than midnight I go to bed.

What was that year in Eiheiji all about?

Sometimes in life you discover the importance of something only when you lose it. During my year in Eiheiji, when I was stripped of all I had and was, I came face to face with numerous questions. As a result of that year, I changed in the following ways:

Afterword to the Japanese First Edition

Now when a mosquito lands on me, I hesitate for a second before killing it.

I no longer eat more than necessary.

I no longer think about things more deeply than necessary.

I have become capable of tears. Once I told someone, "A man who can cry is a lucky man." I never could, before. I used to think what a relief it must be to let yourself go and cry, but I just couldn't. Now I can cry in great gulping sobs.

That's about it, I think. Then again, I could be completely wrong.

Lately I've started to forget my year at Eiheiji. But forgetting is a sign of life, a principle of nature. In time, the days of that year will no doubt be buried under a host of other memories, just as a shell washed up on shore is battered by waves until it breaks into tiny pieces and disappears into the sand. That's all right. Even if we forget the past completely, it lives on in the present. The present is born out of the past and in turn gives birth to the future. At Eiheiji I learned the courage to affirm everything in the past and the joy of living mindfully in the present, out of which the future will be born. I like to think that that courage and joy will stay with me, somewhere inside, and that someday when I burst into sudden loud weeping or wish out loud for death I may remember them. Then I think I'll know what my year at Eiheiji was all about.

Kaoru Nonomura
October 10, 1996

AFTERWORD TO THE JAPANESE PAPERBACK EDITION

I wrote this book on the commuter train between Zushi, the seaside town about an hour outside Tokyo where I used to live, and Shibuya, in the bustling heart of the city. Every morning I would set out at the same time and board the same train at Zushi Station. As soon as the wheels started to roll, I would carefully take the writing paper out of my bag. From then until we pulled into Shibuya I would scribble with a red pen, sometimes hanging onto a strap, sometimes leaning against a door. Between the shaking of the train and my naturally bad handwriting, what came out was a pretty awful scrawl.

After working all day in a design office in a corner of Shibuya, I would head straight for a nearby municipal pool and swim my usual twenty laps. For dinner I would go to one or another of the many little restaurants in the neighborhood there before getting on the train home. Then I'd take out the manuscript again and pick up where I'd left off in the morning—sometimes getting a seat, sometimes nodding off—

writing in the same hideous scrawl until the train pulled into Zushi Station.

At my house in Zushi—a quiet place without radio or TV—only a family of stray cats would be there to welcome me. My first order of business when I got in the door was always to feed the cats. Then, while playing some kind of music that didn't disturb the evening quiet, I would try to decipher what I'd scribbled on the train that day and type it up on a word processor. When the clock hands passed twelve I'd turn in, and soon it would be morning all over again.

That went on for a long time, until after five years my scribbles amounted to nearly seven hundred pages of manuscript. Needless to say, it wasn't some fanciful notion of becoming a writer that motivated me. As we get older, our memories inevitably fade, but some of them we'd like to keep. I decided that before I forgot all about my year at Eiheiji I would set it down on paper. That's how this book got started. When I made that decision, I had just started living again in Zushi, where I was before I went to Eiheiji. The town of Zushi has played a significant role in my life.

Before the idea of going to Eiheiji had entered my head, I moved to this quiet summer resort town facing the ocean because I wanted to live somewhere an hour from Shibuya. Until then I'd been riding my bike to work from Ebisu, a neighboring area of Tokyo. An hour from Shibuya . . . Mount Takao, Chichibu, the southern Boso Peninsula . . . among all the place names that ran vaguely through my head was Zushi. Why I should have thought of it I don't know, since I'd never been there, but somehow it came to me. That very weekend I set off in high spirits to check it out, and ended up picking a place to live the first day. It was a two-story rental home, really too big for one person, located in a peaceful residential neighborhood midway between the station and the sea.

So began my quiet life in Zushi. I would spend weekend afternoons alone doing yard work. "Yard" is a stretch; when I first moved in it was a weed-grown empty lot with no trees, stuck on my cheaply built house as an afterthought. Little by little I planted whatever trees I liked and put down grass, making it into a yard. I always did my weeding in a methodical way: I started from the towering, thick-stemmed bamboo, then went under the maple tree, along the azaleas, and on toward the latticed bamboo gate beside the front entrance. With no one to crack the whip, I worked at my own pace, stopping when I grew tired and starting up again when I felt like it. The only sounds that came to my ears were the twittering of wild birds in the branches of neighboring trees and, riding on an occasional breeze filled with the tang of salt, the gleeful shouts of children at the beach. I owed the tranquility to my remote location, far from main street traffic.

That day I took two breaks from my yard work, and by the time I reached the latticed bamboo gate, the sun was already beginning to set in the sky. At the end of the afternoon's weeding, following my usual custom, I made coffee and sat on the porch with nothing particular to do except look out alone at my yard until the sun vanished below the horizon.

Afterword to the Japanese Paperback Edition

Then the doorbell rang. No one ever came to call at my house except the mailman, but on this Sunday evening I had an unexpected visitor. I opened the door to find a police officer standing there.

He said, "I'm from the police box by the station. The other day we had a report of some stolen silver grass, and the victim says you're the one who stole it. Would you know anything about this, sir?"

For a moment I couldn't think what he was talking about, but then I remembered. It had been just a week ago.

That day, too, I'd finished my afternoon weeding and then sat alone on the porch sipping coffee and looking out at my garden. The moon had been visible in the still-light sky. After I'd looked unconcernedly at the moon for a while, an idea came to me: why not plant some feathery silver grass, one of the seven grasses of autumn, to go with the autumn moon? Having decided to do this, I went out for supper and swung around on the way back to check out a nearby abandoned lot where silver grass was growing. The building there had once been a store of some kind, apparently. The shutter at the entrance was wide open, and piles of scrap wood lay around. Weeds grew thickly around the outside of the building, and I had the swift impression that the place had been long neglected. There was an armful of silver grass growing in a clump, and without any hesitation I had leaped over a scrap-wood fence, pulled it up, and taken it home.

"That might have been me, actually," I told the police officer.

"I see. The other party says that if you put it back tomorrow, he won't press charges, so will you do that?"

How could this be happening? I was appalled at this unexpected trouble. But I felt an urgent need to apologize to the owner of the silver grass as soon as I could, and hastily followed after the departing police officer. At the police box, the officer produced a smallish old man wearing gym clothes and a beret who, the moment he saw me, turned purple and unleashed an angry tirade:

"So it's you, is it, who stole my grass! Sunday morning I went by and saw something had been dug up. I knew right away I'd been robbed. I found clods of dirt in the street and followed the trail—it led straight to your house. I looked around the side, and what do I see in your yard but silver grass! I knew it was mine. Well, what have you got to say for yourself? If you want silver grass, next time steal somebody else's! Stay away from mine!"

I let him have his say, and apologized. If he had gone to the trouble of following a trail of dirt clumps to track his property down, it must have meant a lot to him. For my part, never dreaming anyone would call the police, I hadn't known or cared if dirt fell in the street. Had I really been out to steal his silver grass, I would have taken the precaution of putting it into some kind of bag to avoid leaving clues.

But the more I thought about his anger, the more sense it made to me. People divide land into blocks for the precise purpose of establishing ownership; help yourself to even a blade of grass from another person's land, and you've committed a crime. I made profuse apologies and promised that I would return the silver grass to its original place the next morning.

Afterword to the Japanese Paperback Edition

The old man thanked the officer for his help and then told him, "I won't press charges this time, but there's always next time, so be sure and get his fingerprints."

By then it was full dark. For a while the officer and I walked side by side under small, walnut-colored streetlights. My mind was dazed, my footsteps heavy.

The officer said, "There are all kinds of people in this world, so you have to be careful. Don't worry, no matter what he says, we don't fingerprint people over a thing like this. Anyway, be sure and see he gets his grass back tomorrow morning." With this final advice, he went back to the police box by the train station.

Criminal. That night I felt branded with that word, and couldn't get it out of my thoughts. I felt as if I had to find someone to blame, or burst into tears. But in the end I did neither. I only sat alone on the porch, looking up at a moonless and starless sky covered with dense, dark clouds, and blamed myself. Not that doing so could change what had happened. I knew all too well that the past was irrecoverable.

In the morning I arrived at the empty lot a little earlier than promised and found the old man already there, standing with his arms crossed, waiting. Using a shovel I'd brought, I quickly replanted the silver grass. With a final deep apology, I turned to go, but he called out to stop me.

"Wait a minute. Stand there next to the silver grass, would you?"

Of all things, he liked to take photographs, it turned out. From the time he first realized he'd been robbed, he'd gone around collecting photographic evidence: the spot where the grass had been dug up, telltale bits of dirt in the street, the grass transplanted in my yard. Now, to cap it all, he wanted a photo of his stolen property safely returned, with me, the thief, standing next to it.

Whatever for? Why make someone so repentant for his misdeed, someone who had apologized for it over and over already, go through such extra humiliation? That's what I thought. But I was clearly in the wrong, and I could think of no real reason to deny him what he wanted. In the end, I let him snap a picture of me standing meekly beside the restored silver grass. I felt myself crumbling away. So this was what people were like. So this was where society's laws left us. This punishment was more than enough to push a frail miscreant like me over the edge and demolish me.

After that I couldn't walk the streets of Zushi with my old pleasure. I was afraid of passing people on the sidewalk, sure that the moment I walked on by they would turn, point their fingers at me, and call me a criminal. Such fears pursued me everywhere.

What had the old man done with his photo of the silver grass and the thief, I wondered. Did he go around showing it to people, bragging about how he'd tracked the culprit down single-handedly? The thought was sickening.

Weeds soon filled in the hole where the silver grass had been, and overhead the autumn moon shed its brilliance on my little yard just the way it was. And so, little by little, my thoughts turned toward Eiheiji. Of course, there was more to it than this, but in the end I felt certain

Afterword to the Japanese Paperback Edition

that the business of the silver grass provided just the nudge I needed. Soon after that, I began to think, *I want to lose myself*, a desire that eventually coalesced in the word *shukke* (leaving home to take Buddhist vows). I would become a Zen monk.

After leaving Eiheiji, why I decided to return to this town where I had such painful memories, I couldn't say. But for whatever reason, I was certain that Zushi was the right place for me to begin life anew.

Now it's been ten years since my year at Eiheiji. During the past five years, the publication of this book provided an impetus for me to return to Tokyo to live, and Zushi has again become a memory. Still, my life is essentially no different from before. (In fact, I haven't told any but a few of my closest friends that I am the book's author.) I no longer have that long commute, but my preferred place to write is still inside the train and bus I take to work. I have penned this afterword in a lurching, swaying bus, writing as before with a red ballpoint pen. As I set down these final sentences, the bus is about to turn right from Roppongi Street onto the rotary in front of Shibuya Station.

Eat Sleep Sit

Notes

PART ONE

The End and the Beginning

1. A lineage chart tracing the transmission of Buddhist teachings through a succession of masters, linking the aspiring acolyte back through previous generations all the way to the Buddha Sakyamuni (563–483 BC).

2. Legend says that the night before Eiheiji founder Dogen (1200–53) left China in 1227, he set out to copy a collection of one hundred Zen koans. When he grew tired, the spirit of Mount Haku (the main peak in the range of mountains where Eiheiji lies) came to him and aided him in completing the task. The scroll, which each applicant has written for him by a Zen priest or mentor, displays calligraphic writing referring to the spirit of Mount Haku as an avatar of Buddha.

3. A collection of ninety-five essays by Dogen, written between 1231 and 1253.

4. About ten US dollars.

5. Zhangweng Rujing (1163–1228). Dogen studied with Rujing for two years, and in 1227 Rujing gave Dogen a certificate declaring him his successor.

6. The cyclic existence of endless suffering that continues for an unimaginably long time until the attainment of nirvana.

PART TWO   Etiquette Is Zen

1. A dharani is a ritual chant similar to a mantra.

2. The three treasures are Buddha, the Dharma (Buddhist law or teachings), and the Sangha (community).

3. It gives the body a healthy color, increases strength, extends life, does not sit heavy on the stomach, makes the voice clear, aids digestion, prevents colds, relieves hunger, relieves thirst, and aids excretion.

4. Those to whom one is beholden for one's spiritual progress: teachers, parents, nation, and the many beings.

5. The three lower realms of devils, hungry ghosts, and animals, and the three higher realms of titans, human beings, and celestial beings.

6. One of the three ages of Buddhism: a time of moral corruption when people are no longer capable of following Buddhist teaching.

7. The three virtues are gentleness, purity, and etiquette; the six flavors are bitter, sour, sweet, spicy, salty, and bland.

PART THREE   Alone in the Freezing Dark

1. Dropwort, shepherd's purse, cudweed, chickweed, henbit, turnip, and garden radish. Porridge cooked with these herbs is traditionally eaten on January 7 to ensure health in the coming year.

2. A Chinese translation of the ancient Sanskrit Buddhist scripture Vinaya Pitaka (meaning "basket of discipline"), which contains monastic rules for monks and nuns.

PART SIX   The Colors of the Peak, the Echo in the Valley

1. A traditional confection made of sweet bean paste in a crisp casing made from glutinous rice.

2. Because the Chinese characters for "eighty-eight" can be combined to make the character for "rice," it is considered a highly auspicious age. The traditional way of calculating age in Japan has people turning a year older not on their birthday but on New Year's Day.

（英文版）食う寝る坐る
Eat Sleep Sit: My Year at Japan's Most Rigorous Zen Temple

2008 年 12 月 22 日　第 1 刷発行

著　者　　野々村　馨

発行者　　富田　充

発行所　　講談社インターナショナル株式会社
　　　　　〒112-8652　東京都文京区音羽 1-17-14
　　　　　電話　03-3944-6493（編集部）
　　　　　　　　03-3944-6492（営業部・業務部）
　　　　　ホームページ　www.kodansha-intl.com

印刷・製本所　大日本印刷株式会社